D1233490

DUNCAN UPSHAW FLETCHER

DUNCAN UPSHAW FLETCHER
Dixie's Reluctant Progressive

Wayne Flynt

FLORIDA STATE UNIVERSITY PRESS
Tallahassee
1971

A Florida State University Press Book

PRINTED FOR THE PUBLISHER BY
THE E. O. PAINTER PRINTING COMPANY,
DE LEON SPRINGS, FLORIDA

To
Dorothy

Preface

POLITICAL BIOGRAPHY creates almost insoluble problems for the historian. When trying to evaluate a man's character and career, the writer must divorce political opportunism from genuine conviction. While striving for objectivity, he must make value judgments involving the most complex motivation. These tasks become infinitely more difficult when unthinking associates of his subject destroy the collected correspondence of a lifetime. Aware of these limitations, the author of this study explores the career of Duncan Upshaw Fletcher, a dominant figure in Florida's fragmented Democratic Party between 1908 and 1936. Primary emphasis is divided between his 27-year career in the United States Senate, with consequent influence on American development, and his interest in rapidly changing Florida. During these years, the "Sunshine State" emerged from rural isolation to become the South's most urbanized, diversified unit, and this transition is an integral part of Fletcher's story. Although it is impossible to attribute a congressman's national posture solely to local pressure, this biography devotes attention to the interaction of constituent and representative in hopes of explaining the otherwise inexplicable paradox of the conservative-progressive.

The destruction of Fletcher's entire files by his secretary after the senator's death constitutes a major research barrier and helps explain Fletcher's obscurity. The absence of any significant primary materials for his early life shrouds this period. Conclusions about early influences are based largely on the reminiscences of relatives and on conjecture. Seldom can the careful historian penetrate with certainty to the motives or transitional forces in Fletcher's early life. Later in his career, when tangential manuscript collections provide assistance, his activity and influence move into sharper focus. Yet even during this later phase, Fletcher's single-minded absorption with maritime and farm problems leaves his career single-dimensional, and his concern for broader issues is episodic and cursory.

A final difficulty arises from Fletcher's private life. This is primarily a study of the Senator's public career, not because his private life is unrelated to it, but because he chose to reveal so little of himself. Perhaps he was so thoroughly politicized during his long career that his private identity became indistinguishable from his public political positions. Possibly family problems may offer a fuller explanation. At any rate, Fletcher offers little candid self-revelation, and what one learns of his private life comes from isolated fragments of information and inference.

During the preparation of this study, I was aided by many people whose names would fill pages. Justice requires that I mention Dr. William W. Rogers of Florida State University, whose interest in southern history and boundless energy have been contagious. I owe special debts to the late Dr. Weymouth T. Jordan, who first suggested the intricacies of Florida politics, and to Dr. Samuel Proctor of the University of Florida, who pioneered the wilderness for all writers of recent Floridiana. The Woodrow Wilson Foundation provided generous financial assistance without which my research would have been impossible. Library personnel at numerous universities and private libraries made research as painless and simple as possible; and I owe special gratitude to the staffs of the P. K. Yonge Library of Florida History, University of Florida, and the Franklin D. Roosevelt Library at Hyde Park, New York. No list of credits would be complete without mention of my wife Dorothy, who hunted through dusty manuscripts, read revisions, and patiently listened to a wide assortment of frustrations.

W.F.

BIRMINGHAM, ALABAMA

Contents

CHAPTER I

The Makings of a Rebel

THE AMERICAN FOREBEARS of Duncan Upshaw Fletcher came to North Carolina in the mid-1770's. They were sturdy, restless folk of Scotch and English lineage and moved frequently in search of a better life. Duncan's great-grandfather, Richard Fletcher, was born in Kentucky where his pioneer family helped push back the frontier in the late eighteenth century. Richard inherited the family's wanderlust and followed the mountains south to Georgia where he married Effie Hardin of Columbus in 1805. The following year the couple christened their first son, John Upshaw Fletcher, and the boy subsequently gained renown in Georgia as a circuit-riding Baptist cleric. John married Indiana McKay in 1811, and she bore Thomas Jefferson Fletcher, Duncan's father, in March, 1830. At age twenty-eight Thomas married Rebecca Ellen McCowan, daughter of a wealthy Monroe County planter.[1]

Monroe County, Georgia, was a center of political power in the 1850's. The county, sixty-five miles south of Atlanta, constituted part of the rich central Georgia cotton belt which possessed the state's highest concentration of Negroes, and consequently enjoyed considerable political and economic power. John Fletcher settled near the town of Forsyth in the early decades of the nineteenth century and took an active place in community life. Though he was blessed with spirituality and respect, wealth came more readily to his McCowan neighbors.

Duncan McCowan dominated the local economy. Aided by

1. Jack K. Fletcher to author, October 31, 1964; Rowland H. Rerick, *Memoirs of Florida*, ed. Francis P. Fleming (Atlanta: Southern Historical Association, 1902), I, 534–35.

peak cotton prices from 1854 to 1857, he increased his plantation from 900 acres to 1,500 acres and 29 slaves; his property was valued at better than $34,000.[2] Thomas Fletcher united the families when he married Rebecca McCowan on January 10, 1858.

Young Fletcher possessed his father's penchant for wandering and forsook Monroe County in favor of the pine-tree country of southern Georgia. Life in Sumter County was difficult, and the birth of Duncan Fletcher on January 6, 1859, only complicated the problems of eking out a minimal existence. While Thomas Fletcher cleared land and planted crops, his infant son feebly clung to life. Duncan's mother wrote that she nursed him "when I nor no other person that sawe [sic] him thought that he would live an hour. . . ."[3] Thomas, faced with poor crops and a sickly son, despaired of the uneven struggle and returned to central Georgia. Rebecca Fletcher requested help in locating good land, and the family settled in Monroe County during the fall of 1860.

Aided by the McCowan family, Thomas Fletcher acquired 530 acres of land on Tobesofkee Creek seven miles west of Forsyth. The new homestead, valued at $8,000, lay in gently rolling hill country. Relatively good soil supported hardwoods and pines for construction and produced good cotton crops when cultivated. The land was devoted almost exclusively to cotton during the boom times of the 1850's. Thomas remodeled the small frame house on the Fletcher farm into an eight-room dwelling, a project necessitated by the birth of Cornelia in November, 1860.[4] By the end of winter the farm boasted eight slaves, and their value added to the land, home, and furnishings amounted to $23,000.[5]

The cannon roar at Fort Sumter climaxed the widening breach between North and South and shattered Thomas Fletcher's dream of prosperity. Duncan McCowan immediately organized and equipped a company of infantry which included Thomas Fletcher, private, Company K, Fifty-Third Georgia Infantry Volunteers. The

2. *Monroe County, Georgia, Tax Digest, 1854–1861*, County Court House, Forsyth, Georgia.
3. Rebecca E. Fletcher to her sister, August 15, 1860, in Fletcher Papers. These papers are in the possession of Mrs. Fred G. Yerkes of Jacksonville, Florida. Hereafter cited as Fletcher Papers.
4. Interview with Mrs. Tom Fletcher, Forsyth, Georgia, October 27, 1964; William James Wells, "Duncan Upshaw Fletcher: 'Florida's Grand Old Man'" (Master's thesis, Stetson University, 1942), p. 8.
5. *Monroe County, Georgia, Tax Digest, 1863–1883*, County Court House, Forsyth, Georgia.

Fifty-Third achieved an illustrious record of gallantry beginning with the Peninsula Campaign and continuing through the battles of Antietam, Chancellorsville, and Gettysburg. Fletcher was wounded in an engagement at Knoxville, Tennessee, on November 28, 1863.[6] He rose to the rank of lieutenant during the war and served as acting colonel of his regiment at Appomattox.

The Fletchers experienced problems typical of southern families in the Civil War. Rebecca bore her second son, Thomas Edgar, in September, 1862, and her third, James McCowan, in November, 1864. In addition to caring for her growing family and the farm, she nursed her husband back to health after he was wounded at Knoxville.

General William T. Sherman brought the war to Monroe County on his march to the sea in the winter of 1864. While the county escaped the full impact of the Union Army, foraging units and deserters roamed through the area. One detachment stopped at the Fletcher home and demanded horses and mules. Learning that the animals had been spirited away by the overseer, the enraged commander fired into the house barely missing Duncan's head. The soldiers spotted the overseer a short distance from the house, shot him as he tried to escape over a fence, and took the animals. The Fletcher children discovered his body minutes later.[7]

The cataclysm of war fell heavily on the family. Of Duncan's eight uncles who fought for the Confederacy, two fell in battle, one died of disease, and three others were seriously wounded. Thomas Fletcher made his way home from Appomattox only to find more grief. His father-in-law paused while driving him to the farm and pointed to Rebecca's grave, providing Fletcher's first knowledge of his wife's death. She died fourteen days after Appomattox and several days before his return. Reconstruction became more than an historical term for Thomas Fletcher who found his home abandoned and wrecked, his gin house with $10,000 worth of cotton burned, his livestock butchered, and his wife dead.[8]

6. The unit won many citations and suffered heavy casualties; i.e. 30 per cent losses in the Maryland campaign. For the general history of the Fifty-Third see U.S., *War of the Rebellion: A Compilation of the Official Records of the Union and Confederate Armies,* 128 vols. (Washington, 1880–91), Series I, vols. XI, XIX, XXV, XXVII, XXXI; see especially vol. XXXI, 522–24.
7. Wells, "Duncan Upshaw Fletcher," p. 15; interview with Mrs. Fred G. Yerkes, Jacksonville, Fla., July 7, 1964.
8. Wells, "Duncan Upshaw Fletcher," p. 15.

He could ill afford time for mourning and rebuilt the farm while his three sisters cared for the children. Duncan's ill health again caused concern, though his recovery and subsequent vitality allowed his father to devote more energy to agriculture.[9] The total assessed value of the farm declined from $23,000 in 1865 to $3,000 in 1867. This loss reflected not only the emancipation of the family's eight slaves, but probably a sympathetic property devaluation to avoid high Reconstruction taxes. Family fortune gradually improved, and Fletcher could afford a Negro laborer by 1870. Cotton prices increased, and Fletcher added ten more hands and another hundred acres in 1872.[10]

The children were old enough to help perform the farm chores by the 1870's, a prospect particularly to Duncan's liking. As the oldest of the four, he received the greatest responsibility. The family used a large white ox, "Old January," in place of expensive horses or mules. The ox, as ornery as he was uncooperative, provided one of the boy's vivid memories. While Duncan was returning with a load of flour from the mill, "Old January" bolted, plunged madly down a hill, and threw boy, cart, and all into Tobesofkee Creek. Duncan was more successful with construction projects and, when sixteen, built a gin house for the farm.[11]

Only education took precedence over chores for the Fletcher clan. Duncan attended four different schools at adjoining farms, and several of his teachers were Yankee immigrants.[12] Thomas Fletcher recognized intellectual curiosity in his oldest son and sent him to Gordon Institute at Barnesville, Georgia. While most subjects came easily and Duncan served as class valedictorian, he literally agonized through elocution. He practiced alone when assigned a speech, and his audiences noted his ruffled composure.[13] Rural isolation had made him introverted and shy, more suited for the independent life of a farmer than for the public scrutiny of politics.

Duncan recognized his distaste for crowds. When Thomas

9. Duncan U. Fletcher to Ruth Huddleston Baxter, undated, in Fletcher Papers.
10. *Monroe County, Georgia, Tax Digest, 1868–1870*; *ibid., 1872–1873*; at County Courthouse, Forsyth, Georgia.
11. Wells, "Duncan Upshaw Fletcher," p. 14; and MS in Fletcher Papers.
12. MS in Fletcher Papers.
13. *Ibid.*; interview with Mrs. Fred G. Yerkes, Jacksonville, Florida, July 7, 1964.

THE MAKINGS OF A REBEL

Fletcher scraped together enough money to send his daughter to Mercer University at Macon, Georgia, Duncan declined higher education. He preferred cotton cultivation to intellectual stimulation. Soon, however, the boy found that although his industry was equal to that of most older farmers, toil alone did not produce crops. Usurious interest rates denied him adequate credit; after he planted and harvested his crop, exorbitant transportation and marketing costs reduced the peak consumer prices to barely five cents a pound. When his income failed to leave enough even for a new plow, the financially insolvent youngster admitted a distaste for farming and turned his attention once more to education.[14]

Duncan Fletcher later recalled the Reconstruction years with mingled nostalgia and frustration. His father's strict discipline and simple integrity made him cherish self-reliance and shun hypocrisy. He had carried from the farm an intense dislike for religious fanaticism, represented in his view by the county's "Hard Shell" Baptists.[15] His Reconstruction legacy also had included an intense affection for the South's regional identity. Years later he still reflected a Rebel's view of the era: "I saw federal soldiers in uniform stationed about the country to see that former slaves had their so-called rights. . . . Carpet-baggers, like vultures swept down upon this stricken and helpless section. They seized the offices, took into their greedy and selfish hands the control of government . . . plundered the public treasuries and oppressed the people."[16] Fletcher shared the same melancholy for the "lost cause" that characterized his generation. Like his contemporaries he defended secession and states' rights. To him—as to Georgia's Hoke Smith, Napoleon B. Broward of Florida, and "Little Jeff" Davis of Arkansas—the Negro was a social and economic liability to the South.[17]

The tenets of political conservatism dominated these early years. From his family he derived respect for religion, education, property, history, and the traditions of the past. His social and political milieu impressed on him respect for law, order, and pro-

14. Clippings from Washington *Post,* May 3, 1932, and the *United States News,* April 30, 1934, in Fletcher Papers.
15. MS in Fletcher Papers.
16. MS speech text by Duncan U. Fletcher, in Fletcher Papers.
17. Smith, Broward, and Davis were contemporary political leaders—Smith in Georgia, Broward in Florida, Davis in Arkansas—who also grew to manhood during Reconstruction.

priety. Reconstruction left him with a fear of unrestrained majority rule and governmental extravagance and power.

The very forces that later softened his view of the Negro and qualified his conservatism also stemmed from Reconstruction. Family difficulty while rebuilding the farm impressed on him the value of cooperation and social democracy. His brief experience as a farmer convinced him that economic injustice resulted not so much from vague inexorable forces or individual failure as from man-made policies which were amenable to change.

The Reconstruction era ended with the contested 1876 presidential campaign between Rutherford B. Hayes and Samuel J. Tilden, but seventeen-year-old Duncan Fletcher was far more interested in choosing a college than in the outcome of the presidential race. He entered Nashville's newly founded Vanderbilt University in the fall of 1877 because he disliked farming, not because he envisioned a career in politics. Vanderbilt brought out the best in the young Georgian, and he blossomed into a popular student and the "eagle orator of the Dialectic Literary Society."[18] The young scholar took justifiable pride in overcoming his distaste for public speaking. He represented the Literary Society as commencement orator his first two years in college.

The boy's money ran low in 1879 when the fourth Fletcher offspring entered college. Thomas Fletcher had expanded the farm to over one thousand acres and this expense, added to the formidable cost of educating four children, caused Duncan to accelerate his studies. The Vanderbilt junior doubled his academic load and finished two years of work in one. His senior classmates elected him to the treasured position of commencement orator in 1880, and he addressed the assembled dignitaries for the third consecutive year.[19]

After receiving his Bachelor of Science degree on June 20, 1880, Fletcher entered the Vanderbilt law school. He again demonstrated his affinity for hard work and long hours, finishing a two-year law course in twelve months. Only a recurrence of mumps which delayed final examinations marred his brilliant law school record. The faculty recognized his achievement by naming him a

18. Jacksonville *Florida Times-Union*, December 10, 1881, quoting *Vanderbilt Observer*.
19. *Deed Book W, 1889, Monroe County, Georgia*, County Court House, Forsyth; clippings from the Washington *Post*, May 3, 1932, in Fletcher Papers.

member of the Moot Court which highlighted law school commencement.[20] Shortly after his graduation in 1881, Fletcher was admitted to the Tennessee bar.

Duncan Fletcher inherited the restless spirit of his family and decided to begin his law practice in some state other than Tennessee or Georgia. Exhausted by three continuous years of school, he accepted the Florida vacation invitation of John M. Barrs, his 1879 Vanderbilt roommate.[21] Jacksonville, Florida, was no great metropolis, but the prospects of urban life together with Barrs' friendship persuaded Fletcher to begin his law career in the port city in the fall of 1881.

Fletcher's new home town experienced epochal and turbulent changes in the decade and a half from Reconstruction to 1890. Money barons and neophyte tycoons found Jacksonville an eager beneficiary of their "conspicuous consumption." The orange industry of northeast and central Florida, drained by the St. Johns River, made Jacksonville a major distributing center. Railroads anxious to tap the treasures of tourism and citrus located there.

When Fletcher arrived, the "Queen City of the St. Johns" numbered 7,650 residents, making it the second largest city in the state. Her only paper, the *Daily Florida Union*, the sole daily in the state, boasted the lone Florida subscription to the Associated Press, and enjoyed the state's largest circulation.[22] This monopoly of the Fourth Estate vanished with the appearance of another daily and two weekly papers by the summer of 1882. The business community reflected the city's growing commercial aspirations by forming a Board of Trade in December, 1881. Politically, a combination of Negro and white Republicans regularly turned out GOP majorities in Duval County and elected their congressional candidate in 1880 with a 1,000-vote plurality.[23] The Barrs, Stockton, Broward, and Taliaferro families provided the town's social, economic, and political leadership. The mobility of the population and the city's rapid growth provided ample opportunity for a lawyer of Duncan Fletcher's ability.

20. Wells, "Duncan Upshaw Fletcher," p. 17.
21. Jacksonville *Florida Times-Union*, December 10, 1881, quoting *Vanderbilt Observer*.
22. Jacksonville *Daily Florida Union*, June 16, 1882. In February, 1883, the *Daily Florida Union* and the Jacksonville *Times* merged to form the *Florida Times-Union*, edited by Charles H. Jones.
23. *Ibid.*, November 5 and 8, 1882.

Fletcher was admitted to the Florida bar shortly after arriving in Jacksonville and joined John M. Barrs to form a new law firm in the fall of 1881. Mrs. Abigail Barrs boarded her son's partner for $10 a month.[24] The financially embarrassed partners purchased a wash basin for their office but could not afford book cases or desks. During their early years of practice, Barrs earned $50 a month working for a judge while Fletcher impatiently awaited clients in the office.[25] The partners attempted to build their practice with newspaper advertisements and qualified to practice in the United States Court.

Cases handled by Fletcher in the first lean years involved everything from arson to licenses for the sale of "spiritous, vinous and malt liquors."[26] He gradually gained a reputation for winning cases, and his practice broadened to include most of north and central Florida. During 1883 he practiced in Duval, Volusia, and Orange counties. The editor of the Lake City *Reporter* heard him argue a case, praised his cogent arguments, and predicted "an enviable reputation as a lawyer before he is many years older. . . ." Fletcher became the United States commissioner for Jacksonville in 1883, and the local paper, observing his argumentative enthusiasm, reported that the new commissioner enjoyed seeing the "pitch made hot."[27]

The compassion for the underdog which characterized his later flirtation with liberalism appeared in these early years. Fletcher criticized a court ruling that relatives of passengers could not collect damages for injuries resulting from railroad negligence. The young lawyer protested to the local press that many states held railroads liable for deaths caused by company neglect and demanded similar action by the Florida legislature to protect passengers and public.[28]

Jacksonville tourism surpassed all expectations when sixty thousand vacationers, including financial tycoons Henry M. Flagler and Jay Gould, crowded the city during the 1884–85 season. Fletcher's law practice shared in the general prosperity, and by

24. Wells, "Duncan Upshaw Fletcher," p. 21.
25. Interview with Mrs. Fred G. Yerkes, Jacksonville, Florida, July 7, 1964.
26. Jacksonville *Florida Times-Union*, March 17, November 16, 1883.
27. *Ibid.*, May 24, 1883, quoting Lake City *Reporter*; *ibid.*, April 22, 1883.
28. Duncan U. Fletcher to editor, Jacksonville *Daily Florida Union*, December 22, 1882.

1885 he had built a large, lucrative practice.[29] He ended the partnership with Barrs the same year and formed a new one with John Wurts, a Yale graduate.

Duncan Fletcher's meteoric rise forced revision of the city's social register. He achieved immediate recognition in Jacksonville when Vanderbilt University invited him to address commencement for the fifth time. The Nashville *American* praised the "distinguished alumni orator," noting that he particularly impressed the young ladies. A Jacksonville paper praised "our popular young townsman," and the Vanderbilt student newspaper predicted that the University would someday take even greater pride "in this rising young man."[30] Apparently romance rather than oratory consumed Fletcher's primary attention at Nashville. John Barrs suggested that Cupid was responsible for visits to Nashville in June and October, 1882. Personal tragedy once again struck when the prospective bride died.[31]

After mourning his loss, the young lawyer returned to the social whirl. A group of prominent socialites organized the Florida Mutual Matrimonial Aid Association with Fletcher as treasurer. John Barrs, Fletcher, and several other eligible men also organized a dancing school. On one occasion Barrs invited Miss Anna Louise Paine, daughter of a prominent New York family drawn south by Jacksonville's climate and economic opportunity. Fletcher won more of the young lady's attention than his former law partner did, and the acquaintanceship blossomed into love.[32] The treasurer of the Florida Matrimonial Association never collected his bachelor's insurance, for on June 20, 1883, he married Anna at Jacksonville's St. John's Episcopal Church.

Mrs. Duncan U. Fletcher, although prominent in Jacksonville society, never really embraced it. In a day when religious orthodoxy was a prerequisite to southern political advancement, Anna deserted the Episcopal Church and converted her husband to Unitarianism. Fletcher subsequently became the chief financial pillar

29. T. Frederick Davis, *History of Jacksonville, Florida, 1513 to 1924* (St. Augustine, Florida: Florida Historical Society, 1925), p. 173; also see court cases in Jacksonville *Florida Times-Union*, 1885.
30. Jacksonville *Daily Florida Union*, June 2, 1882, quoting Nashville *American;* Jacksonville *Daily Florida Union*, June 25, 1882, quoting *Vanderbilt Observer.*
31. Jacksonville *Daily Florida Union*, May 7, 1882; interview with Mrs. Fred G. Yerkes, Jacksonville, Florida, July 7, 1964.
32. Wells, "Duncan Upshaw Fletcher," p. 22.

of the Unitarian congregation in Jacksonville.[33] Anna was later attracted to spiritualism and shocked Washington society by defending mediums at a 1926 congressional hearing.[34] Perhaps the unpredictable conduct of his wife helps to explain Fletcher's aloofness. In his long career, the senator was circumspect in conduct and decorous in language. Even private correspondence with his family and friends reveals only the public man, seldom his candid thoughts, family matters, or personal warmth. Though Fletcher was himself a shy man who never sought center stage, his wife's embarrassing involvements no doubt help to explain his reticence toward even his closest friends. Throughout his career, Anna remained discreetly in the shadows of his public life, and their private relationship was never discussed with others.

For all her quirks, Anna was a dedicated wife and the center of Fletcher's attention. The young couple erected a two-story house on their lot in Springfield, part of rapidly expanding East Jacksonville. It was finished before the birth of their two daughters, Ellen Abey or "Nell" in June, 1884, and Louise in November, 1886.

Politics attracted Fletcher's interest after only a few months in his adopted state. Florida's transition from Republican to "Bourbon" Democratic politics brought little economic change, and the post-Reconstruction administrations of Governors George F. Drew, William D. Bloxham, Edward A. Perry, and Francis P. Fleming encouraged the activities of railroads, corporations, and land speculators.[35] Although Florida became solidly Democratic after 1876, Jacksonville maintained a spirited two-party system throughout the 1880's. Liberal and conservative Democrats united to oppose Republicans in the general elections, then fragmented into intraparty factionalism. Jacksonville Democrats, properly called "Conservative-Democrats," adopted a platform calling for economic retrenchment, tax reduction, cessation of corruption, and states' rights.[36]

33. Interview with Miss Sally Puleston, Monticello, Florida, May 27, 1963; interview with Mrs. Fred G. Yerkes, Jacksonville, Florida, July 7, 1964. Mrs. Yerkes suggests that Fletcher's "conversion" to Unitarianism was partly to maintain domestic tranquility. It is a fact that he was a close and lifelong friend of Dr. W. A. Hobson, pastor of Jacksonville's First Baptist Church.
34. Tampa *Morning Tribune*, May 22, 1926.
35. C. Vann Woodward, *Origins of the New South*, vol. IX of *A History of the South*, eds. Wendell Holmes Stephenson and E. Merton Coulter, 10 vols. (Baton Rouge: Louisiana State University Press, 1943–67), pp. 19–20, 115–117.
36. Jacksonville *Daily Florida Union*, October 27, 1882. For an excellent survey

The Barrs family introduced Fletcher to politics. John Barrs was a Fourth Ward delegate to the city Democratic convention, while C. C. Barrs and A. W. Barrs served as alternates. At the Fourth Ward meeting in July, 1882, Fletcher won his first office as one of six alternate delegates. The popular young lawyer was subsequently chosen representative to the district Democratic convention and considered for the state legislature.[37] Few single-year residents of Duval County could match Fletcher's propitious debut.

Duval politics remained complicated throughout the decade, with the Republican Negro vote a dominant feature. In 1884 the GOP congressional delegate carried the county by a two-to-one margin, and James G. Blaine rolled over Democrat Grover Cleveland 3,332 to 1,679 in the presidential contest.[38] Democrats united only for the general elections, then dissolved into haggling factions. Fletcher served as a delegate to ward meetings but avoided this internecine party conflict.

Ward control and consequent dominance of the Democratic county conventions lay in the hands of conservatives led by Mayor William M. Dancy and James P. Taliaferro, who headed the Jacksonville, Tampa, and Key West Railroad. Labor and farm representatives directed the vaguely defined but vocal liberal minority. The Knights of Labor had made substantial progress among Jacksonville workers, and the typographical union, perhaps the strongest of the local unions, staged a bitter strike against city newspapers in the spring of 1886. Labor supported the strike by boycotting uncooperative merchants. *Florida Times-Union* editor Charles H. Jones blasted this "Communism run mad" and prepared to crush the labor forces at the county Democratic convention in July.[39] When the battle ended, the vanquished liberal insurgents deserted the party and held a rump convention to protest conservative suzerainty. Conservatives such as Jones sometimes crossed factional lines in the succeeding years to support reform candidates, but the basic philosophical clash continued into the

---

of the political and social life of Jacksonville to 1900, see Samuel Proctor, *Napoleon Bonaparte Broward: Florida's Fighting Democrat* (Gainesville: University of Florida Press, 1950).

37. Jacksonville *Daily Florida Union*, July 19 and October 1, 1882. Fletcher withdrew his name from consideration in the legislative race.

38. *Ibid.*, November 6, 1890.

39. *Ibid.*, April and May, 1886; June 5, 1886.

1900's. Fletcher increasingly became identified with the insurgent reform wing of the party, apparently more because of his revulsion at clique politics than because of his nascent liberalism.

Negro voters dominated Duval County politics in 1887, but a white majority kept Democrats in firm control of Jacksonville affairs. As a result Democratic factionalism surfaced first in city government. The initial challenge to the conservative oligarchy which controlled metropolitan policy appeared with the March, 1887, organization of the Young Men's Burbridge Club. One hundred aspiring young politicos, united by their desire to broaden the city's power structure, purposed to elect Colonel John Q. Burbridge mayor. They chose Duncan Fletcher as president, and he submitted to the city's Democratic bosses a list of election reforms designed to eliminate voting corruption. The Democratic Executive Committee, controlled by conservative William M. Dancy, rejected these reforms. Fletcher consequently advised the reformers to ignore the Democratic primaries and run in the general election as candidates of a Citizen's Party.[40] He defended the party bolt by arguing that Democratic ranks included men who acquiesced to voting corruption, while the Citizen's ticket comprised young men united "in an earnest effort to lend their aid toward purifying our city politics."[41]

Regular Democrats nominated William Dancy for mayor. When the Citizen's Party met five nights later, Chairman Fletcher praised the crowd of six hundred (including many Negroes) as comprising the best men of both Republican and Democratic parties. The Citizen's platform called for strict and impartial law enforcement, election reforms, equitable taxation, creation of a nonpolitical and salaried fire department, and extension of the city limits.[42] The convention nominated Burbridge for mayor and Fletcher for second ward city councilman.

Campaigning for the next few days reached a crescendo of charge and countercharge. Burbridge demanded reform, expanded public institutions, new manufacturing, and a bipartisan approach

40. *Ibid.*, March 7 and 24, 1887.
41. Duncan U. Fletcher to editor, Jacksonville *Florida Times-Union*, March 26, 1887.
42. Jacksonville *Florida Times-Union*, March 31, 1887. Impartial law enforcement, taxation reforms, and extension of city limits were designed to win Negro support. Extension of the city limits was especially attractive since this would provide a Negro voting majority in the city.

to politics. Dancy leaders tried to split the Negro vote by persuading Republicans to nominate candidates, but GOP leaders rejected this stratagem. Prominent Negro leaders, the local Negro paper *Southern Leader,* and the *Florida Times-Union* endorsed the Citizen's ticket; the Jacksonville *Evening Herald* and the city's elite backed the Dancy slate.

Another powerful Burbridge ally in the election was organized labor. One anti-labor source verified the Knights of Labor claim of three thousand members in Jacksonville. The Knights had tapped the large Negro labor force and prospered enough to build its own hall. M. B. Bartholomew edited the Knights' weekly paper *Palladium,* which called for land, labor, and financial reform.[43]

Both factions did much maneuvering on election day with white bands blaring for the Democrats and a colored ensemble whipping up Citizen's Party enthusiasm. It was rumored that Dancy lieutenants allotted $6,000 in "crisp new silver certificates" to buy votes, but the Burbridge camp possessed a few surprises of its own. A Dancy spokesman, according to one story, was seeking funds for the purchase of sixty Negro votes when a resourceful "reformer" happened by, correctly grasped the situation, and bought every vote by doubling the Democratic bribe. The Citizen's ticket swept all offices but one, and Duncan Fletcher carried every ward, finishing second highest in the eight-man council race.[44] Jubilant Burbridge mobs surged into the streets and marched to the home of the mayor-elect. Colonel Burbridge responded with a speech remarkable by 1887 southern standards: "I shall know no one on account of his color and I shall make no distinctions. (Loud cheers and cries of 'Hurrah for Burbridge!'). The Colored man can get justice from me as well as the white. . . . Why? Because they have rallied around us in this fight and saved us from a government not of the people but of a clique. They have rallied around the standard of good government. . . . Had it not been thus, the opposition would have over-ridden us and driven us from the field."[45] The crowd roared its approval and amid tumultuous enthusiasm chanted for Fletcher; he echoed the mayor-elect's sentiments and praised the cooperation of the people. Negro leaders were invited to join

43. *Ibid.,* September 29, October 11, and April 12, 1887.
44. *Ibid.,* April 5, 1887.
45. *Ibid.*

Fletcher and other reformers at the Burbridge home for a victory party; they incredulously remembered the event as an "incident which had never before occurred in their recollection." The New York *Evening Post* pronounced Jacksonville's municipal election "another victory for non-partisanship" which showed that "Mugwumpism [liberal reform] is growing in the South. . . ."[46] The new government contained a *potpourri* of Democrats and Republicans, whites and Negroes.

Burbridge convened the city council on April 5, 1887, and Fletcher was appointed council president *pro tempore* and a member of the Committee for Support and Relief of the Poor. First business for the new city government involved a demand for the "enforced collection of unpaid taxes."[47] This proved to be the chief problem facing the new administration, since large property owners refused to pay their assessments. Taxes in arrears from 1876 to 1884 amounted to $17,539, while $12,098 of the 1885–86 tax levy remained uncollected. The council unsuccessfully pressured the collector to provide funds for the new $54,500 budget.[48]

Largest council appropriations went for sanitary improvement. Yellow fever epidemics in Key West, Tampa, and Palatka panicked the city during the summer of 1887. The council appointed Fletcher to the Board of Health, and he instituted programs of sewer repair, street cleaning, and mail fumigation. When the sanitary program faltered for lack of funds, the city council voted to turn the delinquent tax cases over to Fletcher for legal action, and he collected enough to complete improvements.

Jacksonville's moral climate also attracted attention. The new government conducted a raid on the city's red light district on April 23, netting eleven white prostitutes and one Negro "lady of pleasure." By May 3 Mayor Burbridge boasted that not one "house of ill-fame" remained in the city. But so many citizens protested this strict enforcement that the Mayor appealed to the city council "for an endorsement of my interpretation of this ordinance or some modification that will permit these houses to remain in the city. . . ."[49] He got the endorsement. Councilman Fletcher

46. *Ibid.*, April 12, 1887, quoting New York *Evening Post.*
47. *Minutes City Council, Book 4*, pp. 436–37, at City Hall, Jacksonville, Florida. Hereafter cited as *Minutes City Council.*
48. *Ibid.*, p. 8. Some of the tax delinquents were the wealthier residents of the city who owed as much as $30,000 in back taxes; see *ibid., Book 5*, p. 12.
49. *Minutes City Council, Book 4*, p. 464.

conducted the prosecution of Miss Lula A. Warner, proprietor of one of the houses. The defendant, "a comely looking blonde," won acquital for lack of evidence, a verdict loudly applauded by the large crowd of male spectators.[50] Administration campaigns against gambling, liquor traffic among minors, and Sabbath saloon sales were more successful.

The most far-reaching change brought about by the Burbridge government was the extension of city boundaries to La Villa and Fairfield, two predominantly Negro suburbs. This extension dramatically altered the city's political structure, for the new city limits left 2,268 white voters to 2,632 Negro registrants; Negroes in the city of 20,004 thus gained a 364-vote margin.[51]

The city council accomplished governmental reform by drafting a new city charter. The document altered election procedures so that city officials, originally elected for two-year terms, faced new elections in December, 1887. Burbridge, Fletcher, and Charles Jones of the *Florida Times-Union* launched another Citizen's movement by negotiating with regular Democrats, Republicans, Negroes, and labor organizations in an attempt to retain their broad support. Regular Democrats had reorganized after the April fiasco and had formed the Jacksonville *News-Herald* to counter the Democratic insurgents.[52] The Citizen's ticket finally arranged an uneasy truce with the regular Democratic party. Republicans were little better organized, with one faction joining a Democratic-Republican "Composite" ticket and another holding the party line. Fletcher represented the Democrats in the Fourth Ward council race.

Four slates of candidates—Composite, Democratic, Republican, and Citizen's—adequately complicated the election, but new voting procedures confused the electorate even more. Under the new charter, councilmen ran in the nine wards rather than at large. The candidate winning the highest total in each ward served a four-year term, while the second highest aspirant received a two-year incumbency.

50. Jacksonville *Florida Times-Union*, May 5, 1887.
51. *Ibid.*, June 26, 1887.
52. Regular Democratic leaders included a conglomeration of liberals such as John N. C. Stockton and conservatives such as John Temple Graves and James P. Taliaferro. Stockholders of the new Democratic paper included seven of the eleven members of the Board of Directors of the National Bank of Florida. Jacksonville *Florida Times-Union*, May 1 and August 28, 1887.

The December 13 election results reflected increased Negro-Republican influence in city affairs and a powerful labor organization. Republican C. B. Smith won the mayor's contest 2,404 to 729, and thirteen Republicans swept into council spots. Of the three Democrats elected, only Fletcher, who profited from Composite-Negro support, led his Republican opponent and won a four-year council term. Four Negroes won council seats, but the real victor was labor. Shrewdly placing union representatives on both Democratic and Republican slates, the Knights of Labor elected a majority of the city council.[53] Fletcher's 311-to-247 triumph was even more remarkable, since both of the other two successful Democrats belonged to labor unions. Fletcher expressed disappointment at the defeat of the Democratic-Citizen's ticket, but avowed his confidence in Republican mayor-elect Smith and the new city council.[54]

Fletcher provided continuity between the Burbridge and Smith city councils and consequently exercised significant influence on the Republican-Labor administration. Conscientious Negro and union councilmen recognized their legislative inadequacies and nominated him as council president, though partisanship prevailed and a Republican finally won the post by a one-vote margin.[55]

Not only did Fletcher cooperate with the new administration, he even defended its electoral victory. The city's Democratic organization fought a desperate legal action against the neo-Reconstruction government by appealing to the state Supreme Court. Fletcher remained loyal to the new city administration and dominated a rancorous debate over council legal strategy.[56] His proposal proved successful, and on March 27, 1888, the court upheld the Smith government.

But the young lawyer soon became disenchanted with his fellow officials. City council election of police commissioner, comptroller, treasurer, recorder, municipal court judge, and marshal provided opportunity for an unhindered spoils system. Decisions

53. One list of Knights of Labor members elected to the council lists eight while two other sources give them thirteen of the eighteen seats. For election results see Jacksonville *News-Herald*, December 14, 1887, and Jacksonville *Florida Times-Union*, December 14, 1887.
54. Jacksonville *Florida Times-Union*, December 16, 1887.
55. *Minutes City Council, Book 6*, p. 3.
56. *Ibid.*, pp. 10–11.

reached at a March, 1888, Knights of Labor caucus united Negro and labor forces, and the coalition dominated council appointments. Selection of fourteen white and eleven colored policemen verified existence of the new cabal. Negroes won appointments as municipal judge and police commissioner, while eight of the eleven officials elected to city jobs on April 3, 1888, were members of the Knights of Labor.[57] Fletcher reacted negatively to such clique politics and used his position as chairman of the city ordinances committee to block salary authorizations. A number of his ordinances limiting council extravagance passed, largely because of Republican frugality and timely aid by Mayor Smith.[58]

City health matters also demanded council attention. With summer and the yellow fever season approaching, Fletcher sponsored legislation which established a Health Department. His ordinance gave the health officer broad power to condemn and quarantine areas of the city and provided for the arrest of anyone who interfered. Protests against the officer's inspection authority were directed at Fletcher, but he replied that breaches of individual property rights were necessary to avoid recurring epidemics.[59] The *Florida Times-Union* pronounced Jacksonville "in excellent sanitary condition," and even the *News-Herald* praised the council's "efficient and vigorous administration of the health department. . . ."[60]

Newspapers were less enthusiastic by the end of the summer when a yellow fever epidemic of devastating proportions swept the city. Fletcher, whose health suffered during most Jacksonville summers, became sick in late June and took his family to more healthful northern regions. When "yellow jack" descended, panic-stricken citizens led by the Mayor and four councilmen swarmed from Jacksonville and cut its population in half. Negroes were not allowed in the hastily constructed refugee camps and constituted most of the remaining citizenry. The epidemic ended in December, leaving 4,704 victims and 427 fatalities.[61]

57. *Ibid.*, pp 11–17. For indication of union strength compare proposed Knights of Labor slate, Jacksonville *Florida Times-Union*, March 31, 1888, with final council election list in *Times-Union*, April 4, 1888.
58. *Minutes City Council, Book 6,* pp. 10–11, 117, 124.
59. *Ibid.*, pp. 23–24.
60. Jacksonville *Florida Times-Union*, July 30, 1888; Jacksonville *Daily News-Herald*, April 14, 1888.
61. Davis, *History of Jacksonville, Florida, 1513 to 1924*, p. 185.

Ironically, yellow fever destroyed Democratic hopes for re-gaining control of Duval County politics. Before the fever's ap-pearance, disgruntled Democrats had formed a new club with Fletcher a member of the five-man central committee. The organi-zation had included such prominent reformers as John M. Barrs and Napoleon B. Broward. Henceforth reform liberalism would be channeled through this rump Democratic organization rather than through coalition with Negroes and bipartisan reformers. Disillusionment with the Smith government partly explained Fletcher's adherence to the new club, but the loss of reform spokes-man Charles H. Jones of the *Florida Times-Union* was another factor. Jones became editor of the St. Louis *Republican,* and Colonel J. J. Daniel combined the *Florida Times-Union* and *Daily News-Herald* into an "uncompromisingly Democratic" paper.[62] Daniel made the newspaper the spokesman of Democratic insur-gents against conservatives, but he felt no sympathy for party-bolting reformers.

Despite physical progress under the Republicans, Jackson-ville's white minority determined to end Negro political su-premacy. Indignant citizens protested that colored policemen were getting "out of their place," and even a Negro council member criticized the police force for "smoking and talking to females and others" while on duty.[63]

Democrats, supported by some white Republicans, intro-duced House Bill Four in the 1889 state legislature. The bill, de-signed to reduce Negro power, authorized Florida's Governor to appoint the Jacksonville city council which would then elect the mayor. Some local papers defended the bill as necessary to obtain business investment, but the editor of the *Florida Times-Union* frankly admitted the bill was designed to end the "rapid approach of absolute negro supremacy in municipal affairs."[64] Fletcher initially sided with the incumbent Republicans, and Mayor Smith appointed him to help formulate administration strategy.[65] Less than a month later Fletcher changed his mind and joined John N. C. Stockton, John M. Barrs, Napoleon B. Broward, and thirty-

62. Jacksonville *Florida Times-Union,* May 2, 1888.
63. See letters to the editor from "W. S. P.," "A. D. C.," and "Five Ladies of Jacksonville, Knocked Off the Sidewalk," Jacksonville *Florida Times-Union,* April 10, 1889; see also *Minutes City Council, Book 6,* pp. 380–81.
64. Jacksonville *Florida Times-Union,* December 29, 1890.
65. *Minutes City Council, Book 6,* pp. 396–97.

three other Jacksonville Democrats in supporting House Bill Four. The bill became law in May, 1889.

Governor Francis P. Fleming implemented the new statute by appointing eleven Democrats and seven Republicans to the city council. At their first meeting the councilmen unanimously chose Patrick McQuid mayor, John M. Barrs city attorney, and Fletcher council president; next, they selected an all-white police force.[66] This new council instituted numerous improvements during the succeeding two years, including construction of new lights and sidewalks, street pavement, regulation of market sanitation, and improvements in the drainage and sewerage systems. The city's economy improved when Jacksonville became the major port for Florida's new phosphate industry. Frugality characterized all projects, allowing a $10,000 reduction in the city budget and a twelve-mill decrease in the tax levy.

Despite these favorable advances, the new government fell short of the predicted utopia. City voters defeated Fletcher's proposed bond issue, and wealthy citizens still refused to pay their taxes; uncollected levies between 1886 and 1889 amounted to $70,000. The pigmentation of the police force changed but not its morality. The city marshal absconded with $2,000 in tax collections, and his replacement, when charged with refusal to serve tax warrants, tried to assassinate Mayor McQuid.[67]

Fletcher served as acting mayor while McQuid recovered and gained statewide recognition by his thorough handling of city problems. When a vacancy occurred on the state Supreme Court, a local editor noted that should the governor appoint a Jacksonville attorney, "members of the bar are practically unanimous in their opinion that the appointment should go either to Mr. C. M. Cooper or to Mr. D. U. Fletcher."[68] The young councilman also figured prominently in the 1890 general elections when one hundred leading Democrats elected him chairman of the Democratic Club of Duval County. Former law partner and reform ally John M. Barrs became chairman of the County Democratic Executive Committee and invited Fletcher to campaign for the county ticket.

House Bill Four had not ended Negro political activity, and

66. *Ibid.*, pp. 480–84.
67. *Ibid., Book 7*, pp. 285, 436.
68. Jacksonville *Florida Times-Union*, December 17, 1890.

local Democrats became increasingly frustrated in the months before the 1890 elections. County newspapers first mentioned disfranchisement as a solution, but some local citizens disdained cumber-
some legal action and advocated economic reprisal against Negroes
who insisted on voting.[69] Such crude proposals may have been employed, for Duval County went Democratic in 1890 for the first time
since the Civil War.[70] With the Negro removed from politics, the
external force binding Jacksonville's liberal and conservative
Democrats vanished.

Jacksonville's politics in the 1880's are remarkable when
considered against the widely held historical view that this era
in the South was dominated by bourbon-oriented, lily-white conservatism. In this Florida city, there emerged a dynamic coalition
of white reformers, blacks, and labor unionists who forged a viable
progressive government and initiated much needed change. Though
their motives differed, reformers of both races proved that they
could cooperate to end corruption and broaden political mobility.

Fletcher's remarkable pre-1890 support of these Negro-Labor-
Reform coalitions defies complete explanation. The reform coalition consisted of philosophically incompatible groups cooperating
temporarily to break the Conservative-Democratic stranglehold on
city affairs, and he undoubtedly acted partly from political expediency. The reformers also expressed legitimate protest against
the lethargic *status quo* approach to Jacksonville's problems and
to clique politics. Fletcher believed that serious issues demanded
solution, even if the remedy meant being tabbed a radical or cooperating with normally undesirable Negroes and unions. Years
later in the United States Senate he would again enter uncomfortable coalitions to relieve pressing economic and social problems.

69. S. A. Jones to editor, Jacksonville *Florida Times-Union*, July 24, 1890.
70. The victory came as a result of a sharp decline in Negro ballots rather
than by increasing white interest, so coercion may explain the triumph. In
1884 the Republican congressional candidate polled 3,292 votes in Duval County
compared to 1,368 in 1890. Jacksonville *Florida Times-Union*, November 6, 1890.

CHAPTER II

"Cracker" Progressivism

$\textbf{A}$GRARIAN REVOLT, Populism, and conservative reaction eclipsed urban reform during the chaotic 1890's. Jacksonville's difficulties merged into a larger struggle, and Fletcher parlayed his local fame into statewide support by vigorously championing the people's interests.

Jacksonville's "mauve decade" reserved a place of honor for the Fletchers. Anna joined the city's feminine elite, organizing a woman's club and serving on numerous committees, while daughter Nell contributed her singing talent to operatic productions. Anna also traveled widely, and Fletcher joined his wife's summer excursions to New York and Michigan when the press of business allowed. He participated fully in the social life of the city, a theme that is not characteristic of his later career. The Lyceum, Library Association, and United Sons of Confederate Veterans made demands on Fletcher's time, and his oratory climaxed many public events.

Civic and financial responsibilities consumed much of his time during the last decade of the century. Tourism fell from its peak of 1885, and the local Board of Trade countered California's tourist promotionalism with a giant "subtropical" exposition. Fletcher coordinated city and county efforts and converted sceptical county officials who had refused to appropriate necessary funds.[1] The brilliantly successful exposition opened in January, 1888, featuring agricultural products from Florida and Latin America. President Grover Cleveland and a party of Washington dignitaries

---

1. Jacksonville *Florida Times-Union*, November 8, 1887.

attended the fair, and Fletcher was a conspicuous figure in the festivities.

The young lawyer's partnership with John Wurts provided income for limited financial speculation. In an attempt in 1893 to diversify the county's economy, Fletcher helped organize a cotton mill and an experimental tobacco company. His most ambitious financial venture was the organization of a hemp fiber company in Dade County. He served as president of the concern and invested part of the $40,000 capital. Returns never fulfilled his lavish predictions, but for a time the company realized profits of fifty dollars an acre.[2]

Legal business still provided most of his income. Apparently Fletcher's chief legal assets were painstaking research, thorough legal knowledge, and a dispassionate but always effective delivery. A large proportion of his cases came from around the state, and he often appeared before the Supreme Court at Tallahassee. Clients included corporations with large stakes in state government, and legal judgments sometimes reached $10,000 with legal fees in the hundreds of dollars.[3] Despite pressure from corporation clients, his involvement with liberalism deepened during the 1890's.

Lucrative civil cases allowed the young attorney to avoid controversial criminal litigation with the exception of the Gato murder, Jacksonville's most sensational crime during the 1890's. Louise Gato was murdered in April, 1897. Fletcher aided the prosecution of Edward Pitzer, the accused slayer, but Pitzer won acquittal when his attorney capped an emotional appeal by fainting into the arms of the deputy sheriff.[4]

John Wurts dissolved the law partnership in 1896, and Fletcher continued his thriving practice in new offices at the First National Bank. The Jacksonville Bar Association, organized in 1897, acknowledged his legal pre-eminence by electing him its first president. Such professional recognition aided his spirited entrance into state politics.

Florida politics veered to the left between 1890 and 1900, although the full tide of agrarian radicalism never swept Florida as it did neighboring states. This was partly attributable to state liberals whose legislative success ameliorated conditions and

2. Duncan U. Fletcher to editor, Jacksonville *Florida Times-Union*, July 3, 1891.
3. Jacksonville *Florida Times-Union*, May 28, 1889.
4. Davis, *History of Jacksonville, Florida, 1513 to 1924*, p. 203.

bridged the chasm between Democrat and Populist.[5] While the progressive movement found its fullest expression in the career of Democratic Governor Napoleon Broward (1904–8), it influenced the programs of most successful politicians.[6] The state also mercifully escaped the reign of Negro-baiting politicians who rode agrarian revolt to power in Alabama, Georgia, Mississippi, and South Carolina. Only Governor Sidney J. Catts (1916–20) approached the demagoguery of Tom Watson, Cole Blease, Theodore Bilbo, and Tom Heflin, and even he was a pale replica of his bombastic contemporaries.

Early rumblings of political discontent arose from liberals in defense of progressive United States Senator Wilkinson Call. Only weeks after this 1890 skirmish, the battle shifted from Tallahassee to Jacksonville.[7] This struggle presents an excellent case study in southern urban progressivism, and Duncan Fletcher played a determining role. The *Florida Times-Union* charged that the "ring" which controlled the state executive committee opposed party nominees in Jacksonville.[8]

Democratic division in Duval County pitted the "straightout" faction against its "antis" adversary. The "straightouts," who opposed railroad and corporation dominance, refused to compromise their pseudo-Populist principles and gained their name for uncompromising or "straightout" Democratic support. When this faction gained control of city affairs in the early 1890's, conservative, pro-railroad forces protested their alleged machine rule of Jacksonville and formed an "anti" machine faction. Jacksonville

5. For detailed support of this thesis, see Kathryn T. Abby, "Florida Versus the Principles of Populism, 1896–1911," *Journal of Southern History*, IV (November, 1938), 462–75; Lloyd Walter Cory, "The Florida Farmers' Alliance, 1887-1892" (Master's thesis, Florida State University, 1963), pp. 77–132. See also Samuel Proctor, "The National Farmers' Alliance Convention of 1890, and its 'Ocala Demands,'" *The Florida Historical Quarterly*, XXVIII (January, 1950), 161–81.
6. Analysis of the Florida political careers of Wilkinson Call, John S. Beard, William B. Lamar, Albert W. Gilchrist, Nathan P. Bryan, Park Trammell, William S. Jennings, Sidney J. Catts, and Fletcher supports this conclusion.
7. Two authorities date the liberal-conservative conflict from 1881 and the Disston land sale. This appears accurate though its peak came in the 1890's. See Samuel Proctor, *Napoleon Bonaparte Broward*, p. 57, and William T. Cash, *History of the Democratic Party in Florida* (Live Oak, Florida: Florida Democratic Historical Foundation, 1936). For the best summary of Florida's ideological-political struggle, particularly in Duval County, see Proctor's study, chs. 4–7, 10, 11.
8. Jacksonville *Florida Times-Union*, November 23, 1890.

"straightouts" allied with state progressives, while "antis" supported the state's conservatives. Florida progressives included rural farmers and urban labor reformers who avoided alliance with the "radical" Populist-Socialist forces, but who did oppose railroad-corporation interests.

Governor Fleming, backed by railroads, controlled Jacksonville's mayor through his appointment of the city council. City Democrats caucused in June, 1891, and nominated Duncan Fletcher for mayor. They approached the council election as a mere formality in view of their eleven to seven majority, but three Fleming-appointed Democrats shocked the liberals by joining Republicans to defeat Fletcher and the Democratic nominee for council president.

Fletcher had lost the election long before the council's 1891 decision. He had sponsored a tax reform bill during 1890 which allowed Jacksonville to assess and tax corporation property. Several Democratic councilmen, influenced by members of the state executive committee, had joined Republicans to defeat his proposal and continue assessment by the state comptroller. This was a convenient arrangement for corporations which could control the comptroller's office through the governor and minimize taxes. Fletcher, president of the council, had called a Democratic caucus in 1890 and insisted on future loyalty on party legislation; but the mavericks had rejected compromise.[9]

Governor Fleming moved to aid his conservative Jacksonville lieutenants after Fletcher won the "straightout" nomination for mayor. Just before the June, 1891, election, the Governor's private secretary and State Democratic chairman, James P. Taliaferro, traveled to Jacksonville determined to defeat Fletcher.[10] Prior collusion became apparent at the council meeting when three Democrats and seven Republicans submitted only one slate of officers and carried every vote by identical ten-to-eight margins. Fletcher attributed the "antis" defection and "straightout" defeat to his 1890 bill "enabling the city to [tax] the property of railroad companies, streetcar lines, telegraph, telephone, and other corporate property. . . ."[11]

9. Duncan U. Fletcher to editor, Jacksonville *Florida Times-Union*, June 11, 1891.
10. Jacksonville *Florida Times-Union*, June 10, 1891.
11. Duncan U. Fletcher to editor, Jacksonville *Florida Times-Union*, June 11, 1891.

Fleming's machinations in local politics enraged Duval "straightouts." Fletcher resigned from the city council, and the liberal county organ declared "open warfare upon Mahoneism [machine rule] in Florida." The paper added that Fletcher was "stronger than ever with his party."[12]

"Straightouts" had the consolation of watching the new conservative government flounder in its own ineptitude. Tax reduction petitions rolled in from wealthy property owners and most were approved. Fifty-two such requests were received on July 23, 1891, fifty-three on July 24, fifty-nine more on July 31.[13] City tax revenue suffered a steady decline for the succeeding two years.

Angry insurgents turned their attention to the county Democratic apparatus. They gained control of the executive committee, elected John M. Barrs chairman, and entered a "straightout" slate of delegates to the county convention. Despite rumored "antis" voting fraud, the "straightouts" apparently won the election. But conservatives James P. Taliaferro, William M. Dancy, and Judge J. B. Christie controlled the convention and seated "antis" delegates from contested wards over the protests of the credentials committee. Conservatives elected their own representatives to the state convention, endorsed state Democratic leadership, and packed the county executive committee. Liberals, concluding that this usurpation "shows clearly the ambition of the F. C. and P. Railroad Company to control the politics of this state . . . ," bolted the convention, established their own executive committee, and called for new elections.[14]

The "straightouts" nominated Fletcher for the state legislature. He and N. B. Broward, liberal nominee for sheriff, campaigned actively before the "rump" election on May 19. Their work resulted in a rousing victory that left no doubt about the progressive zeal of Jacksonville Democrats. Despite a conservative boycott, 1,319 of the county's 1,800 registered Democrats voted the "straightout" ticket.[15] Insurgents interpreted returns as a mandate to oppose corporate domination and selected their own delegates to the Tampa Democratic convention.

12. Jacksonville *Florida Times-Union*, June 10, 1891.
13. Most petitions were accepted, including one assessment reduction from $7,000 to $4,000, and another from $22,000 to $15,000. See *Minutes City Council, Book 7*, pp. 53-70, and *Book 8*, pp. 47–52.
14. Jacksonville *Florida Times-Union*, April 17, 1892.
15. *Ibid.*, May 20, 1892.

James P. Taliaferro and the state executive committee held firm control at Tampa and seated the "antis" faction from Duval. Henry L. Mitchell, a man with corporation ties and a foe of Jacksonville progressives, won the nomination for governor. But Florida agrarians finally united to write a liberal platform calling for unlimited coinage of silver, state banking systems, a graduated income tax, government regulation of railroads, and legislation to end speculation in agricultural futures.[16]

Defeated at Tampa, the Duval progressives took their fight to the district Democratic convention at Gainesville. The "straightout" paper gave them little chance of winning; however, Fletcher argued their case before the Gainesville credentials committee, and its members voted ten to seven to accept his logic. Jacksonville progressives were ecstatic. The staid *Florida Times-Union* rejoiced: "Fletcher did things up brown. His argument was eloquent, logical, magnificent."[17]

Fletcher's eloquence so impressed the delegates that they chose him chairman *pro tempore* of the convention. Supporters of Charles M. Cooper persuaded Fletcher to second Cooper's congressional nomination, and Fletcher responded with a bold declaration of reform principles. Cooper was a Duval County liberal who entered the race as a distinct dark horse but finally won on ballot number 140. Fletcher won votes on the one-hundred-and-nineteenth ballot but remained loyal to his Jacksonville colleague. When Cooper finally gained the nomination, his forces chanted "Fletcher, Fletcher, Fletcher," and the young Jacksonville attorney responded with another tribute to reformism.[18]

The "straightouts" initiated a vigorous campaign against Duval conservatives following their triumphant sojourn in Gainesville. Fletcher and Broward again directed the effort. Broward Clubs mushroomed across the county, and Fletcher made a notable speech at one of these. "There was no party for the working man," he said, "whose principles were better for him, or under whose banner he could fight more successfully than that of the ['straightout'] democratic party."[19] This was effective oratory since conservative failure to appoint unionists to city jobs had alienated a power-

16. For text of the Tampa platform, see *ibid.*, March 28, 1894.
17. *Ibid.*, August 4, 1892.
18. *Ibid.*, August 6, 1892.
19. *Ibid.*, July 30, 1892.

ful bloc of voters. Fletcher also had endeared himself to laborers by his warm praise of Terence V. Powderly when the General Master of the Knights of Labor had visited Jacksonville in 1890.

The October, 1892, Democratic primaries proved disastrous to corporation candidates. Fletcher lost only one of Duval's twenty-four districts while winning a seat in the state legislature, 1,281 to 534. He spent the remaining weeks before the November general elections blasting Republicans in general and Ohio's William McKinley in particular. Election returns confirmed almost total Negro disfranchisement. Of the 2,365 residents who paid their poll tax, only 137 were colored.[20] Fletcher predictably swamped his Republican opponent.

Agrarian revolt, which was a more serious local menace than the GOP, disturbed Florida Democrats. General James B. Weaver, the Populist presidential nominee, visited Florida and encouraged farmer protest. Fletcher's performance at Gainesville had won favorable comment, and Democratic leaders enlisted him to stump with Senator Wilkinson Call to stem discontent in the hinterland. Despite their efforts, four Populists and one Independent won seats in the 1892 state legislature. Had the Democrats not written a liberal platform and nominated liberals Stephen R. Mallory and Charles M. Cooper for Congress, Populist gains would have been even greater.[21] Fletcher spent much of his term in the House of Representatives minimizing farmer defection by securing legislative reform.

The Florida legislature convened on April 4, 1893. The *Florida Times-Union* considered the freshman representative from Duval "one of the brightest of the many bright young men of Florida," a "thoughtful, dispassionate, broadminded man" who would honor the county.[22] Fletcher justified this confidence during the first session by nominating George M. Nolan of Orange County speaker *pro tempore* of the House. Nolan won and rewarded Fletcher with appointment to the potent Judiciary Committee.

Legislation sponsored by Fletcher reflected his advanced progressivism. He introduced bills establishing a state board of medical

20. *Ibid.*, September 18, 1892.
21. Samuel Proctor, "Napoleon Bonaparte Broward: The Portrait of a Progressive Democrat" (Master's thesis, University of Florida, 1942), p. 189. This pioneer study in Floridiana appears in published form in Proctor's *Napoleon Bonaparte Broward*, but the thesis contains more detail in certain areas.
22. Jacksonville *Florida Times-Union*, September 23, 1892.

examiners and broadening the power of the state health board. A Fletcher bill allowing Duval County to issue bonds for city improvements became law, but a statute to regulate party primaries, which received his endorsement, lost. He was one of only eighteen representatives supporting creation of a state penitentiary and abolition of the state's infamous convict lease system; the bill was defeated 18 to 41.[23]

Repeal of House Bill Four, which gave Florida's Governor control of Jacksonville affairs, headed Fletcher's list of priority legislation. N. B. Broward, John M. Barrs, and the "straightout" organization considered this second only to railroad regulation, since Governor Henry L. Mitchell promised more conservative appointments. Labor unions, allied to the progressives, also endorsed repeal. Fletcher led the crucial fight in the House.

The liberals' plan was officially designated Senate Bill Three and provided for an elective city government. This bill passed the Senate on May 2 and went to the House, where Fletcher maneuvered it past obstructionists and into a neutral committee. James P. Taliaferro attacked the bill as a move to restore Negro mastery. "Straightouts" shrewdly anticipated this argument and restored the poll tax, which had been excluded from the original version. Fletcher argued that the poll tax disfranchised Negro voters and dismissed Taliaferro's objection as a ruse to maintain railroad rule.

The bill came to the floor on May 5 amid great excitement. Conservatives attempted to amend the measure, but Fletcher blistered them with charges of "bad faith or buncombe." Opponents of the bill paraded the Negro with "glaring eyeballs, horns, talons, hoofs and a spiked-tail" to "frighten the members of the house."[24] Fletcher's motion to kill amendments passed 36 to 22, and Governor Mitchell signed Senate Bill Three into law on May 16, 1893.[25] Lobbyists John M. Barrs and James P. Taliaferro concluded the struggle with a brawl outside the House chamber. "Straightouts" had their bill and Taliaferro returned to Jacksonville with empty hands and a bloody nose.

23. Florida, *Journal of the House of Representatives, 1893* (Tallahassee: State Printing Office, 1893). For the struggle to end Florida's convict lease system, see Gordan N. Carper, "The Convict Lease System in Florida" (Ph.D. dissertation, Florida State University, 1964).
24. For text of debate, see Jacksonville *Florida Times-Union*, May 6, 1893.
25. Florida *House Journal, 1893*, pp. 431–34.

Railroad regulation consumed Fletcher's remaining attention. An investigation in 1887 by the *Florida Times-Union* had revealed railroad malfeasance and kindled fierce opposition to freight rates. The paper had discovered that it cost $1.05 to ship an 85-cent box of Florida hardware to Savannah, Georgia. One editor had recalled a car of freight sent one thousand miles over competing railroads for one-third the cost of fifteen miles over noncompeting track.[26] Florida had granted railroads seven million acres of land worth fifty-one million dollars following the Civil War, and state editors insisted that the state require fair rates.[27] As a result of this agitation, the legislature of 1887 had established a railroad commission to regulate charges.

Railroads had successfully demanded that the legislature abolish this commission in 1891. The commission's abolition had resulted from a number of factors: political retaliation by supporters of Senator Wilkinson Call against the senator's pro-commission opponents; opposition by railroad companies; an economy drive by Farmers' Alliance legislators.[28] Before the commission's defeat in 1891, freight rates on phosphate from central Florida to Jacksonville had amounted to $1.39 per ton, compared to $1.70 per ton to Savannah. Jacksonville rates had leaped to $3.05 and Savannah's to $2.95 per ton as soon as the commission was abolished.[29] Increased freight levies in Duval County had driven the Highland, Columbia City, and Branford mills into bankruptcy.[30] Small entrepreneurs had viewed repeal with alarm and had joined farmers demanding re-establishment of the railroad commission.

Fletcher, Goree Nelson of Sumter County, George D. Matthews, Jr., of Marion County, and E. A. Wilson of Lake County introduced a bill on April 24 to regulate railroads. The proposal would have prevented unjust rate discrimination, established a state railroad commission, and punished violators.[31] Corporations directed enormous pressure against the bill, and Tallahassee was

26. Jacksonville *Florida Times-Union*, February 3, 1887, quoting Cedar Key *Gulf View*.
27. Jacksonville *Florida Times-Union*, May 10, 1887.
28. Durward Long, "Florida's First Railroad Commission, 1887–1891," *Florida Historical Quarterly*, XLII (January, 1964), 255.
29. Lower Savannah rates spelled the end of Jacksonville's monopoly as a phosphate shipping center and provoked angry protests. See Jacksonville *Florida Times-Union*, March 21, 1894.
30. "Justice" to editor, Jacksonville *Florida Times-Union*, May 13, 1892.
31. Florida, *House Journal, 1893*, p. 258.

so full of railroad representatives that "if you throw a stick at a pointer dog . . . you are likely to hit several railroad lobbyists."[32] The Florida Senate, which considered the bill on May 10, echoed with anti-railroad philippics as bitter as any hurled by a southern populist. When the invective ended, the railroad commission died by a 10-to-16 vote. Progressives tried to salvage the bill in the lower house on May 23 with Fletcher pleading eloquently for regulation; but a motion to postpone the bill indefinitely carried over his protests 24 to 20.

Progressives lost most battles in the 1893 Florida legislature; failure of railroad, election, tax, and prison reforms left their major aspirations unfulfilled. Governor Mitchell even compromised the new Duval election code by appointing five conservative county commissioners. Despite these legislative defeats the session was a personal triumph for Representative Duncan Fletcher. His fame spread across the state, and his consistent support of progressive legislation endeared him to Florida "crackers" and urban reformers. Whether his actions resulted from pragmatism or his attachment to liberalism remains uncertain. Jacksonville's phosphate shipping industry and Florida's prosperity depended on commission regulated freight rates; effective self-government in Jacksonville demanded cessation of corporation control. Yet concern for human dignity clearly motivated his support of medical and prison reforms. His desire for progress, fear of unharnessed agrarian radicalism, and genuine revulsion at economic and social injustice inextricably meshed.

The legislative session also enhanced his reputation as an ethical but effective strategist. The *Florida Times-Union* concluded that he dominated the House "by sheer force of character and ability in argument. . . ."[33] The Tallahassee correspondent of the Savannah *Morning News* praised him highly: "First among these [in high popular favor] I am inclined to place Fletcher of Duval, who, long known as a successful and high-minded lawyer, has shown himself endowed with remarkable abilities as a legislator. . . . Mr. Fletcher may not be seen here again, but it is safe to say that he has before him the brightest of futures. . . ."[34]

The young legislator returned to Jacksonville as the darling

32. Jacksonville *Florida Times-Union*, May 8, 1893.
33. *Ibid.*, April 24, 1893.
34. *Ibid.*, June 8, 1893, quoting Savannah *Morning News*.

of the progressives. City officials set elections for July 18 to implement Senate Bill Three, and "straightouts" rewarded Fletcher with nomination for mayor. One local paper observed that "there never was a candidate for public office more nearly the unanimous choice of his party."[35] Conservative Democrats offered only token opposition in the primaries, then joined a rump labor faction in the general election.

Fletcher promised to make Jacksonville the commercial and shipping center of Florida and to recognize the rights of labor. Conservative Democrats borrowed from the reform movement of the 1880's and attempted to construct a Republican-Negro-Labor coalition. Led by William M. Dancy, they persuaded some labor leaders to join the "antis" cabal. The labor ticket appeared strong until J. J. Holland, state union leader and author of the victorious labor strategy of 1887, was dropped from the ticket. Coupled with labor's natural reluctance to ally with its traditional antagonists, this spelled doom for the "antis" faction. Large numbers of workingmen defected, repudiated the so-called labor ticket, and endorsed Fletcher. At one Dancy rally, most of the union members walked out.[36] Laborite-conservative Democrats elected four councilmen to twelve for the "straightouts" in the July election. Fletcher won strong union support, carrying three of the four wards which elected labor councilmen, and swept to a 759-to-552 victory.[37]

Mayor Fletcher provided Jacksonville's most progressive leadership between the Civil War and the twentieth century. The election broke years of fusionist-"antis" government and placed "straightouts" in firm control. Fletcher consolidated this advantage by securing John M. Barrs for city attorney and John N. C. Stockton for the Board of Public Works.

The new mayor proposed ambitious renovation involving hundreds of thousands of dollars in revenue. Since the projects benefited the city's future population, he favored bonding as the most equitable method of financing. City councilmen endorsed the plan, and Fletcher submitted a one-million-dollar bond issue to the people. He organized a bipartisan drive based on the argument that bonding was the only alternative to higher taxation. The

35. Jacksonville *Florida Times-Union,* July 8, 1893.
36. See letters to the editor, Jacksonville *Florida Times-Union,* July 16–18, 1893, from "Carpenter," "Workingman," and "Workman."
37. *Minutes City Council, Book 9,* p. 84.

program, which had been soundly defeated only a few years before, passed by a vote of 734 to 211. Atlanta and Montgomery viewed the bond issue with envy, and the New York *Commercial Advertiser* noted that Jacksonville thereby incurred an obligation "equal to one-fourth the total increase in ten previous years of all the cities of the South." This betokened "an enterprise new and —in view of the excellent uses to which the money is to be put— commendable."[38]

Fletcher not only provided new revenue, he also enforced tax collection with a passion. When the city collected only $966 of $131,000 in back taxes, he and City Attorney Barrs initiated 139 suits.[39] Citizens Gas and Electric Company and the Florida Central and Peninsula Railroad typified companies requesting tax reductions, but their pleas brought no response. City councilmen passed effective enforcement legislation, and tax collections climbed from $188,000 in 1893 to $282,000 in 1894. At the same time governmental efficiency allowed reduction of property taxes from 13.8 to 10.1 mills. The Mayor increased police and fire department salaries, paid bond interest, and still reduced the city budget from $149,500 in 1893 to $134,300 in 1894.[40]

Physical progress accompanied financial reform. Fletcher designated $300,000 of the bond revenue for construction of municipally owned electric and water plants. Jacksonville labor unions backed the project and the mayor hurried construction. The Jacksonville Electric Light Company sued to halt city provision of commercial power but failed to halt progress.[41] Electric lights soon brightened the main streets, and electric street cars replaced horse drawn vehicles. Completion of the city owned facilities in 1895 brought cost reduction for electricity, free public lighting for the entire city, and an annual profit of $18,000. Erection of municipal water works also permitted cheaper and more efficient service.

Street pavement, sewer extension, and public buildings accounted for $450,000 of the bond issue. Regulation of food markets and sanitation improvements nearly eliminated Jackson-

38. Jacksonville *Florida Times-Union*, October 14, 24, and 31, 1893, quoting New York *Commercial Advertiser*, Atlanta *Journal*, and Montgomery *Advertiser*.
39. *Minutes City Council, Book 9*, pp. 110–14.
40. *Ibid.*, pp. 475–81, and *ibid.*, *Book 10*, pp. 61–74.
41. *Ibid.*, *Book 9*, p. 579, and *Book 10*, pp. 61–74; and Jacksonville *Florida Times-Union*, September 16, 1896.

ville's annual epidemics. Dirt streets had plagued the city and only one block had been paved in the four years preceding the Fletcher administration. Under his direction, six miles of street were paved and ten more miles were contracted.[42]

Fire department improvement, waterfront expansion, and municipal construction absorbed $150,000. Extension of fire protection reduced insurance rates by 25 per cent and minimized fires such as the holocaust of 1891, which had nearly destroyed the city. The department attained its most efficient operation, and fires totaled only $11,000 in property loss during his administration.[43] Wharf and dredging improvements allowed large ships to dock at Jacksonville, and new city buildings dotted the skyline.

Jacksonville's morals concerned the mayor as vitally as her prosperity. He ordered a secret investigation of the police department to eliminate bribes for gambling and prostitution, dismissed several officers, and reorganized the force.[44] Raids on local gambling houses virtually eliminated that Jacksonville pastime. The city council passed laws against pornography and prize fighting, which Fletcher viewed as equally opprobrious. He opposed the city fathers in a futile effort to prevent Jacksonville's world championship boxing match between James J. Corbett and Charles Mitchell. Fletcher identified pugilism with "gambling, drinking, carousing, brutality and immorality" and pledged to save Jacksonville from such temptation.[45] Jacksonville declined salvation and Corbett disposed of Mitchell in the third round of the match in January, 1894.

Fletcher demonstrated his compassion for unfortunate Jacksonville residents when the depression of the 1890's brought high unemployment. He expanded aid to the poor and created a city unemployment agency. The mayor aided Jacksonville manufacturers and unions by requiring local labor and materials for all city contracts. His administration also initiated a maximum nine-hour day for city employees.[46]

Progress during Fletcher's two-year term surpassed the most optimistic "straightout" predictions. People united so completely behind the administration that one paper pronounced the end of

42. Jacksonville *Florida Times-Union*, January 3, 1895.
43. *Ibid.*, January 3, 1895.
44. *Minutes City Council, Book 9*, pp. 286–91.
45. *Ibid.*, p. 192.
46. *Ibid.*, pp. 166–67, 429.

partisanship.[47] When a minority of recalcitrant conservatives challenged Fletcher's bond issue in court, two thousand citizens of both factions filled the opera hall to overflowing in tribute to their mayor. The *Florida Times-Union* pronounced him the spokesman for a new era, predicting prophetically that "in due time his clarion voice will be heard as the colleague of the lawmakers at Washington. . . ."[48]

The reformism which swept Jacksonville "straightouts" to power reverberated across the state. Fletcher attempted to unify the Florida insurgents by inviting reform leaders to his office on February 28, 1894. C. B. Collins, Alexander St. Clair-Abrams, Alston W. Cockrell, Frank Clark, and Fletcher drafted a reform credo at the conference. It charged transportation companies with exorbitant levies, undue political influence, and unfair monopoly, while scolding the Democratic Party for refusing to pass effective regulation. The assembled progressives urged Florida voters to make railroad control the central issue in forthcoming elections.[49] The reformers organized in every Florida precinct to check corporation power, and Fletcher stumped the state for candidates who supported a railroad commission. Progress came slowly and the corporation-dominated Democratic convention refused to endorse regulatory legislation in 1894.

The 1894 campaign in Duval County brought a renewed conservative challenge. "Straightouts" nominated Fletcher for the state Senate, and he made railroad regulation his principal issue. This race prompted the most coherent and forceful statement of his early political philosophy: "It seems to me clear that at present the railroads are in control of the democratic party, and that they are making it the instrument . . . to control the internal affairs of the state. . . . To say democracy has spoken when democracy was made the mouthpiece of railroads, is to say that we must submit to their domination. . . . As a democrat I object to the party being handled by any one interest in the state for its particular use and benefit."[50]

N. B. Broward, Fletcher, and John M. Barrs carried the brunt

---

47. Jacksonville *Florida Times-Union*, January 5, 1894.
48. *Ibid.*, January 28, 1894.
49. *Ibid.*, March 11, 1894.
50. Duncan U. Fletcher to editor, Jacksonville *Florida Times-Union,* August 19, 1894.

of the Duval campaign. Several "straightout" Negro clubs supported them; and many unions, led by the cigar workers, also endorsed the ticket. Fletcher's speeches abounded with facts and statistics. He brandished endorsements of railroad regulation by southern dignitaries and cited affidavits from Florida shippers to illustrate exorbitant freight rates.

Evaluated on the basis of oratorical forcefulness, "straightouts" should have swept the election. But "antis" county commissioners eliminated the rhetorical advantage by appointing election inspectors with not a single Populist or "straightout" representative. Eleven of the twenty-eight inspectors reportedly worked for Jacksonville railroads. Mayor Fletcher countered by invoking a law which allowed policemen at election booths. When Sheriff Broward's deputies moved to halt illegal voting practices, "antis" inspectors simply closed the booths. Precincts containing half the city's population and most "straightout" strength reported no returns whatever. Fletcher lost to John E. Hartridge, 1,011 to 868.[51] Governor Mitchell removed Sheriff Broward from office and ignored obvious "antis" corruption.

The new conservative city government reversed Fletcher's progress, raised taxes 51 per cent, and reduced tax assessments on railroads and corporations by $250,000. Despite these Duval reversals, the statewide reform slate launched in February swept to victory. This liberal nucleus expanded until it won enactment of a new railroad commission in 1897.

The spectacular ascendancy of William Jennings Bryan in 1896 diverted Florida's attention from railroads to currency legislation. As late as 1892 the *Florida Times-Union* had advised the party to ignore silver coinage in favor of tariff revision, but the new apostle of the Democratic Party made free silver his gospel. Fletcher joined the silver bandwagon even before Bryan's Democratic convention triumph. He nominated a free silver advocate as temporary chairman of the county convention in June, 1896, but the silverites lost to a gold "bug." In July he addressed an audience of Jacksonville citizens and advocated unilateral free coinage of silver.[52]

Fletcher, Barrs, John N. C. Stockton, and other "straightouts" organized a Bryan and Sewall Central Silver Club in 1896

51. Jacksonville *Florida Times-Union*, October 3, 1894.
52. *Ibid.*, July 7, 1896.

to campaign for Democrats and free silver. Democratic conservatives countered with a nonpartisan Duval Sound Money Club
backing Republican William McKinley and the gold standard.
Barrs and Fletcher charged that even the state Democratic executive committee considered Bryan a dangerous Populist.[53] Conservatives, rent with dissension over currency, presented only half-
hearted opposition in the county elections, and "straightouts"
launched a decade of political control. Fletcher remained an ardent
"straightout" through the remainder of the decade, but his ardor
for politics waned, and he devoted more time to his legal career
and teen-age daughters.

It was during these same years that a nonpolitical event
occurred which reflected Fletcher's openness on racial relations,
openness at least when judged by contemporary American standards. In the last months of 1897 James Weldon Johnson, later to
become a prominent writer and official of the National Association
for the Advancement of Colored People, applied to become the
first Negro admitted to the bar in Duval County since Reconstruction. Fletcher served as a member of a three-man committee, presided over by Judge R. M. Call, which examined Johnson.
According to the Negro applicant, Fletcher was reputed to be "one
of the outstanding members of the Jacksonville bar," a man known
in the black community for his fairness and justice. When Major
W. B. Young demonstrated racial bias against Johnson, Fletcher
championed the black man's cause. After Young stalked from the
courtroom remarking, "I'll be damned if I'll stay here to see him
admitted," Fletcher made the motion to admit Johnson to the bar,
then offered his congratulations to the young lawyer.[54]

The complicated political strife in Jacksonville had its impact on rural areas of the state. Agrarian revolt in most southern
states took the form of third-party movements, but Florida farmers
largely ignored Populism because the Democratic Party responded
sympathetically to their demands.[55] Duncan Fletcher, N. B. Broward, Wilkinson Call, Stephen R. Mallory, and other progressives

53. *Ibid.*, July 29, 1896.
54. James Weldon Johnson, *Along This Way* (New York: The Viking Press
Edition, 1968), pp. 142–43. This autobiography also contains an interesting account by a perceptive black man of the "straightout" faction of the Democratic
Party in Jacksonville, pp. 140–45.
55. Proctor, *Napoleon Bonaparte Broward*, pp. 59–60. Proctor suggests a Democratic response to agrarian demands.

offered an alternative to both agrarian radicalism and standpat corporation rule. Unlike other southern states in the 1890's, liberal leadership came from Florida's urban areas as well as from her isolated rural hamlets. Labor-urban progressives combined with agrarian mavericks to win party leadership in the late 1890's. Fletcher's legislative innovation, leadership in forming a cohesive progressive faction, and imaginative mayoralty helped transform the Democratic Party into this responsive, broadly based alliance. He reaffirmed his belief that government must be sensitive to public problems if it was to be effective.

If Fletcher's pre-1900 political career is measured by the issues he endorsed, he must be judged a thoroughgoing progressive nearly a decade before progressivism swept the South. He opposed the convict lease system, conservative machine politics and attendant corruption; he endorsed railroad regulation, an equitable tax system bearing more heavily on corporations, extension of city services, reduced hours for labor, regulation of health practices, municipal control of utilities, and even a degree of racial justice.

When his motives for such positions are analyzed, a collage emerges constructed of political pragmatism, humanitarian liberalism, and his desire for moderate middle-class reform. No doubt Fletcher felt uncomfortable in coalition with Negroes and Knights of Labor even when he shared their political objectives. He slid out of such arrangements whenever political conditions allowed. But his political success before 1900, like his U.S. Senate career afterwards, hinged on his accurate analysis of the public climate of opinion and a philosophical elasticity which accommodated shifting ideologies.

CHAPTER III

Two Roads to Armageddon

FLORIDA'S POLITICAL STRUCTURE during the early twentieth century has been defined as "an incredibly complex melange of amorphous factions" characterized by dispersion of leadership and factional discontinuity.[1] Allies in one campaign became opponents in the next, and voters appeared unable to transform philosophical positions into consistent voting patterns. For a time, the liberal-conservative dichotomy gained pre-eminence; then this factionalism faded into a gray political twilight. Temporal political organization replaced ideological rigidity and aided Duncan Fletcher's career during the first bewildering decade of the new century.

Fletcher's brief political retirement was ended by a conflagration that destroyed most of Jacksonville. Beginning on the night of May 3, 1901, the fire raced through frame buildings in the heart of the city, destroying 146 city blocks with 2,368 buildings. People in Savannah, Georgia, reported the flare, and the smoke was observed in Raleigh, North Carolina. Every public building except one disappeared along with twenty-three churches and ten hotels. Ten thousand people, more than one-third of the population, lost their homes, and total property losses amounted to $15,600,000. A Jacksonville historian called it the largest fire in area and property loss experienced by any southern city up to that time.[2] Fletcher's office and house burned, but an alert clerk loaded

1. V. O. Key, Jr., *Southern Politics in State and Nation* (New York: Alfred A. Knopf, 1949), pp. 82–87.
2. Jacksonville *Florida Times-Union*, May 4, 5, 1901; T. Frederick Davis, *History of Jacksonville, Florida, 1513 to 1924*, pp. 219–28.

his law books in a wheelbarrow and saved them. The family salvaged only the silverware and a valuable violin from their home.[3]

With municipal elections scheduled for June 18, city leaders agreed that the new mayor must represent a general consensus. J. D. Burbridge and Fletcher clashed in the June 6 Democratic primary, and Fletcher carried every precinct on the way to a 959-to-425 vote triumph. His election restored the confidence of citizens who recalled his brilliant 1894–95 mayoralty.[4] Fletcher prefaced his administration with a ringing appeal for unity: "There is no room for thought of 'spoils,' or the reward of political adherents or punishment of political opponents. The all absorbing idea now is the restoration of Jacksonville."[5] Pleasant A. Holt, "straightout" leader in the 1890's, won the presidency of the city council, John N. C. Stockton returned to the Board of Public Works, and John M. Barrs became city attorney. A large Democratic majority on the city council assured implementation of the new mayor's program.

The city's immediate problem concerned general order and provision for ten thousand homeless residents. Mayor Fletcher relied on Governor William S. Jennings' declaration of martial law until the local Relief Association could restore stability. The federal government provided twelve thousand tents to house destitute citizens, and Jennings, a progressive friend of the mayor, offered state resources.[6] Donations of $225,000 poured into the city, and Fletcher utilized these funds to purchase rations, 477 sewing machines, and 172 sets of carpenter's tools. Fletcher's public works program put women to work sewing, men rebuilding, and 1,600 unemployed clearing and improving the city.[7]

Financing the monumental rebuilding required expanded revenue. Fletcher once again submitted a bond issue to his fellow citizens, and they demonstrated their confidence by accepting it 344 to 34. The mayor utilized the $400,000 bond issue to construct a

3. Wells, "Duncan Upshaw Fletcher," p. 25.
4. For example, see Edwin Hansford Rennolds' Diaries, No. 14, P. K. Yonge Library of Florida History, University of Florida. Hereafter cited as E. H. Rennolds' Diaries.
5. *Minutes City Council, Book 15*, pp. 151-52.
6. William S. Jennings to Duncan U. Fletcher, May 13, 1901; in William S. Jennings Letterbooks, P. K. Yonge Library of Florida History, University of Florida. Hereafter cited as Jennings Letterbooks.
7. Davis, *History of Jacksonville, Florida, 1513 to 1924*, p. 227.

new city hall and city market, extend the waterworks, improve the fire department, and construct bridges and viaducts; railroad extension to the city docks also enlarged Jacksonville's port capacity. Fletcher established an emergency hospital after the fire and considered it so valuable that he made it a permanent service. Destruction of half the city's taxable property necessitated financial retrenchment, and he reduced city employees and expenditures.

Fear of devastating fires spurred building reform. The council controlled new construction with building permits which allowed only brick structures in the central area; brick veneer and wooden buildings were permitted toward the edge of town. Between 1901 and 1903, 3,096 structures replaced those destroyed by fire; and the population increased by 6,000.[8]

Fletcher also conducted a vigorous campaign to enlarge the city-owned electric facilities. Partisanship revived over this issue, and the old "antis" faction, aided by council president P. A. Holt and John W. Dodge, proposed selling the electric plant to the Jacksonville Street Railway Company. City Attorney John M. Barrs blasted this proposal, and Fletcher supported him. Thanks to their fervor the facility remained under municipal control, and the council actually expended $74,000 to extend electric service during Fletcher's two-year term. On leaving office Fletcher commended the council for standing "emphatically . . . for municipal ownership of public utilities . . . which gives them deeper root in public esteem and confidence. . . ."[9]

Jim Crow visited Jacksonville during the Fletcher administration. Two Negro councilmen failed to kill an ordinance permitting streetcar conductors to assign seats and segregate cars. Negro representatives asked Fletcher to veto the measure when it passed the council. The mayor professed sympathy and agreed to champion repeal if the bill provoked trouble, but he finally approved it.[10]

Fletcher correctly summarized his own administration as one of action rather than rhetoric. Despite fragmentation of the old "straightout" organization, he maintained public control of city utilities. He constructed a modern city during his first term as mayor and rebuilt it in his second.

8. *Minutes City Council, Book 17*, p. 91.
9. *Ibid.*, p. 92; *ibid., Book 15*, pp. 158–61.
10. Jacksonville *Florida Times-Union*, November 9, 1901.

Education competed with local politics for Fletcher's attention. He served as a trustee of Stetson University during a period
of turmoil and chaired the Duval County Board of Public Instruc-
tion from 1900 to 1907.[11] When Jacksonville's schools vanished in
the 1901 fire, the school board owed $30,000. Relying on an in-
sufficient county tax levy and public donations, Fletcher pushed
construction of a $42,000 grammar–high school. He extended the
school term to eight months, unusually long for southern towns in
1903, and increased teachers' salaries.[12] At his direction, the county
constructed 40 wagons to transport country children to school, an
innovation which increased high school attendance from 100 to 321
between 1903 and 1905. By 1905, 2,500 white children were en-
rolled in county schools, and the educational debt had declined
from $71,800 to $32,000. He was particularly proud that his
system of transportation had made schools available to poorer
children.[13]

Mayor Fletcher sponsored additional taxes and educational
bond issues to construct Duval High School. Jacksonville citizens
invited him to speak at the cornerstone ceremony, and he stated
that free public schools constituted an absolute necessity, that there
could be no excuse for ignorance in America.[14] Curriculum concerned him and he requested his niece to fill what he considered a
critical gap by teaching Latin classes in the Fletcher home. He
finally persuaded school officials to hire a Latin and algebra teacher
at a salary of $80 a year.[15]

Fletcher softened the impact of Jim Crow legislation by providing education for Negroes. As a result of his urging, the school
board constructed an academy to accommodate 1,200 Negro stu-
dents. He promoted a Negro industrial training school to furnish
job skills and recommended that all philanthropic citizens help
finance it.[16]

The first decade of the new century also brought Fletcher
legal and financial success. As a civil lawyer, state government rep-

11. William S. Jennings to Duncan U. Fletcher, January 26, 1903, in Jennings
Letterbooks.
12. The average southern school term was 100 days in 1900, 130 days in 1910.
13. Jacksonville *Florida Times-Union*, May 16 and November 22, 1905.
14. *Ibid.*, April 5, 1907.
15. Duncan U. Fletcher to Ruth Huddleston, December 31, 1904; and Duncan
U. Fletcher to Francis Yerkes, undated, in Fletcher Papers.
16. Jacksonville *Florida Times-Union*, August 22, 1906.

resentative, and corporation attorney, he developed a practice netting $40,000 a year.[17] Financial success allowed him to invest in Fort Lauderdale real estate, erect a two-story home, and construct a six-unit apartment building. In addition he organized and served as president of the Citizens' Bank of Jacksonville. This wealth enhanced his political credentials.

The year 1900 was a turning point in Florida's political history. Conservative domination of state politics ended, and moderately liberal William S. Jennings launched a new era of Florida progressivism.[18] Governors Jennings, Broward, Albert W. Gilchrist, and Park Trammell initiated and expanded reform.

In Jacksonville "straightouts" ruled the county convention in May, 1900, and selected Fletcher as delegate to the state Democratic convention. William S. Jennings, campaigning for the gubernatorial nomination, suggested Fletcher as temporary chairman of the state gathering. Fletcher declined but agreed to accept the job of permanent chairman.[19] Progressive newspapers across the state endorsed him, and Jennings became so certain of the election that he suggested an outline for Fletcher's keynote speech. The two progressives planned to attack conservative ex-president Grover Cleveland, the gold standard, and Democratic "bossism," while endorsing silver, William Jennings Bryan, and state progressivism.[20]

Judge B. S. Liddon, former justice of the Florida Supreme Court, nominated Fletcher for permanent convention chairman on June 19, and seconding speeches praised his impartiality and parliamentary skill. But he lost the chairmanship to Thomas Palmer by a razor-thin 139½-to-137½ vote. Counties in every portion of the state supported him, with noticeable strength in the progressive stronghold of northwest Florida. Despite Fletcher's defeat, liberals controlled the convention and nominated Jennings for governor. Their platform endorsed control of trusts, a graduated income tax,

17. Washington *Post,* May 3, 1932; clipping in Fletcher Papers.
18. Jennings set the stage for Broward's program and remained a state drainage lawyer during Broward's administration. He also corresponded with state liberal leaders. See Austen Shuey Mann Papers, 1901–3, P. K. Yonge Library of Florida History, University of Florida. Mann was a Florida Populist leader.
19. Duncan U. Fletcher to William S. Jennings, June 8, 1900, in Jennings Letterbooks.
20. William S. Jennings to Duncan U. Fletcher, June 6 and 7, 1900, in Jennings Letterbooks.

unlimited coinage of silver, government control of transportation, direct election of United States Senators, municipal ownership of public utilities, an inheritance tax, and reform of the state convict lease system.[21]

Fletcher devoted his time for the next four years to the renovation of Jacksonville, but he maintained close ties with Governor Jennings. Both men served as trustees of Stetson University, and their friendship deepened. Jennings sought Fletcher's advice on patronage and funneled lucrative state legal business to his firm.[22]

Despite Fletcher's continued support of Jennings and progressivism, his corporation ties also increased, notably through his friendship with Joseph R. Parrott. Parrott, a Maine native, had met Georgian S. Price Gilbert at Yale University. When Parrott expressed a desire to practice law in the South, Gilbert had introduced him to Fletcher, a former undergraduate friend at Vanderbilt. Parrott had arrived in Jacksonville in 1885, and aided by the local attorney, had become counsel for the Jacksonville, Tampa, and Key West Railroad. Railroad baron Henry Flagler had hired Parrott in 1890, and he had served as head of Flagler's legal department for many years. He had become general manager of Flagler Enterprises in 1899, vice-president in 1909, and then president.[23] Parrott had enlarged his financial empire, serving as president of the Mercantile Exchange Bank, vice-president of the Florida National Bank, and director of the Jacksonville *Florida Times-Union*. Political and financial connections linked Parrott to the conservative faction dominated by James P. Taliaferro.

Fletcher had served frequently with Parrott in civic affairs and profited from the friendship during the 1890's when Parrott channeled a number of railroad cases to his benefactor. This personal link became official in 1902 when Parrott retained Fletcher as counsel for the Florida East Coast Railway Company. Fletcher also represented several Georgia railroads in Jacksonville.[24]

21. Jacksonville *Florida Times-Union*, June 21, 1900.
22. William S. Jennings to Duncan U. Fletcher, October 21, 1902, and July 25, 1901, in Jennings Letterbooks.
23. Sidney W. Martin, "Flagler's Associates in East Florida Developments," *Florida Historical Quarterly*, XXVI (January, 1948), 256–58.
24. J. E. Hall to J. B. Hodges, May 5, 1936, Box 107, in James B. Hodges Papers, P. K. Yonge Library of Florida History, University of Florida. Hereafter cited as Hodges Papers.

Conservative spokesmen from other parts of the state met and apparently liked the personable attorney. Peter O. Knight became one of Fletcher's closest friends. Knight, a Pennsylvania native, exercised great influence on Tampa politics. He had organized the Tampa Phosphate Company (1890), Tampa Tribune Publishing Company (1891), a street railway and electric light company (1892), Exchange National Bank (1894), Tampa Gas Company (1895), Florida Brewing Company (1896), and numerous other enterprises.[25]

According to the political tradition, Fletcher's most heinous capitulation came in April, 1901. On April 9, a railroad spokesman introduced a bill in the state legislature making incurable insanity grounds for divorce. Henry Flagler reportedly instigated the bill to permit the divorce of his mentally disturbed wife and spent $20,000 bribing legislators to pass it.[26] Coincidentally, Flagler donated $10,000 to build a gymnasium at Florida Agricultural College on April 11. The bill passed both houses and Governor Jennings signed it into law on April 25. The seventy-one-year-old Flagler filed divorce proceedings under the bill's provisions on June 3, and seven days after his divorce married a thirty-four-year-old North Carolinian. The bill provoked a storm of controversy, especially from religious groups, and many legislators who voted for it subsequently lost their seats.[27]

Some Floridians contended that Fletcher helped purchase the state legislature.[28] Since these events occurred a year before his formal retention by the Florida East Coast Railroad, such charges appear to have been politically motivated. Possibly he did lobby for the bill; he arrived in Tallahassee on April 8, the day before the bill was introduced, and remained for several days.[29] At any

25. Peter O. Knight to James W. Morris, March 6, 1936, in Scrapbook M, Peter O. Knight Collection, P. K. Yonge Library of Florida History, University of Florida. Hereafter cited as Knight Collection.
26. Sidney W. Martin, *Florida's Flagler* (Athens, Georgia: University of Georgia Press, 1949), pp. 186–91.
27. W. E. Mabry to Austen Shuey Mann, undated, in Austen Shuey Mann Papers.
28. Jerry W. Carter, Fletcher's 1926 opponent, maintained this position. State Librarian Dorothy Dodd recalls this charge in Fletcher's subsequent campaigns. Perusal of the Broward papers reveals several letters mentioning this reason for not supporting him. Interviews with Dr. Dorothy Dodd, June 22, 1964, and Jerry W. Carter, May 15, 1964, at Tallahassee, Florida.
29. Jacksonville *Florida Times-Union*, April 11, 1901.

rate, in Fletcher's later career he was innocent of unethical conduct. Napoleon Broward, a member of the legislature and an unquestioned liberal, voted for the Flagler bill out of conviction.[30] Fletcher conceivably represented Flagler as a lobbyist with an equally clear conscience.

Though Fletcher's conservative bent became more pronounced after 1902, railroad affiliation and political reaction were not necessarily synonymous. Florida progressives often invested in and represented railroads, since the lines offered lucrative investment and substantial legal fees. John N. C. Stockton served as president of the Jacksonville and Mayport Railroad Company, and John M. Barrs was a leading stockholder in the Jacksonville and Atlantic Railroad. Corporation opponents of John M. Barrs and even Napoleon Broward portrayed them as pawns of the railroad barons.

Fletcher's conservative clients and political supporters unquestionably influenced his political views. They accounted in part for his contradictory voting record in the United States Senate and reinforced his conservative view of federal regulatory power and his aversion to central government. Yet they did not alter his basic philosophy that government must respond to public needs even if this meant disturbing otherwise inviolate state or private prerogatives. He remained convinced that order and progress could be maintained only by insuring broad economic opportunity and social mobility.

The "straightouts" achieved their ultimate goal in 1904 when Napoleon B. Broward won the governorship. John M. Barrs opposed Frank Clark for Congress and John N. C. Stockton announced for Taliaferro's United States Senate seat. Opponents dubbed Broward-Barrs-Stockton the "three friends" and blasted their "machine." The three candidates often campaigned together, attacking corporations and railroads. Robert Davis, a pro-railroad conservative, opposed Broward in the governor's race. Fletcher stayed out of the contest until the runoff and then scheduled a speech at a Broward rally in St. Augustine. One Davis speaker at the rally parried charges of corporation dominance by referring to Fletcher, a railroad attorney who supported Broward.[31]

State editors subsequently recalled Fletcher's support of

30. Broward's railroad political opponents in 1904 even accused him of duplicity for supporting the bill. See *ibid.*, May 24, 1904, quoting Punta Gorda *Herald*.
31. Jacksonville *Florida Times-Union*, June 2, 1904.

Broward in 1904. The DeLand *Record*, a pro-Broward paper, indicted the governor in 1908 for ridiculing Fletcher, "who went to the stump for Broward when [he] was running for governor."[32] Editors of the Gainesville *Daily Sun*, DeSoto County *News*, and Dade City *Star* published similar opinions. Former Broward adherents charged the governor with ingratitude for opposing a man who had always remained loyal.[33]

Broward and Fletcher maintained mutually cordial relations in the interim after 1904, and the new governor wasted no time in rewarding his old "straightout" ally. During the 1904 elections, Fletcher defeated twenty-four Duval aspirants for a place on the State Democratic Executive Committee. Shortly after the election, William James Bryan, Broward's Jacksonville lieutenant, launched a letter-writing campaign to gain control of the state committee. He wrote that rumors of Democratic defection in the forthcoming general election necessitated control of the state campaign apparatus by a Broward loyalist. Fletcher, he argued, while a fair and impartial Democrat, "is at the same time a loyal friend and ardent supporter of Mr. Broward . . . and it is believed by the friends of Mr. Broward that his campaign should be in the hands of his friends."[34] The letter encouraged each member either to attend the state committee session or forward his proxy.

When the state committee met at Jacksonville on July 9, 1904, Bryan nominated Fletcher as chairman of the Florida Democratic Party. John M. Barrs seconded the nomination, maintaining that the chairmanship should go to a man who had backed Broward in the Democratic primary.[35] Conservatives tried to delay the vote, but the well-organized progressives rolled over them and elected Fletcher chairman by a 31-to-20 vote.

Fletcher responded by organizing the most vigorous Democratic campaign in years. He and Broward spoke in every part of the state, concentrating on areas with Socialist and Republican strength. He attacked Theodore Roosevelt and the Republican

---

32. Tampa *Morning Tribune*, May 17, 1908, quoting the DeLand *Record*.
33. Gainesville *Daily Sun*, April 26, 1908; Jacksonville *Florida Times-Union*, April 18, 1908, quoting DeSoto County *News* (Arcadia); and Tampa *Morning Tribune*, April 5, 1908, quoting Dade City *Star*. See also Arthur Lee to Napoleon B. Broward, undated, in Napoleon B. Broward Papers, P. K. Yonge Library of Florida History, University of Florida. Hereafter cited as Broward Papers.
34. For text of letter, see Jacksonville *Florida Times-Union*, July 10, 1904.
35. *Ibid.*

Party for weakening the Interstate Commerce Commission, promoting colonialism in Asia, "big stick" diplomacy, militarism, and appointing unqualified Negroes to federal office. Floridians heeded their appeal by voting for Alton B. Parker over Roosevelt, 27,046 to 8,314, and gave Broward an even larger margin.

The Democratic Executive Committee, under Fletcher's guidance until 1908, reflected Broward's liberalism. In March, 1905, Fletcher, Stockton, and Raymond D. Knight drafted a new election code. The law prohibited large corporation contributions to candidates on penalty of annulment of the corporation's charter. Other provisions forbade wholesale payment of poll taxes and allowed the state committee to appoint one election inspector for each precinct.[36] Only a proposal to abolish the poll tax failed. Fletcher formulated strategy for the election reforms in consultation with Broward.[37]

Progressives on the executive committee also controlled state Democratic policy. Fletcher torpedoed a conservative effort to nominate William Randolph Hearst as the party's 1908 presidential candidate by winning committee endorsement of William Jennings Bryan. In August, 1906, Fletcher addressed a crowd of 20,000 which gathered to honor the "Great Commoner" at New York City's Madison Square Garden.[38]

While relations with Stockton and Broward remained placid, John M. Barrs began to question Fletcher's fidelity. The controversy developed over a bill in the state legislature extending railroad track to Key West. Fletcher and other members of the Jacksonville Board of Trade endorsed the bill, but Barrs wrote an angry denunciation. He argued that the bill, by reassessing railroad taxes, would transfer cost of the extension from Henry Flagler to the taxpayers. Such action would virtually destroy the state railroad commission.[39]

Broward dismissed this protest and supported the bill. When Fletcher learned of Barrs' attack, he attempted to resign as chairman of the state committee, but Broward dissuaded him:

36. *Ibid.*, March 24, 1905. Multiple payment of poll taxes by large companies was a particularly iniquitous practice. One source paid poll taxes for 1,500 Jacksonville voters in 1904, and liberals Broward, Barrs, and Stockton were massacred in their home county. See *ibid.*, June, 1904.
37. Duncan U. Fletcher to N. B. Broward, July 12, 1904, in Broward Papers.
38. Jacksonville *Florida Times-Union*, June 23, and September 2, 1906.
39. John M. Barrs to N. B. Broward, April 20, 1905, in Broward Papers.

I am glad to know that you are pleased at my action in regard to the railroad extension bill for Key West.

I do not see the logic of your resigning the chairmanship of the State Democratic Executive Committee, because you chance to represent a railroad company as attorney. I fear that you are too thin-skinned. You, perhaps, would not appreciate the very delicate position you occupy, [as Broward's spokesman?] unless your attention was called to it in some way, and I certainly do not approve of your resignation. No one has any doubt about your political integrity, and while persons in their comments are sometimes careless, I am satisfied that I express the sentiment of all your friends. . . . Sometimes we are misjudged, sometimes we are reported wrong, which temporarily affects our reputation, but our character remains the same and the heart and integrity are not affected, they will triumph in the affections of our friends, though we may spat and squabble at times.[40]

This tactful vote of confidence apparently soothed Fletcher's ruffled feelings, for he remained as state chairman.

Florida newspapers reported in the fall of 1907 that friends of Fletcher were urging him to campaign for the United States Senate. William James Bryan announced his candidacy on November 15, and Fletcher followed two days later. Boredom and a fatiguing law practice influenced his decision to run.[41] Persistent rumors suggested that Governor Broward would enter the race, but he declined because three personal friends—Fletcher, Bryan, and John S. Beard—had announced, and his candidacy would further disperse the moderate-liberal vote. He preferred to delay until 1910 and oppose railroad spokesman James P. Taliaferro.[42]

Incumbent Senator Stephen R. Mallory died on December 23, and Broward appointed W. James Bryan to replace him. Broward supported Bryan for the nomination and believed the appointment would aid him in the campaign.[43] The governor's decision reflected personal preference for Bryan rather than an-

---

40. N. B. Broward to Duncan U. Fletcher, May 9, 1905, in Broward Papers.
41. Washington *United States News*, April 30, 1934, and Washington *Post*, May 3, 1932, in Fletcher Papers. For a detailed discussion of the 1908 senatorial primary, see Wayne Flynt, "The 1908 Democratic Senatorial Primary in Florida" (Master's thesis, Florida State University, 1962).
42. N. B. Broward to John C. Wills, December 20, 1907, and N. B. Broward to J. W. Brady, February 19, 1908, in Broward Papers.
43. N. B. Broward to Albert H. Roberts, December 27, 1907, in Broward Papers.

tipathy toward Fletcher. When former Governor Jennings endorsed Fletcher, Broward wrote a political confidant "that the friends of the people are seriously divided [between Fletcher and Bryan], while the corporations present a solid front."[44]

Broward's dilemma intensified when interim Senator Bryan died of typhoid fever in March, 1908. For several weeks Fletcher dominated the race. He instructed his political aides to enlist former Bryan supporters, while his managers launched a propaganda barrage unprecedented in previous state politics.[45] The governor ended this political monopoly by appointing W. H. Milton, a wealthy west Florida banker, to fill Bryan's unexpired term. Appointment of a man who possessed no personal political aspirations renewed rumors that Broward planned to enter the race. He ended the speculation by announcing his candidacy on March 27.

The most obvious factor in the subsequent campaign was the fragmentation of progressive strength. Candidates in the Senate race reflected this internecine struggle, for Broward's three opponents—William B. Lamar, John Beard, and Fletcher—all had supported him in the 1904 governor's contest. Weekly papers, largely Broward advocates in 1904, split with over half opposing him in 1908.[46] The Jacksonville *Floridian*, Milton *Index*, and DeLand *Record*, all influential papers, changed allegiance between 1904 and 1908. Other liberal papers solved their dilemma by endorsing John N. C. Stockton, Broward's close ally, for governor and Fletcher for senator. Many progressive Floridians voted straight liberal tickets, substituting Fletcher for Broward in the senate race.[47] One irate former Broward supporter condemned the governor for entering the campaign after writing him that Fletcher was "without a pier [*sic*] in Florida today."[48]

Fletcher also suffered from the split. The official organ of the state Farmers' Union exemplified Florida's political schizophrenia by praising Fletcher before Broward's candidacy, and damning him as the spokesman for Jacksonville's "saloons, bar-

44. N. B. Broward to W. R. Carter, February 5, 1908, in Broward Papers.
45. Duncan U. Fletcher to J. B. Hodges, April 2, 1908, Box 3, in Hodges Papers. See advertisements in Daytona *Gazette-News*, March, 1908, and Panama City *Pilot*, April 9, 1908.
46. Tampa *Morning Tribune*, April 10, 1908, quoting Miami *News-Record*.
47. Duval County farmer Edwin H. Rennolds voted for Stockton, Park Trammell for Attorney General, and Fletcher. E. H. Rennolds' Diaries, Number 14.
48. Arthur Lee to N. B. Broward, April 21, 1908, in Broward Papers.

rooms and hell holes" afterward.[49] Individual progressives praised
Fletcher while switching to Broward.[50]

The platforms of the two principal candidates were models
of progressive reform. Broward proposed federally enforced freight
rates, tariff revision, financial reform, trust busting, free rural mail
delivery, coastal development, and national drainage legislation.
Fletcher endorsed railroad regulation, arbitration of labor disputes,
Philippine independence, graduated income tax, tariff revision, and
governmental appropriations for harbors, rivers, and waterways; he
opposed nationalization of railroads and American colonialism.
Since Floridians suffered from the general financial recession, he
attacked trusts and battered Wall Street. His speeches abounded
with excerpts from the muckraking writers Ida M. Tarbell, Upton
Sinclair, and Thomas Lawson. "Gambling sharks and rascals in
Wall Street," he told the throngs, "soaked millions of dollars out
of the South."[51] He proposed regulation of the Treasury Department during financial panics and the prevention of certain Wall
Street practices.

With little to choose from in the similar platforms, the
voters' attention was diverted to personalities and peripheral issues.
Broward assumed a defensive posture from the outset and controversy raged around his gubernatorial programs. Fletcher condemned the "Broward political machine" and charged that the
governor's Everglades drainage scheme would take five hundred
years to complete. Farm spokesmen complained that Broward
spent more time draining swamps than tending to agricultural
problems.[52] Labor disputes and controversy over relocation of the
University of Florida also cost Broward votes. Floridians tradition-
ally frowned on incumbents seeking office, and one paper satirized
Broward's absence from the capital by proposing that the state
pay his secretary and rent the governor's mansion for a factory.[53]

Paradoxically, alleged corporation collusion proved Broward's Achilles heel. When the governor's drainage program floun-
dered in litigation, attorney William S. Jennings had negotiated a

49. Jasper *News*, March 27 and June 12, 1908.
50. Juan C. Edmundoz to N. B. Broward, April 13, 1908; Edward J. Leonardy
to N. B. Broward, June 10, 1908; D. C. Keys to N. B. Broward, April 30, 1908;
W. B. Forman to N. B. Broward, April 17, 1908; in Broward Papers.
51. Tallahassee *Weekly True Democrat*, June 5, 1908.
52. Gainesville *Daily Sun,* June 6, 1908.
53. Jacksonville *Florida Times-Union*, April 17, 1908.

compromise which recognized railroad claims to $125,000 and 440,000 acres of land. Fletcher castigated this "surrender" to the railroads. Broward's controversial appointment of Milton as interim senator further identified him with conservative interests, and Fletcher reminded "cracker" audiences that Milton had served as president of two national banks, four state banks, and as director of a railroad. Anti-Broward forces charged that the governor contracted his dredging and towing company to the Florida East Coast Railroad for $5,000.[54]

First primary results supported the accusation of Broward's corporation duplicity. His spokesmen had predicted before the vote that he would lose every eastern county dominated by the Florida East Coast Railroad. Instead, he carried the east coast counties of St. Johns, Volusia, Brevard, St. Lucie, and Dade. One conservative paper concluded that the railroad interests had knifed Fletcher and supported Broward.[55] In a final ironic twist, the railroad-dominated *Florida Times-Union* maintained a mystifying neutrality in the runoff. This ruse compromised Broward's reform reputation and blunted his allegation that railroads controlled Fletcher.

Broward continually charged that Fletcher owed his first loyalty to the corporations. Hubbel's *Law Dictionary* listed Fletcher as counsel for the Georgia Southern and Florida Railroad, the Florida East Coast Railroad, and the Fidelity and Deposit Company of Maryland. According to Broward, he had supported his opponent for chairman of the state executive committee only after Fletcher had pledged to ignore corporation demands. Fletcher had used his influence instead, said the governor, to end regulation of the Florida East Coast Railroad.[56]

Fletcher retorted that he represented corporations like any other client. Representing murderers did not make him a co-conspirator and representing railroads did not make him their pawn. No railroads attempted to "dictate my politics, interfere with my vote . . . or my political principles."[57] Fletcher met the

54. Duncan U. Fletcher, *What Has Broward Done for the People?* 1908 campaign document, in Broward Papers.
55. Tallahassee *Weekly True Democrat*, June 12, 1908.
56. N. B. Broward, "Absolute Facts Regarding Duncan U. Fletcher," 1908 campaign document, in Broward Papers.
57. Duncan U. Fletcher, *Fletcher Replies to the Malicious Misrepresentations of Broward*, 1908 campaign document, in Broward Papers.

issue squarely in a Tampa speech: "Is a railway or capital necessarily an evil? Shall we say to the capitalists and developers that
we look upon them as interlopers and interferers? I believe that
railroads and corporations should not dabble in politics, but
the man who labors for them is not contaminated any more than
if he were engaged by any other private or public interest."[58] This
approach endeared him to the businessmen and left him little
worse among Florida "crackers."

A clandestine and less sophisticated charge against Fletcher
involved his religion. Rumors circulated that Fletcher was an
atheist, and he incorrectly attributed the rumors to Broward. The
explosive reports were quieted by a denial from his old friend,
Pastor W. A. Hobson of Jacksonville's First Baptist Church.[59]

Fletcher's well-financed campaign clearly surpassed Broward's
tardy effort. Master organizer Pleasant A. Holt devised an in-
genious strategy for blitzing the rural areas; teams distributed
posters and recorded each undecided voter for follow-up letters.[60]
By the time Broward entered the campaign, numerous political
leaders owed allegiance to his opponent. In addition, Broward was
hopelessly in debt and could hardly match Fletcher's financial
support.[61]

Broward hoped to compensate for lack of funds by winning
the endorsement of Thomas E. Watson, Georgia agrarian leader.
When spokesmen for Broward requested Watson's endorsement in
The Jeffersonian, the Georgian responded with ringing praise. He
wrote that no state had a better governor than Broward and "no
state will have a better Senator . . . if [Florida] chooses him for
that place."[62] Watson distributed 250 free copies of The Jeffersonian to his wavering Florida readers and wrote follow-up articles
for state newspapers.

Broward led the first ballot with 19,038 votes, compared
to 17,208 for Fletcher and Lamar's 12,572. Most conservatives supported Lamar, with Fletcher and Broward dividing the liberal

58. Tampa Morning Tribune, May 8, 1908.
59. Gainesville Daily Sun, June 9, 1908.
60. P. A. Holt to J. B. Hodges, April 2, 1908, Box 3, in Hodges Papers.
61. Broward's correspondence reveals dozens of unpaid debts, and he protested
that money was "almost obsolete." N. B. Broward to F. M. Simonton, December
13, 1907, in Broward Papers.
62. J. S. Blitch to Thomas E. Watson, May 23, 1908, in Thomas E. Watson
Papers, Southern Historical Collection, University of North Carolina. Also
see The Jeffersonian, May 28, 1908, in the Flowers' Collection, Duke University.

vote.[63] Broward's lieutenants attempted to neutralize Fletcher's advantage in the runoff by paying poll taxes for prospective voters, but corporations surpassed their belated effort by qualifying 1,200 Jacksonville residents with one check.[64] Both John Beard and Lamar endorsed Fletcher, and reluctant conservatives joined enthusiastic progressives to elect him senator in the runoff, 29,151 to 25,563. Broward attributed his defeat to Fletcher's campaign chest, insufficient time to organize, and the division of the progressive vote between himself and Fletcher. Bitterly disappointed, he confided privately that in his opinion the railroads had elected Florida's senator.[65]

The liberal Pensacola *Journal*, a pro-Broward paper, regretted the governor's defeat but reaffirmed its faith in Fletcher's democracy and progressivism. Two other Broward journals, the Ft. Myers *Press* and St. Petersburg *Independent*, considered Florida's senator-elect an advocate of the common man.[66] Even Broward reached a reconciliation in the following years.

The 1908 senatorial primary demonstrated the fragmentation of the progressive movement into several factions. This, rather than basic philosophical divergence, resulted in Broward's defeat. Progressive coherence before 1908 was an exception to the "every man for himself" principle of Florida politics. Unionists, farmers, urban reformers and conservatives reasserted Florida's penchant for defeating incumbent politicians.

Fletcher overwhelmed his Republican opponent in the general election. During the campaign he endorsed direct election of United States senators, the income tax, publication of campaign contributions, federal guarantee of bank deposits, free trade, and states' rights. Concluding on a more conservative note, he indicted Republicans for suggesting that "we have grown beyond the Constitution; that courts should, by construction, make law. . . ."[67]

Florida's senator-elect utilized the months before the congres-

63. The conservative Tallahassee *Weekly True Democrat* opposed Fletcher's former "straightout" identification and praised Lamar, March 13, 1908.
64. Tom Lecherty to N. B. Broward, May 4, 1908, in Broward Papers. The primary law forbidding this practice passed in May, 1909.
65. N. B. Broward to Claude L'Engle, June 25, 1908; and N. B. Broward to James H. Jones, June 24, 1908; in Broward Papers.
66. Pensacola *Journal*, June 21 and 26, 1908, quoting Ft. Myers *Press* and St. Petersburg *Independent*.
67. Jacksonville *Florida Times-Union*, October 20, 1908.

sional session to encourage southern waterway development, a project which had attracted his interest for many years. Waterways agitation comparable to that of the 1820's had engulfed the nation. The revival, which had begun about 1895 and which lasted well into the new century, was sustained by three factors: Theodore Roosevelt's emphasis on conservation, the desire for commercially navigable rivers, and concern for exorbitant railroad freight rates. Claims that water transportation permitted cheaper movement of products attracted farm-state backing. Peak activity came between 1906 and 1910 when a series of waterway conferences convened.[68]

Waterway agitation in Florida stemmed from coastal businessmen and farmers. Florida pineapple growers complained that the Florida East Coast Railroad used its monopoly to discriminate against them. Only railroads conducted organized opposition to Florida waterway development.[69]

The Mississippi to Atlantic Inland Waterway Association met at Columbus, Georgia, in November, 1908. Its leaders planned an inland route from the Mississippi to Apalachicola, Florida, then across the peninsula by canal to Jacksonville. Delegates elected Fletcher president, and he responded with a large donation.[70] Fletcher envisioned the cross-Florida canal as a means of cutting 1,000 miles from United States–Latin American trade routes, thus opening this lucrative market.

The new congressional session interrupted this grandiose commercial scheme. Senator Fletcher loosely allied with southern progressives in the Sixty-first Congress, but vacillated on tariff reduction. Rapidly growing St. Lucie County produced the largest pineapple crop in the world, and Fletcher's constituents opposed admission of competitive Cuban citrus. Fletcher denounced tariffs as an unlawful tax on consumers, then spent hours convincing colleagues—and presumably himself—that Florida products deserved special consideration and protection.[71] Senators Taliaferro and Fletcher won Republican support and passed an amendment to the Payne-Aldrich Tariff increasing Florida pineapple rates. However,

68. Harold G. Moulton, *Waterways Versus Railways* (New York: Houghton Mifflin Company, 1926).
69. Jacksonville *Florida Times-Union,* June 7, 1909; Pensacola *Journal,* July 16, 1908, and July 23, 1908, quoting Albany (Georgia) *Herald.*
70. D. U. Fletcher to N. B. Broward, September 14, 1909, and a pamphlet in the Broward Papers.
71. U.S., *Congressional Record,* 61st Congress, 1st Session, 1911, XLVI, 1624-29.

the freshman senator maintained some consistency with his principles by then opposing the tariff bill, which passed on July 8, 1909. President William Howard Taft liked Florida's junior senator and ended the session by dubbing him "old pineapples" in honor of the Floridian's advocacy of restrictive duties on Cuban citrus.[72]

Conservative Floridians praised Fletcher's protection of state products and declared that they did not "care a continental what the Democratic platform declaimed . . ."; but the junior senator was considerably more popular with conservatives and President Taft than with state progressives.[73] Moderate papers such as the Tampa *Tribune* and Orlando *Reporter-Star* declared for "Democratic principles first, and for . . . Sea Island cotton and pineapples second. . . ."[74] Tom Watson could hardly contain his wrath: "Fletcher and Taliaferro have followed Rhode Island's Mary [Senator Nelson W. Aldrich] like two little docile and affectionate lambs. . . . *Everytime* that Aldrich cried '*Sheep! Sheep!*' there went Fletcher and Taliaferro . . . bleating with the Republican flock and swelling the tuneful chorus of the standpat '*Ba-a! Ba-a!*'"[75]

Fletcher's senatorial record for the next three years remained inconsistent. He rigorously adhered to the time-honored tradition that freshmen United States Senators should be seen and not heard. Though he sought funds for Florida waterways and harbors, he seldom commented on priority legislation before the Senate. One searches the *Congressional Record* in vain to find his comment on tax reform, government regulation of business, and other significant matters.[76]

Two clues to Fletcher's early senatorial philosophy can be found. One emerges from his regular and faithful service on the Senate's special committees. Florida's Governor Albert W. Gilchrist had continued Broward's Everglades' drainage project.[77] Fletcher, assigned to participate in an investigation of Agriculture Department expenditures, changed his position from scathing criticism

72. Interview with Miss Sally Puleston, Monticello, Florida, May 27, 1963.
73. Jacksonville *Florida Times-Union*, July 3, 1909, quoting Ocala *Star*.
74. *Ibid.*, August 28 and 31, 1909, quoting Tampa *Tribune* and Orlando *Reporter-Star*.
75. *The Jeffersonian*, July 15, 1909, in Flowers' Collection.
76. See U.S., *Congressional Record*, 61st and 62d Congresses, 1909–13, XLIV–XLIX.
77. For information on Gilchrist's program, see manuscript of press release by Albert W. Gilchrist in A. W. Gilchrist Papers, copies at Florida State University.

of the program while opposing Broward in 1908 to senatorial defense of the project by 1912.[78] He did not subsequently oppose
federal "pork barrel" expenditures—unless they benefited his political enemies.

Another special committee assignment involved the struggle
between Secretary of Interior Richard A. Ballinger and progressive
Forestry Department chief Gifford Pinchot. When Congress
launched an investigation of the Interior Department's handling
of national conservation policy, Fletcher was appointed to the committee.[79] Counsel Louis D. Brandeis attempted to broaden the
scope of the investigation by considering the political involvements
of Ballinger's appointees, but conservative Republican congressmen protested. Fletcher, aided by progressive Republicans on the
committee, argued that since Ballinger had collected funds for
party purposes, this constituted a legitimate sphere of concern.[80]
When a congressman chastised Brandeis for trying the case before
the press rather than before the committee, Fletcher again sprang
to the counsel's defense. He maintained that the case was not only
being tried before the committee but was indeed open to the
press and country. The majority report of the committee completely exonerated Ballinger of any misconduct and attributed opposition to him to narrow partisanship and disagreement over conservation policy. However, Senators Fletcher and William Purcell
of North Dakota joined Representatives Ollie M. James of Kentucky and James M. Graham of Illinois in a blistering minority report. They accused Ballinger of fraudulently transferring valuable
public property from the government to private firms, conflict of
interest, and of purposely allowing unskilled attorneys to handle
government cases where he had private financial interest in the
outcome of litigation. After a lengthy list of indictments, the
minority concluded that the Secretary had "not been true to the
trust reposed in him . . . that he should be requested by the proper

78. See U. S., Committee on Expenditures in the Department of Agriculture,
Everglades of Florida, 62d Congress, 1st Session, 1912, Rept. 12.
79. For a condensed summary of the hearings and Fletcher's part in them, see
ch. 7, "The Ballinger-Pinchot Conservation Feud," in Alpheus T. Mason,
Brandeis: A Free Man's Life (New York: Viking Press, 1946), pp. 254–81. For
a more detailed study, see U.S., Congress, *Investigation of the Department of the
Interior and of the Bureau of Forestry*, 61st Congress, 3d Session, 1910–11,
I–XIII.
80. U.S., Congress, *Investigation of Interior Department and Forestry Bureau*,
61st Congress, 3d Session, 1910–11, VII, 3793–94.

authority to resign. . . ."[81] Brandeis' concern for the national welfare so impressed Fletcher that the senator later became a key congressional spokesman for the lawyer's appointment to the Supreme Court.

His experience with special committees presaged his lifelong concern for home state patronage and federal grants. It also suggested his idealistic priority for what he defined as the national welfare, whether viewed from the perspective of conservation of natural resources in 1910, maritime policy in the teens and twenties, national agricultural credits, or depression era relief.

Another index to his future career in the Senate is found in sometimes misleading roll-call votes. Some of the contradictions which later characterized his political philosophy appeared in the Sixty-first and Sixty-second Congresses. He voted with liberals in favor of a federal income tax and split on two votes to expand government regulation of railroads. He hedged on direct election of United States Senators, fearing federal supervision, though he favored the principle of direct vote, and opposed a children's bureau to curtail child labor; yet he also joined liberals in advocacy of Canadian tariff reciprocity and a maximum eight-hour day for government workers. One careful student of southern progressivism identifies six southern senators who voted consistently "progressive" between 1909 and 1912; six other southerners, including Fletcher, frequently joined their more liberal colleagues.[82]

Southern progressivism has been defined as the impulse toward social, political, and economic reform, which included agrarian radicals, middle-class reformers, utopianists, and political realists. Some espoused southern radicalism while others remained essentially conservative, seeking order and progress by controlled and gradual change.[83] Fletcher fits properly if not comfortably into the latter category. His educational and metropolitan reforms demonstrated commitment to progressivism. Florida liberals acknowledged Fletcher's leadership early in the decade, later questioned his advocacy of corporate interests, and finally labeled him an enemy of the people. Napoleon Broward, foe of exploitation and leader of the masses, damned his former ally. Fletcher, aided by interests

81. *Ibid.*, I, 145–47.
82. For an excellent study of southern progressives from 1906 to 1916, see Anne Firor Scott, "The Southern Progressives in National Politics, 1906–1916" (Ph.D. dissertation, Radcliffe College, 1957).
83. *Ibid.*, pp. 1–20.

he once castigated, defeated Florida's most liberal spokesman. Intemperate charges, based on some facts and many half-truths, clouded Fletcher's earlier reputation as reformer and progressive. As a railroad lawyer he unquestionably modified his liberalism. Corporate conversion, though, explained his success less than Florida factionalism. He opposed Broward out of political chance and personal ambition, not because of philosophical conflict. Disintegration of progressive unity rather than railroad money launched his twenty-seven-year senatorial career. Fletcher carried a smaller stick and spoke in softer tones, but he remained with Broward at Armageddon battling for the Lord and the people.

CHAPTER IV

Florida and the New Freedom

National politics underwent considerable change during the first decade of the twentieth century. Urban progressives assumed a more prominent role in the Democratic Party as agrarian liberals lost influence. Middle-class reformers challenged boss-controlled political machines and catapulted new figures into national prominence. Such a man was New Jersey's Governor Woodrow Wilson. Born and raised in the South, Wilson chose to launch his presidential bid with a 1911 address to the Southern Commercial Congress meeting in Atlanta where he also conferred with Georgia progressives. Wilson hoped to enter the 1912 Baltimore Democratic Convention with formidable if not monolithic southern backing.

Wilson's chief opposition in the South came from Oscar W. Underwood, a genial Alabama conservative. Southern conservatives endorsed Underwood, oftentimes as much to defeat Wilson as to elect the Alabamian. Missouri's James B. "Champ" Clark, the Democratic presidential aspirant favored by many of the old Bryan forces, ignored the southeastern primaries in an effort to avoid fragmenting the anti-Wilson vote. Underwood hoped to win a block of southern delegates, deadlock the convention between Clark and Wilson, and then emerge victorious as a compromise candidate.[1] To forge such a coalition of dissimilar units, the Alabamian emphasized his southern genealogy rather than specific issues. For his part, Wilson attempted to steer a middle course

1. Evans C. Johnson, "Oscar W. Underwood: The Development of a National Statesman" (Ph.D. dissertation, University of North Carolina, 1953), pp. 266–69.

between Bryan's "radicalism" and Underwood's "conservatism," though his personal philosophy closely paralleled Underwood's.[2]

Florida's presidential primary was another confrontation between the liberal and conservative elements in the state's amorphous Democratic Party. William B. Crawford of Kissimmee, Florida, scion of a powerful political family, and Dr. T. S. Anderson of Live Oak championed the progressive wing of the party while A. V. Long of Starke and Frank J. Fernside of Palatka defended the conservative element. These Democratic spokesmen fought an indecisive skirmish at an executive committee meeting in January, 1912, then squared off in the gubernatorial and presidential primaries.[3]

Initial response heartened Wilson's Florida lieutenants. William B. Crawford persuaded the Democratic Executive Committee to replace the factional caucus with a state-wide presidential primary. Wilson stood a better chance with "cracker" voters than with conservative members of a party caucus. United States Senator Nathan P. Bryan, a Broward protégé, endorsed the New Jersey governor in February, 1912, and other prominent Floridians soon joined the Wilson camp: W. P. Watson, state labor leader; Secretary of State H. Clay Crawford of the Crawford family; and Frank L. Mayes, editor of the Pensacola *Journal*. Wilsonian newspapers included the Pensacola *Journal*, Tampa *Times*, Volusia County *Record*, Ocala *Star*, and Ft. Lauderdale *Sentinel*.

Grass roots enthusiasm greeted Wilson organizers. Woodrow Wilson clubs sprang up at the University of Florida, in Tampa, and in Jacksonville during January and February, 1912.[4] Wilson rallies heard prominent local citizens, and on April 18, 2,200 cheering Jacksonville Democrats attended Wilson's only Florida appearance. Judge William H. Price toured Florida in March and reported that state sentiment favored Wilson. Even the conservative *Florida Times-Union* recognized a strong Wilson impetus in the state.[5]

Conservative disarray vanished as attention centered on Underwood. Most Florida papers endorsed the Alabamian, and state officials, led by Governor Albert W. Gilchrist, joined the

2. Arthur S. Link, *Wilson: The Road to the White House* (Princeton, New Jersey: Princeton University Press, 1947), p. 335.
3. Jacksonville *Florida Times-Union*, January 7, 1912.
4. *Ibid.*, January 12 and 17, February 28, 1912.
5. *Ibid.*, interview in March 17, 1912, and March 25, 1912.

Underwood bandwagon. Alabama's Senator John H. Bankhead visited Jacksonville on February 27 to gauge Underwood sentiment and establish a campaign headquarters.

Pleasant A. Holt, a Fletcher confidant, helped official chairman Frank E. Chase direct the Underwood campaign. They built an effective organization with local offices in ten cities. Money apparently constituted no barrier, and they exceeded their original allocation by $2,300. National manager Bankhead considered Florida vital to Underwood's strategy and promptly forwarded the extra money.[6]

Duncan Fletcher, partly out of friendship and regional identity, supported his congressional colleague. Fletcher declined open endorsement until late in the race but used every opportunity to aid Underwood. As president of the Southern Commercial Congress he invited Underwood to address the annual meeting. This gathering attracted ten thousand southern business and civic leaders in April, 1912. Fletcher confidentially explained to Underwood that southern leaders would gather in one place, thus reducing the extensive campaigning necessary to contact them. He added in a footnote that the Chicago *Tribune* planned sixteen pages of pre-convention coverage which would provide free Underwood publicity to two million midwestern subscribers and thirty thousand southern leaders who would receive free copies. Fletcher also served as liaison between Senator Bankhead and Underwood's Florida managers.[7]

Superior organization, together with overwhelming press and financial support, gradually overcame the enthusiastic Wilsonians. Underwood pulled ahead until William Jennings Bryan toured Florida attacking the congressman as reactionary. Fletcher panicked and, three days before the primary, broke his public neutrality with a cautious endorsement: "Mr. Wilson is a man of learning and abilities of the highest order, but it seems to me he ignores or treats indifferently the tariff issue, and the trust question. . . . The Democracy needs Underwood—the country needs him."[8] This last-

6. P. A. Holt to Duncan U. Fletcher, June 3, 1912, and Thomas M. Owen to Frank E. Chase, June 11, 1912, in Remittances File, Oscar B. Underwood Papers, Department of Archives and History, Montgomery, Alabama. Hereafter cited as Underwood Papers.
7. Duncan U. Fletcher to Oscar W. Underwood, February 23, 1912, P. A. Holt to Duncan U. Fletcher, June 3, 1912, in Remittances File, Underwood Papers.
8. Jacksonville *Florida Times-Union*, April 27, 1912.

minute support helped swing undecided Democrats, and Underwood carried the state 28,343 to Wilson's 20,482.

The pre-eminent Wilson scholar has concluded that the primary presented a straight progressive-conservative test.[9] This explanation only partly explains Underwood's victory. In the same primary Park Trammell—a liberal who advocated abolishment of the convict lease system, state anti-trust laws, and a state labor commissioner—won the governorship; and Claude L'Engle, labor spokesman and Broward aide, won a congressional post. Progressives won spectacular victories except in the presidential race.

Accurate analysis of Florida's 1912 presidential primary must weigh the influence of what V. O. Key called the "friends and neighbors" vote in southern politics. Many papers joined the Perry *Herald* in praise of Wilson but endorsed Underwood as a lifelong southerner who deserved sectional support.[10] The two Toms, Watson of Georgia and Heflin of Alabama, stumped for Underwood, and their names worked magic among the old Populists and "crackers" of west Florida. Support by Fletcher and other respected reformers further enhanced Underwood's credentials. One careful observer attributes Underwood's triumph to an ironic combination of the conservative press, a large "friends and neighbors" vote, and Populist remnants stirred by Watson and Heflin.[11]

At the Baltimore Democratic convention, Fletcher spent his energy formulating platform resolutions. Powerfully backed by the Southern Commercial Congress, he introduced planks pledging the federal government to Mississippi waterway development, swamp drainage, vocational training, and agricultural extension programs. His most significant proposal committed the party to the investigation of European agricultural credit systems and legislation establishing farm loans.[12] All four planks were written into the 1912 Democratic platform.

Fletcher made his peace with Wilson after the convention

---

9. Arthur S. Link, "The South and the Democratic Campaign of 1912" (Ph.D. dissertation, University of North Carolina, 1945), p. 311.
10. Jacksonville *Florida Times-Union*, February 15, 1912.
11. George N. Green, "Florida's Politics and Socialism at the Crossroads of the Progressive Era, 1912" (Master's thesis, Florida State University, 1962), pp. 35–40.
12. Jacksonville *Florida Times-Union*, July 7, 1912; and U.S., *Congressional Record*, 63d Congress, 2d Session, 1914, LI, 16299.

and returned to stump Florida for the Democratic nominee. He addressed Wilson rallies in Jacksonville and Tampa, helped organize a Woman's Democratic League in his home city, and campaigned with N. P. Bryan, the state's junior senator. Wilson easily carried Florida and, aided by division in the Republican Party, won an overwhelming majority of the nation's electoral votes.

The next year, as Wilson's inauguration approached, Fletcher arrived in Washington unsure of his status with the man he had fought in Florida's presidential primary. Predictions concerning his reception differed markedly; one published account mentioned a federal judgeship, while others speculated that Fletcher would become Secretary of Agriculture.[13] Liberal papers, recalling the bitter 1908 struggle and the recent clash in Florida presidential politics, prophesied his eclipse.

Liberals who forecast Fletcher's political isolation misread the New Freedom and misunderstood the personalities of Fletcher and Wilson. President Wilson conceived his program as the implementation of laissez-faire economics. He opposed both special class legislation and monopoly. At first the New Freedom did not envision positive federal aid to farmers or laborers, since Wilson considered this class legislation. Only when Democratic liberals rebelled did Wilson adopt the positive governmental concepts of Theodore Roosevelt's New Nationalism. One authority concludes that Wilson built the New Freedom on the "bedrock of conservatism."[14]

Wilson's personal political philosophy also lacked the essential ingredients of liberalism. Wilson—the traditionalist, the moralist, the constitutionalist—sought to restore opportunity in a free and competitive society.[15] He believed, as did Fletcher, that moderate progressivism was essential to the preservation of American institutions. Wilson betrayed no philosophical liberalism when he defined his New Freedom: "Are those thoughtful men who fear

13. Rumors that he would become Secretary of Agriculture were generally accepted, and Fletcher issued no denial. See Jacksonville *Florida Times-Union*, January, 1913, quoting Fort Myers *Press*, Orlando *Reporter-Star*, and Panama City *Pilot*.
14. Clinton Rossiter, *Conservatism in America* (New York: Random House, 1962), p. 90. See also Arthur S. Link, "The South and the 'New Freedom': An Interpretation," *The American Scholar*, XX (Summer, 1951), 316.
15. Rossiter, *Conservatism in America*, pp. 90–91.

that we are now about to disturb the ancient foundations of our institutions justified in their fear? I believe, for one, that you cannot tear up ancient rootages and safely plant the tree of liberty in soil which is not native to it. I believe that the ancient traditions of a people are its ballast. . . . You must knit the new into the old. . . . If I did not believe that to be progressive was to preserve the essentials of our institutions, I for one could not be a progressive."[16]

Fletcher and Wilson were alike in more ways than either imagined in 1912. Like Wilson, Fletcher espoused a nineteenth-century laissez-faire liberalism; he would defend human dignity by diffusing power and fragmenting governmental authority. Of the two factions into which southern congressmen divided—pro-administration regulars and agrarian mavericks to the left of Wilson—Fletcher clearly belonged to the former.

Fletcher's practical effectiveness during the years from 1912 to 1920 depended largely on skills refined by a lifetime of political activity. He was a moderate, a consummate diplomat capable of both deep conviction and pragmatic compromise. He held the middle ground between factions without losing the respect of either. The Floridian was a methodical but thorough worker, a party man but not a political hack; a man of culture and erudition who could still communicate with the people. A progressive, he represented the conservative tradition of nineteenth-century liberalism rather than Populist radicalism. Humorless, even aloof on the stump, he won the respect and admiration of the people. Although often allied with conservatives, he shrewdly recognized the needs and aspirations of the masses. Fletcher, who had remained loyal to William Jennings Bryan during years when Wilson had viewed "the Commoner" as a dangerous radical, proved no less loyal to Woodrow Wilson.

The Sixty-third Congress convened in 1913 eager to hear Wilson's legislative proposals. Southern congressmen divided into two factions. The administration group consisted mainly of committee chairmen such as Carter Glass who were somewhat conservative but loyal to Wilson. A large faction of southern agrarians, including Mississippi's James K. Vardaman, advocated positive government intervention in the economy and was frequently to

16. Woodrow Wilson, *The New Freedom* (New York: Doubleday, Page and Company, 1914), pp. 43–44.

the left of the administration.[17] Fletcher's role in the Wilsonian era was determined by the President's decision to work through the Democratic Party rather than through a progressive Democratic–insurgent Republican coalition.[18] Fletcher was catapulted to prominence as a liaison between party maverick liberals and regulars.

During congressional organization, the senator yielded his right to the chairmanship of the Commerce Committee to Senator James P. Clarke of Arkansas. Yet he remained active by serving on the Judiciary Committee, the Military Affairs Committee, as second ranking member of the Commerce Committee, and as chairman of the Senate Committee on Printing.

An early item on the Presidential agenda was the revision of tariff rates. Wilson summoned a special congressional session on April 7, 1913. Agrarian senators wholeheartedly endorsed reform, but southerners came under considerable pressure from fruit, cotton, and lumber interests. Nathan P. Bryan, Florida's junior senator, unequivocally endorsed lower rates, while Fletcher ignored conservative pressure and also fought for tariff reduction. Wilson persuaded Fletcher to delay an important rural credits investigation because he considered the senator's vote and influence crucial in passage of the Underwood tariff bill.[19]

Fletcher adhered to the straight administration line on other high priority legislation. The Smith-Lever or Agricultural Education Extension Act of 1914 implemented Fletcher's plank in the 1912 Democratic platform; it provided federal funds for agricultural education and, except for a provision including Negro schools in the program, received Fletcher's complete support. He voted for the Federal Reserve Act, the Clayton Antitrust Act, and the Federal Trade Commission, measures which extended governmental authority over currency and corporate organization. Fletcher favored the graduated income tax, arguing that "placing the tax-

17. Link, "The South and the 'New Freedom,'" p. 316. See also Dewey W. Grantham, Jr., "Southern Congressional Leaders and the New Freedom, 1913–1917," *Journal of Southern History*, XIII (November, 1947), 439–59. Grantham concludes that southern congressmen were both progressive and conservative depending on the particular issue, but were generally more nationalistic under Wilson.
18. Arthur S. Link, *Wilson: The New Freedom* (Princeton, New Jersey: Princeton University Press, 1956), p. 153.
19. Woodrow Wilson to Duncan U. Fletcher, March 21, 1913, in Woodrow Wilson Papers, Series II, Box 34, Manuscript Division, Library of Congress, Washington, D.C. Hereafter cited as Woodrow Wilson Papers.

ation on those most able to bear it and enabling relief to come to those who have heretofore borne the burden, will prove a great blessing to the people."[20]

The Floridian's most advanced progressivism emerged in the struggle for maritime reform. Fletcher served on the committee investigating the *Titanic* disaster and was appalled by the living conditions of seamen. President Wilson recognized Fletcher's request for remedial action by appointing him to an international conference to draft rules for maritime safety. Some Wilson advisers considered Fletcher the Senate leader on such matters.[21] Wilson approved an international treaty which set minimum safety standards, but Fletcher pronounced these provisions inadequate and lent support to more fundamental changes.

Senator Robert La Follette, progressive Wisconsin Republican, introduced a bill to mitigate wretched maritime conditions, control working hours, and regulate safety standards. The American Federation of Labor backed the bill, but conservative shipping interests opposed the measure, and Wilson considered it unnecessary. Even some progressives, including Nathan P. Bryan and Georgia's Senator Hoke Smith, opposed the legislation. After much soul-searching Fletcher broke with Wilson and fought effectively for the La Follette seaman's bill. As second ranking member of the Commerce Committee, he marshaled wavering Democrats and became the majority spokesman for the bill.[22]

Despite an occasional foray into the La Follette brand of liberalism, Fletcher consistently maintained his traditional aversion to government encroachment on state prerogatives. Like Wilson he opposed federal intervention to abolish child labor or guarantee woman suffrage. While supporting the objectives of such legislation, he maintained that these were state and not federal matters.

His constituents profited indirectly from New Freedom legislation, but they were far more impressed with Fletcher's proficiency in manipulating the congressional pork barrel. He served as president of a waterway association and maintained his deep concern for southern navigation. His position on the Commerce Com-

20. Jacksonville *Florida Times-Union*, November 20, 1913.
21. E. G. Chamberlain, "Memorandum for Secretary Redfield," September 12, 1913, in Wilson Papers, Series VI, Box 385.
22. See U.S., *Congressional Record*, 63d Congress, 1st Session, 1913, L, 5670, 5748–51.

mittee, which drafted the annual Rivers and Harbors Bill, gave him powerful influence over waterway appropriations.

No single factor explained Fletcher's mastery of Florida politics more adequately than his effectiveness in passing local river and harbor bills. Florida possessed the longest coast line of any state, and the large majority of her population lived in Atlantic and Gulf port cities or along inland rivers. Fletcher thoroughly understood the political potential of this fortuitous circumstance and devoted inordinate effort to waterway legislation. He guided a bill through the Sixty-second Congress which provided two million dollars for Florida projects; and the March, 1913, Rivers and Harbors Bill contained appropriations of $800,000 for work on the St. Johns (affecting Jacksonville), Indian, Crystal, Withlacoochee, Caloosahatchee, and Boca Grande rivers, and on Key West, Sarasota, and Tampa bays.[23] Before facing the 1914 senatorial primary, he won an appropriation of $730,000 for a trans-Florida canal.

Patronage also strengthened his political power. President Wilson chose to dispense political spoils through state congressmen and parties. Where the Democratic organization was conservative, he preferred to win the congressional delegations rather than use patronage to build separate progressive factions. Fletcher utilized this policy to reward political adherents.[24] He won appointments for his friends in the customs service and as federal judges. As chairman of the Committee on Printing with 4,500 employees, he controlled many lucrative positions. He frequently besought Wilson for appointments and was usually successful.[25] The Palatka *Times-Herald* accurately observed that "Mr. Fletcher believes in looking out for the interests of worthy Floridians."[26]

Washington social life absorbed little of Fletcher's time but

23. Jacksonville *Florida Times-Union*, March 3, 1913.
24. J. B. Hodges to Duncan U. Fletcher, May 14, 1914, Box 16, in Hodges Papers.
25. William G. McAdoo to Woodrow Wilson, April 22, 1913; Duncan U. Fletcher to Woodrow Wilson, March 27, 1913; in Wilson Papers, Series VI, Box 283. And Bryan R. Newton to Duncan U. Fletcher, September 13, 1913, in William G. McAdoo Papers, Letterbook 6, Box 479, Manuscript Division, Library of Congress. Hereafter cited as McAdoo Papers. See also Duncan U. Fletcher to Woodrow Wilson, April 11 and March 17, 1913, in Wilson Papers, Series VI, Box 14.
26. Jacksonville *Florida Times-Union*, September 19, 1913, quoting Palatka *Times-Herald*.

intrigued his family. Anna Fletcher was elected vice-president of the Woman's National Democratic League and frequently entertained local politicians. Louise and Nell joined the capital's social whirl where Louise met and, in 1912, married a prominent Washington physician, Thomas J. Kemp. Unfortunately, Dr. Kemp became involved in breaches of medical ethics and in 1914 was convicted of informing patients where illegal operations might be performed. A rumor spread in Washington that Fletcher had interceded with Wilson on behalf of his son-in-law. For whatever reason, Wilson intervened and commuted Kemp's two-year prison sentence. One congressman demanded an investigation, but his motion died in committee.[27] The Senator's Florida opponents either never discovered or ignored the affair, which was not made an issue in the 1914 senatorial race.

Fletcher could hardly have approached a campaign with more advantages that he enjoyed in 1914. His waterway programs aided Florida businessmen, and his support of Wilsonian reform endeared him to farmer-progressives. The Key West *Journal* called him the strongest man in the state; other papers praised his record of waterway development.[28]

Some Floridians expected Fletcher to retire, and south Florida conservatives privately mentioned Peter O. Knight of Tampa as a likely person to "succeed" him.[29] Governor Albert W. Gilchrist, backed by state conservatives, entered the race and campaigned actively for four months before suddenly withdrawing. Business interests feared that the Bryan primary law of 1913, by eliminating runoff elections through provision for first and second choice votes, might splinter conservative strength and give the election to John N. C. Stockton. Stockton, former "straightout" and Broward protégé, had run for the Senate in 1904, the governorship in 1908, and the Senate again in 1910, losing each race. He had come close to victory in 1910 when fellow progressive Nathan Bryan had defeated him by only five hundred votes. Political unknown Fred M. Hudson also entered the 1914 campaign as the south Florida candidate, prompting one editor to quip that Florida

27. New York *Times*, July 21, 1914.
28. Jacksonville *Florida Times-Union*, October 14, 1912, March 4, 1913, February 18, 1914, quoting Key West *Journal*, Dade City *Star*, Hastings *Journal*.
29. Frank Bentley to Peter O. Knight, December 18, 1913, Scrapbook A, in Knight Collection.

"crackers" did not know whether he was a man or an automobile.[30]

The most noticeable feature of the 1914 race was the fade-out of the old progressive-conservative dichotomy. Dozens of liberal papers echoed the sentiments of the Leesburg *Commercial*: "John Stockton is a man we have always liked. Under ordinary circumstances we would be willing for him to have most anything in reason, but the sacrifice of Senator Fletcher is too great a favor to ask."[31] The incumbent senator frequently quoted a letter of 1913 from Stockton which praised Fletcher's record as progressive and far-sighted.[32] Many Florida progressives clearly opted for the incumbent.

Conservatives also united behind Fletcher when Governor Gilchrist withdrew. The Punta Gorda *Herald*, whose strongest claim to progressivism was its advocacy of a law prohibiting cows on Punta Gorda's main street, unhesitatingly endorsed Fletcher. J. B. Hodges aided Fletcher's campaign while helping the Florida East Coast Railroad elect conservatives to the state legislature.[33]

Organizational genius P. A. Holt joined James M. Cathcart, former city editor of the Tampa *Tribune* who served as Fletcher's private secretary, in organizing the campaign. Holt contacted Fletcher lieutenants to determine Stockton's strength and Fletcher's weakness. Local observers claimed that Stockton's record as the "original progressive" was his best weapon, while Fletcher's principal handicap stemmed from opposition by popular Jacksonville politician John W. Martin and the Lorimer affair.[34]

William Lorimer, Republican senator from Illinois, had been accused of corrupt election practices. Fletcher had served as a member of the investigating committee and had opposed impeachment on the grounds of insufficient evidence. He drew heated criti-

30. Jacksonville *Florida Times-Union*, September 11, 1913, quoting Kissimmee *Journal*.
31. Jacksonville *Florida Times-Union*, April 17, 1914, quoting Leesburg *Commercial*. For identical views by progressive papers which praised Stockton but supported Fletcher, see Jacksonville *Florida Times-Union*, July 17, August 13, 15, and 26, September 8 and 23, November 3, 1913, quoting Wauchula *Advocate*, Bartow *Courier-Informant*, Santa Rosa *Star*, Stuart *Times*, Bronson *Times-Democrat*, Tarpon Springs *Progressive*, and Ocala *Banner*.
32. Jacksonville *Florida Times-Union*, November 17, 1913, quoting Tampa *Tribune*; and May 26, 1914.
33. J. B. Hodges to Morton Riddle, June 11, 1914, and J. B. Hodges to Duncan U. Fletcher, May 29, 1914, Box 16, in Hodges Papers.
34. P. A. Holt to J. B. Hodges, January 27, 1914, and J. B. Hodges to P. A. Holt, January 29, 1914, Box 16, in Hodges Papers.

cism in Florida which he met squarely in his address before the state legislature in May, 1913. Arguing persuasively against Lorimer's politics, he added that political expediency must not obscure evidence exonerating the Illinois senator. Legislators received his speech with a standing ovation despite their rumored displeasure over his vote.

Stockton geared his campaign to the confused issue of progressive identity. Fletcher, he argued, was a progressive-come-lately, a reactionary who only feigned support for President Wilson. He disparaged Fletcher's rural credits program[35] as a Wall Street hoax to allay farmer discontent. Stockton advocated direct government loans to farmers which Fletcher rejected as socialistic.

Fletcher demolished Stockton's primary issue by a combination of shrewd logic, reference to his senatorial voting record, and timely aid from the President. The senator won disgruntled union members by reviewing his consistent support for shorter hours and better working conditions. Of the sixteen measures officially endorsed by the American Federation of Labor, Fletcher had voted for fifteen and was paired in favor of the other.[36] He defended his rural credits bill by citing the approval of President Wilson, the Secretary of Agriculture, William Jennings Bryan, and numerous farm leaders. Farmers generally applauded Fletcher's agricultural program; when he addressed the Putnam County Farmer's Convention, six hundred farmers filled the hall and gave their champion a tumultuous welcome.[37]

Ironically, Woodrow Wilson, who was supported by Stockton and opposed by Fletcher in 1912, administered the *coup de grace* to Stockton's campaign. Arthur T. Williams, former state Democratic Executive chairman and a Fletcher aide, challenged Stockton's claim to Wilson's covert endorsement. He wrote President Wilson on March 19, 1914: "Senator Fletcher's opponent claims that the Senator should be classed as a reactionary and that his record in the senate has been favorable to special interests and that he is not in accord with the policies and principles of your administration. I should be glad if you would give me the benefit of your views on this matter, and allow me to use the same in respect to these charges."[38] Wilson replied on March 24: "I am sur-

35. Discussed in Chapter VI.
36. Jacksonville *Florida Times-Union*, May 28, 1914.
37. *Ibid.*, November 16, 1913.   38. *Ibid.*, April 12, 1914.

prised that anyone should charge Senator Fletcher with being a reactionary. Certainly during the time I have been able to observe his course of action, he has supported the progressive policy of the party not only with unvarying loyalty but with real energy, and has shown at every turn a desire to promote the best interests of the people. . . . I have learned to feel the highest regard for him and am glad to have this opportunity of expressing my confidence in him in answer to your question."[39]

Stockton dismissed the reply as a politically motivated statement to retain Fletcher's support of key administration measures. Stockton's analysis was partly correct, for Fletcher had directed Democratic maritime strategy after Senator Clarke, Democratic chairman of the Commerce Committee, deserted the administration. Wilson desperately needed the senator's persuasive counsel. Apart from this, Wilson apparently developed genuine admiration for the amiable Floridian whose political views so nearly paralleled his own.

Regardless of the motivation for Wilson's letter, it annihilated Stockton. John Beard, venerable Pensacola progressive, referred to Wilson's endorsement in his appeal for Fletcher's re-election. Fletcher triumphantly read the letter at every rally, and its effect was electric. The DeLand *News* neutralized the issue of anti-progressivism even more by characterizing the senator as a lifelong liberal: "Mr. Fletcher was recognized for many years as the leader of the old 'straightout' faction. . . . He was elected repeatedly as a mayor of Jacksonville as a progressive leader; he was sent to the state senate as a progressive; he was chosen as the chairman of the state executive committee by the Progressive Democrats, and was in sympathy and full accord with them and with the late Gov. Broward. In the senatorial campaign in 1908 . . . Fletcher received many votes from Progressives; Broward's friends were not able to line up the Progressives entirely for even the great commoner Broward himself."[40]

By a strange twist of political fate, a vote for Stockton became synonymous with rejection of Woodrow Wilson, and in 1914 Floridians adored Wilson. Stockton carried only Brevard, Dade, DeSoto, Gadsden, Monroe, Nassau, and Taylor counties,

39. *Ibid.*
40. Jacksonville *Florida Times-Union*, September 18, 1913, quoting DeLand *News.*

while losing a close race in his home county of Duval 3,006 to 2,995. Fletcher rode his farm bill and Wilson's popularity to a 32,042-to-21,733 victory. Paradoxically, many urban Wilsonian progressives applauded Fletcher's re-election, while Morton Riddle, conservative general manager of the Florida East Coast Railroad, also could privately rejoice at Stockton's defeat and the demise of "this breed of self-seeking demagogues, calling themselves Progressives."[41] Only the agrarian loyalists of the old Broward persuasion damned Wilson's "stab-in-the-back" and deserted Florida's senior senator to vote for Stockton.

Fletcher recuperated from the grueling senatorial campaign on a European tour. The continent's military convulsion of August, 1914, caught him in Paris. The French government refused to allow currency to leave the country, and many Americans were left destitute. Fletcher and a Bishop Hamilton organized unofficial committees which collected $25,000 for impoverished American citizens stranded in Europe.[42] He finally made his way to England and set sail for America aboard the *New Amsterdam*. A German cruiser intercepted the ship and ordered it searched for contraband. The *New Amsterdam*'s captain treated the American senator to a bit of wartime melodrama by trying to outrun the warship, but changed his mind when the German craft fired two shells over the deck.[43]

Washington presented a tranquil contrast to the hectic summer months in Europe. Diplomacy vied with domestic reform for attention, and Fletcher enunciated a consistently progressive approach to foreign policy. He deplored American intervention in Latin America and championed absolute independence for the Philippine Islands. When Britain protested the fee exemption for United States ships using the Panama Canal, Fletcher supported Wilson's bill for repeal of the American immunity.

Domestically, Fletcher redoubled his efforts to pass the La Follette seaman's bill. He considered the measure essential to "abolish involuntary servitude and prevent men aboard ships from being locked up in the ships jails [*sic*] for infractions and without an opportunity of being heard."[44] Conservative papers such

41. Morton Riddle to J. B. Hodges, June 12, 1914, Box 44, in Hodges Papers.
42. T. Bentley Mott, *Myron T. Herrick, Friend of France* (Garden City, New York: Doubleday, Doran and Company, 1929), p. 129.
43. Jacksonville *Florida Times-Union*, August 19, 1914.
44. *Ibid.*, February 28, 1915.

as the New York *Times* blasted the bill, and President Wilson continued his opposition. When the bill finally became law in 1915, conservative shippers directed a torrent of private criticism at Fletcher; but he defended the La Follette Act in a series of brilliant letters. To shippers who argued that the bill made their companies uncompetitive, he replied that archaic laws and poor management, not fair salaries for seamen, explained company inefficiency. He refuted charges that pampered crews deserted ships by suggesting that maritime companies pay equitable wages and serve better food if they desired more loyal crews.[45] Simple morality and justice dictated federal regulation, and Fletcher ignored the constitutional qualms of many opponents of the Act.

Another progressive-conservative affray involved the appointment of liberal jurist Louis D. Brandeis to the Supreme Court in 1916. Fletcher had first encountered the lawyer during hearings on the Ballinger-Pinchot Affair in 1910. Brandeis had impressed him, and when a major struggle developed in the Senate Judiciary Committee Fletcher came to Brandeis' defense. During subcommittee meetings the senator directed devastating questions at opponents of Brandeis' appointment.[46] He then broke a 2–2 deadlock by voting for confirmation. Of the five southerners on the full Judiciary Committee, only Fletcher and one other senator unreservedly endorsed Brandeis.[47] By contrast, Georgia's progressive Senator Hoke Smith opposed the appointment and capitulated only when labor unions and other groups pressured him.[48] Brandeis won committee approval by a narrow two-vote margin, 10 to 8.

Fletcher justified the support of Florida labor unionists by favoring the 1916 Adamson Act, which provided a maximum eight-hour day for railroad employees engaged in interstate commerce. He implemented the financial demands of Florida "crackers" by

45. Duncan U. Fletcher to A. H. McLeod, January 31, 1916; Duncan U. Fletcher to P. A. S. Franklin, February 2, 1916; Box 154, McAdoo Papers; and Duncan U. Fletcher to Captain Robert Dollar, January 19, 1916, General Records of the Department of Commerce, Office of the Secretary, National Archives, Washington, D.C.
46. For an excellent summary of Fletcher's role in the Brandeis struggle see Alpheus T. Mason, *Brandeis: A Free Man's Life* (New York: The Viking Press, 1946), pp. 463–505.
47. New York *Times*, April 4, 1916. Also see Scott, "The Southern Progressives in National Politics, 1906–1916," pp. 110–33.
48. Dewey W. Grantham, Jr., *Hoke Smith and the Politics of the New South* (Baton Rouge: Louisiana State University Press, 1958), p. 298.

endorsing the 1916 Revenue Bill establishing graduated income and inheritance taxes. Florida conservatives viewed this record with considerable misgiving; for example, the powerful *Florida Times-Union* opposed the La Follette Seaman's Act, the Brandeis appointment, the Adamson Act, and the 1916 Revenue Bill.

Florida's senior senator finally parted ways with progressives over the issue of child labor. The Keating-Owen Bill, prohibiting the interstate shipment of goods manufactured by children, drew withering fire from southern congressmen. Some opposed it in order to protect southern textile manufacturers who thrived on child labor, while others considered the bill an unconstitutional infringement on states' rights. Fletcher applauded the objective of the bill but questioned its constitutionality. His constitutional reservations appeared strangely inconsistent, for he argued during the same month that the commerce clause justified governmental control of the merchant marine. Such control involved a far more expansive interpretation of the proviso than the one maintained by advocates of the Keating-Owen Bill. In subsequent debate Fletcher protested that federal child labor inspectors would regulate individual liberties. It was not always bad, he added, for sixteen-year-old children to work, and whenever it was detrimental the state should initiate reform.[49] Fletcher's lack of concern for child labor contrasted noticeably with his humanitarian fervor on behalf of American seamen. Other southern progressives demonstrated the same contradictions, with Florida's Nathan Bryan and Georgia's Hoke Smith also opposing the bill. Perhaps reform that affected the South very little was more palatable than legislation which threatened the traditional social or economic patterns.

Wilson's conservative New Freedom became the liberal New Nationalism between 1914 and 1916. Americans demanded a government neutral in foreign affairs but active in domestic matters, even to the point of intervening on behalf of the people. Fletcher joined the vanguard of this transition, supporting eight of nine key progressive proposals and defecting only on the issue of child labor.[50]

The Floridian's progressive friends did embarrass him on one

49. U.S., *Congressional Record*, 64th Congress, 1st Session, 1916, LIII, 12201-8.
50. Scott, "The Southern Progressives in National Politics, 1906–1916," pp. 110–33. Analysis of the 64th Congress roll calls on nine of Mrs. Scott's representative measures reveals Fletcher's affirmative vote on eight. See U.S., *Congressional Record*, 64th Congress, 1st Session.

sensitive matter. Despite administration pressure, sixteen liberals bolted party leadership and filibustered the 1914 Rivers and Harbors Bill. They won a battle to recommit the bill, then sliced it from the original $34 million to $20 million.[51] Fletcher, who chaired the subcommittee on commerce, watched many Florida projects die at the hands of his Democratic allies.

This 1914 clash irked Fletcher, and he determined to marshal every vote necessary to pass the 1915 waterways bill. He confidentially pleaded with Wilson for a public statement favoring the bill. Wilson agreed to buttonhole individual senators on behalf of the bill but declined to endorse it publicly.[52] Wilson's persuasion proved inadequate and the 1915 measure was again mutilated. Fletcher's fortunes changed in 1916 when a $43 million Rivers and Harbors Bill survived a three-week filibuster and passed 35 to 32. The senator conducted a national speaking tour in 1916 to convince the public that waterway systems contributed to national defense. They also served an important commercial purpose, he argued, providing cheap transportation for farmers.[53]

Appointment of P. A. Dignan as Jacksonville's postmaster also tarnished Fletcher's home state prestige. Since both Florida senators lived in Jacksonville, local patronage frequently created dissension. Wilson solved the problem by requiring joint consent on local appointments. Trouble had developed when a Nathan Bryan appointee helped direct Stockton's 1914 campaign against Fletcher. Shortly after the spring primary, Bryan nominated P. A. Dignan for the position of Jacksonville postmaster. Dignan had vigorously opposed Fletcher in 1908 though he claimed to have supported him in 1914. Fletcher dismissed Dignan's alleged endorsement and absolutely refused to acquiesce in his appointment. The senator confided to friends that he would take his fight to the Senate floor if necessary to defeat Dignan.[54] Wilson refused to intervene on either side and Dignan received a favorable committee report. Fletcher fought the report on the floor, but he declined to invoke senatorial privilege, and the Senate confirmed the appointment on July 6, 1914. Fletcher seldom forgot a political enemy, as P. A. Dignan later learned to his regret.

51. Jacksonville *Florida Times-Union*, September 22, 1914.
52. Woodrow Wilson to Duncan U. Fletcher, February 26, 1915, in Wilson Papers, File II, Box 76.
53. Jacksonville *Florida Times-Union*, September 13, 1916.
54. Duncan U. Fletcher to J. B. Hodges, July 2, 1914, Box 16, in Hodges Papers.

Fletcher demonstrated considerably more statesmanship during Florida's 1916 governor's race. Sidney J. Catts—a one-eyed, Catholic-baiting, Baptist preacher—stirred the caldron of state politics to a frothy boil. After his narrow and perhaps fraudulent loss in the Democratic gubernatorial primary, he bolted the party and entered the general election as the nominee of the Prohibitionist Party. Fletcher detested Catts' religious bigotry and held party loyalty even more sacrosanct than theological tolerance. He openly took sides in the state election, urging support of the regular Democratic nominees. But Catts won the election, and many Fletcher enthusiasts, caught in the aura of Catts' mysticism, renounced their senatorial champion.[55]

The political fortunes of Duncan Fletcher had tumbled from their 1914 pinnacle. In an outburst of temper he attacked the press for misstating his role in the Lorimer affair. The Dignan controversy made him appear petty to many observers, and his long-promised rural credits bill languished in committee. Progressive allies axed his political panacea, river and harbor appropriations, and some erstwhile friends made ugly noises of discontent. In 1916 northern journalists acknowledged the importance of his rural credits bill by mentioning him for vice-president; but the Key West *Journal*, which months before had called him the strongest man in Florida, admonished him to forget the vice-presidency and worry about Florida waterways.[56] Fletcher regrouped his political fortunes by exploiting the ever vexatious American farm problem.

55. Jacksonville *Florida Times-Union*, October 27, 1916. Among these deserters was J. B. Hodges, a Fletcher stalwart, who castigated the senator after 1916.
56. Jacksonville *Florida Times-Union*, August 21, 1915, quoting Key West *Journal*.

CHAPTER V

A Progressive Approach to Agriculture

SOUTHERN INDUSTRIAL COOPERATION had begun in the ante-bellum attempt to exploit latent commercial wealth and to end northern economic colonialism. A new and more positive approach had followed the Civil War when Georgia's Henry W. Grady and Henry Watterson of Kentucky had measured the South's future in terms of northern capital and economic diversification. Far from protesting "Yankee" investment, they enthusiastically had welcomed it. This effort, though accompanied by furious activity, had caused no economic revolution, and the South retained her ancient vassalage to the soil.

Duncan Fletcher helped initiate a new economic thrust beginning in 1908. In that year the senator assisted in organizing the Southern Commercial Congress, which held its first meeting in Washington. He told the delegates that the South must achieve industrial equality if American sectionalism were to end.[1] The ill-defined objectives of the 1908 conference left the Congress little more than a sectional chamber of commerce; but the delegates did demonstrate their willingness to examine basic economic shortcomings.

Fletcher was elected as the first president of the Congress in 1911 and headed it until 1918. During his years as president, the Congress reflected his concepts of southern development. The Floridian believed that the primary function of the Commercial Congress was educational. When other sections of America saw the

1. Jacksonville *Florida Times-Union*, December 8, 1908.

enormous resources and potential of the South, old antagonisms would disappear. The organization, Fletcher argued, must project the South into the mainstream of national debate on controversial issues. His 1915 presidential address contained his most incisive view of the group's objectives: "The controlling forces, the dominating influences of this life, are ideas. The meetings of the Southern Commercial Congress have brought forth and put into exercise ideas. . . . These meetings call for the expression of ideas on the great questions of the day. . . . Ideas will be let loose to energize the forces set to work for the common good. Creative ideas will be generated and later utilized. . . . That is the essence of our mission —the dissemination of useful creative ideas and giving them effective application."[2] The Congress had moved a long way from the original supra–chamber of commerce to Fletcher's expansive 1915 organization.

The senator recognized pragmatic demands by diverting primary emphasis from industry to agriculture. Between 1912 and 1916 rural credits dominated Fletcher's politics and the agenda of the Southern Commercial Congress. Secondary projects included waterway development and a government-owned merchant marine, both permitting inexpensive transportation of farm produce. The Congress established a Washington office and, with Fletcher as its senatorial champion, became a powerful lobby.

After assuming presidency of the Congress, Fletcher outlined a five-year, semi-centennial program contrasting southern conditions in 1861–65 with those of 1911–15.[3] The Atlanta meeting in 1911 stressed southern industrial recovery and attracted ten thousand people; Woodrow Wilson, campaigning for the presidency, addressed the delegates. The 1912 convention at Nashville, Tennessee, emphasized agricultural progress and produced the Congress' most significant achievement, impetus for a national rural credits system. The Nashville conference catapulted Fletcher into national prominence as chief spokesman for agricultural credit legislation.

Commercial development and Latin American affairs provided the theme for the Mobile Congress in 1913. Fletcher invited the President to speak, and Wilson obliged with his famous decla-

2. For speech text, see *ibid.*, April 27, 1915.
3. Duncan U. Fletcher to Oscar W. Underwood, February 23, 1912, in Underwood Papers.

ration of policy toward Latin America. He announced the end of United States colonialism south of the border and pledged a new diplomacy based on morality. Fletcher's presidential address called for federal rural credits legislation, and the Congress drafted resolutions supporting this program. The woman's auxiliary met for the first time in 1913 and emphasized education and woman suffrage. Floridians noted the growing prominence of their senior senator, and one paper called him the central figure in southern development.[4]

Fletcher arranged another blue-ribbon agenda for 1914. He procured leading figures in numerous fields led by President Wilson. Under Fletcher's prodding, the 1914 conference endorsed federal control of the merchant marine and opposed the Republican alternative of government subsidies for private shipping companies.[5]

In 1915 the Congress shifted to the Southwest, meeting in Muskogee, Oklahoma. Fletcher stirred debate with a bold challenge to isolationists who felt America should ignore the European conflagration: "All nations are more or less inter-dependent. No country can long prosper isolated and alone. . . . The ideal relationship is international cooperation."[6] Possibly his keynote speech enunciating an idea-centered credo for the Congress was designed to gain a tolerant audience for the controversial speeches which followed. A University of Texas professor called for land distribution to tenant farmers, and the president of the University of Arkansas advocated compulsory education for Negroes. Arkansas Commissioner of Agriculture John H. Page attributed small farmer difficulties to usurious interest rates, while other speakers called for federal rural credits, curbs on real estate speculation, and a national department of health with cabinet status. William G. McAdoo, Secretary of the Treasury and chief cabinet liberal, recognized this stimulating debate by calling the Congress a "militant and effective organization."[7]

4. Jacksonville *Florida Times-Union*, October 29–31, 1913.
5. For an example of his diligent arrangements, see Duncan U. Fletcher to Woodrow Wilson, March 26, 1915, and Woodrow Wilson to Duncan U. Fletcher, March 31, 1915. See also Duncan U. Fletcher to Woodrow Wilson, January 31, 1914, in Wilson Papers, Series VI, Box 422.
6. Jacksonville *Florida Times-Union*, April 27, 1915.
7. William G. McAdoo to Duncan U. Fletcher, April 27, 1915, in McAdoo Papers, Box 485, Letterbook 22.

The Southern Commercial Congress attracted national atten-
tion after 1912, and the December, 1915, meeting in Charleston,
South Carolina, drew many groups concerned with southern life.
Eleven organizations—including the Southern Governors' Con-
ference, Southern Cotton Congress, National Drainage Congress,
and the National Marketing Committee—met concurrently with the
Congress. Speakers included Treasury Secretary William G. Mc-
Adoo, Secretary of the Navy Josephus Daniels, Secretary of War
Lindley M. Garrison, former Secretary of State William Jennings
Bryan, United States Surgeon General William C. Gorgas, and
Secretary of Labor William B. Wilson. Among the nongovernment
speakers were the presidents of Harvard and Columbia Universities, and the Chinese Minister to the United States. Dr. Abbott
Lawrence Lowell, Harvard President and chairman of the League
to Enforce Peace, appealed eloquently for the resolution of international problems without recourse to war. United States Commissioner of Education P. P. Claxton provoked controversy by
advocating universal high school education "for every boy and
girl, black and white," in America.[8]

The Charleston congress went further than any other in
advocating domestic reform. Delegates endorsed a rural credits bill
and government ownership of the merchant marine. The woman's
auxiliary favored abolition of child labor, compulsory education,
factory inspection, minimum wages, and reduced hours for female
factory employees. The ladies also launched a campaign to create
state and local branches of the League to Enforce Peace.

The 1916 meeting in Norfolk, Virginia, accomplished
nothing of major importance, but the 1917 New York convention
demonstrated the Congress' influence outside the South. The New
York General Committee of the Southern Commercial Congress
included such disparate figures as William G. McAdoo; William
C. Redfield; John Temple Graves, editor of the New York *Ameri-
can*; William Randolph Hearst; former President William Howard
Taft; and financial barons Otto H. Kahn, J. P. Morgan, Frank
Munsey, George F. Peabody, Meyer D. Rothschild, and Samuel
Untermyer.[9] In New York Fletcher reaffirmed his belief that the

8. "Program of Seventh Annual Convention of the Southern Commercial Congress," in Wilson Papers, Series VI, Box 422. And Jacksonville *Florida Times-
Union*, December 18, 1915.
9. Clarence J. Owens to Woodrow Wilson, April 9, 1917, in Wilson Papers,
File VI, Box 422.

Congress must "put forth ideas . . . advance ideals, which constitute the basis for sound and certain progress." He also predicted that a new world order would emerge out of European chaos: "New international relations will be established," with "the feature of interdependence among nations" dominating future affairs.[10] In an attempt to attract northern investments, he established a $1,200,000 advertising fund. Delegates proposed federal power plant development on American rivers and requested that southern states end the convict lease system.[11]

Congress delegates re-elected the Floridian president in 1917, but senatorial duties forced his resignation the following January. The press lauded his efforts to prod the South into the center of national affairs, and the Nashville *Tennessean* could hardly contain its praise of his financial program:

> As chairman . . . of the Southern Commercial Congress, he has done very much toward bringing to the attention of the investing world the almost unparalleled natural wealth of the south. . . . He has shown a most intiment [*sic*] personal knowledge of the sources of this wealth; has made these known in a desirable way, and . . . has pointed out the best means of development. . . .
>
> When a man has thus devoted to a large section of the country as many years of hard and intelligent labor as has Senator Fletcher . . . he has the clear right . . . to compare present conditions with those which existed when his work began. With even his genius for assembling statistics . . . Senator Fletcher would be hard put to it even to mention all the things which he has fostered. . . .[12]

Such laudatory comment usually took notice of agricultural credit, where Fletcher performed the most notable service of his long Senate career. The nation's banking machinery suited the needs of urban producers but left farmers in a desperate plight. They paid interest on long-term loans ranging from 5 per cent in older agricultural states to 10 per cent or more in states such as Florida; interest on short-term loans usually ranged from 7 to 15

10. Jacksonville *Florida Times-Union*, October 16, 1917.
11. "Resolutions Adopted at the Ninth Annual Convention of the Southern Commercial Congress," in Wilson Papers, Series VI, Box 422.
12. Jacksonville *Florida Times-Union*, February 5, 1918, quoting Nashville *Tennessean*.

per cent.[13] Farmers in eastern Oklahoma complained of extreme interest rates as high as 160 per cent.[14] One Virginia small farmer protested that he could not secure loans at any rates and reported that hundreds of farmers in his county had lost their farms because of exorbitant interest.[15] In the midst of prosperity, the "New South" still wrestled with her old agrarian problem.

Fletcher felt particular concern for Florida, one of the states worst affected by the prevailing financial system. Ninety per cent of all loans in the state were based on terms of one year or less at an average interest rate of 10 per cent. In 1910, 15 per cent of all Florida farms were mortgaged, and 27 per cent (involving 110,000 farmers) were worked by tenants who did not own their land.[16]

Farm organizations had suggested remedial action before 1912, but Americans were absorbed with urban reform. Fletcher conducted his own investigation of the problem between 1909 and 1912, then launched a national campaign at the Nashville meeting of the Southern Commercial Congress. The senator attributed his early farming failure to excessive interest rates and responded angrily to what he considered exploitation of the farm population. In 1911 he contacted David Lubin, a Californian who had invested his life and fortune in agricultural research. Lubin, who represented the United States at the International Institute of Agriculture in France, agreed to speak, provided the Congress devoted a week to discussion of the rural credits problem. His conditions met, Lubin spoke at Nashville suggesting a possible solution based on European credit experience. Enthusiastic delegates authorized a commission, including two representatives from each state, to conduct a comprehensive European study. Fletcher won commission approval from conservative groups as well as from the Farmers'

---

13. David F. Houston, *Eight Years with Wilson's Cabinet, 1913–1920* (Garden City, New York: Doubleday, Page and Company, 1926), I, 207.
14. "Petition from Citizens of Harper and Ellis Counties, Oklahoma," Legislative Division, Record Group 46, National Archives, Washington, D.C. Hereafter cited as Record Group 46. Numerous petitions complained of interest rates of 10 per cent or more.
15. Edward Daniels to Carter Glass, January 5, 1916, Box 50A, in Carter Glass Papers, University of Virginia Library. Hereafter cited as Glass Papers.
16. U.S., *Congressional Record*, 64th Congress, 1st Session, 1916, LIII, 3545–46. For a brief summary of the entire issue of long term credit, see Theodore Saloutos, *Farmer Movements in the South, 1865–1933* (Lincoln: University of Nebraska Press [1964?] reprinted from the University of California Press 1960 edition), pp. 217–23.

Union and National Grange. He attended all three political conventions in 1912, persuading Republicans, Progressives, and Democrats to include rural credit in their platforms. President Taft discussed the subject with Fletcher, then instructed American ambassadors in Europe to conduct separate surveys on the subject.[17] Meanwhile, the director of the Southern Commercial Congress visited individual states to explain the proposed European inquiry.

Optimistic response greeted this activity, and Senator Francis G. Newlands introduced a congressional resolution endorsing the commission. The Senate appointed its own seven-man committee to accompany the American Commission established by the Commercial Congress. The President praised Fletcher's work on behalf of farmers and appointed him to the Senate group. Committee members chose Fletcher chairman, but Wilson persuaded him to forego the European trip in order to bolster administration forces engaged in tariff revision.[18]

The American Commission, comprised of 70 delegates from 29 states and from 4 Canadian provinces, joined the senatorial committee in Europe. Their investigation revealed that both France and Germany provided 25- to 75-year loans at 4½ per cent interest. European farmer cooperatives received state loans and were subject to governmental supervision. American papers published periodic commission reports which popularized European credit systems and heightened demand for legislation.

Fletcher began formulating proposals even before the commissions returned. He corresponded with Secretary of Agriculture David F. Houston, suggesting farmer cooperatives as the first step toward alleviating conditions. Such cooperatives could market products and finance farming operations by pooling economic resources.[19] Houston viewed this proposal without enthusiasm, but Fletcher continued his correspondence with leading farm experts.[20] In the Senate he called for rapid enactment of a rural credits system and summarized his plans for agrarian cooperation. The Wis-

17. Jacksonville *Florida Times-Union*, December 8, 1912.
18. Woodrow Wilson to Duncan U. Fletcher, March 21, 1913, in Wilson Papers, Series II, Box 34.
19. Duncan U. Fletcher to David F. Houston, June 11, 1913, Records of the Office of Agriculture, Record Group 16, National Archives. Hereafter cited as Record Group 16.
20. Duncan U. Fletcher to David F. Houston, June 14, 1913, Record Group 16, National Archives.

consin Board of Public Affairs applauded his speech as the best delivered on the subject and distributed one thousand copies to influential Wisconsin citizens.[21]

Fletcher exploited this growing interest by introducing the first long-term farm credits bill on August 9, 1912. The subject proved so popular that seventy other bills establishing credit systems were eventually introduced. The National Governors' Conference, organized in 1912, recognized Fletcher's role in agricultural finance and invited him to discuss the matter at its first gathering.

The two commissions studying European agriculture returned from their tour on July 26, 1913, and established headquarters in Washington. Fletcher, chairman of both groups, supervised analysis. After digesting the massive research, both delegations issued comprehensive reports. The American Commission praised European credit systems, especially their cooperative feature. The Senate committee concluded that direct government aid was unnecessary but maintained that "it is highly proper that the Government should be the agency" to establish rural credits.[22] These reports, which formed the basis for Fletcher's subsequent bills, contained four basic features: private credit was insufficient to solve farm needs; direct government grants were unnecessary; federally supervised but independent regional banks should provide farm credit; the new banks should provide long term loans of 35 years at a maximum 5 per cent interest.[23] The final 1916 law adopted each principle with the single exception of direct government participation.

Fletcher summarized the proposals for Wilson who expressed particular pleasure that the Floridian envisioned no direct government financing.[24] The senator conferred with cabinet officials, and his plan gained support among administration leaders.[25]

21. Jacksonville *Florida Times-Union*, September 14, 1912.
22. American Commission, *Agricultural Cooperation and Rural Credit in Europe*, 63d Congress, 2d Session, 1914, Senate Document 261, p. 28.
23. U.S., *Congressional Record*, 63d Congress, 2d Session, 1914, LI, 2487–99.
24. Duncan U. Fletcher to Woodrow Wilson, April 6, 1915, in Wilson Papers, Series VI, Box 205. Intimates had called the problem of rural credits to Wilson's attention earlier in 1912; see Burton J. Hendrick, *The Life and Letters of Walter H. Page* (Garden City, New York: Doubleday, Page and Co., 1922), I, 108–9.
25. William G. McAdoo, *Crowded Years* (New York: Houghton Mifflin Company, 1931), pp. 436–37.

There can be no doubt that Fletcher and the Southern Commercial Congress deserved primary recognition for the 1912–14 national crusade for rural credits. Prior to the 1914 publication of government documents on the subject, the Departments of State and Agriculture referred all inquiries on rural credits to the Southern Commercial Congress.[26] Two leading agricultural historians contend that the Nashville Congress of 1912 was responsible for the most important work on rural credits. The foremost historian of the Wilson era also credits the Southern Commercial Congress with originating the first nationwide movement for long-term rural financing.[27] What has been overlooked is Fletcher's driving energy which contributed so much to final passage.

Senator Fletcher revised his original bill in 1913 and wrote Secretary Houston that the Department of Agriculture should take the initiative in recommending legislation. Houston preferred to leave responsibility with Fletcher and a group of Congressmen organized by the Senator to champion rural credits.[28] Department officials reacted coolly to agricultural credit legislation throughout the entire controversy, and congressional leaders completely dominated the conflict.[29]

With this preliminary work accomplished, Fletcher reintroduced his bill in August, 1913. His defense of the measure indicated the depth of his protest against the financial status quo. He argued that a small group of men controlled 18 financial institutions which directed 134 corporations with an aggregate capital of $24 billion. These narrowly based institutions dominated the nation's capital and credit rates. Fletcher maintained that "no body of men responsible only to themselves can, in safety and justice . . . possess such power or possibilities of control over the destinies . . ." of the American people. He thought it better "to have the Government look after that control, if it is to be vested anywhere. . . ."[30] While admitting that some farmers enjoyed prosperity, he pleaded

---

26. Clarence J. Owens to Woodrow Wilson, December 18, 1914, in Wilson Papers, Series VI, Box 205.
27. Theodore Saloutos and John D. Hicks, *Agricultural Discontent in the Middle West, 1900–1939* (Madison: University of Wisconsin Press, 1951), p. 85; and Link, "The South and the 'New Freedom,'" p. 322.
28. Duncan U. Fletcher to David F. Houston, July 2, 1913, Record Group 16, National Archives.
29. RWS to T. N. Carver, June 14, 1913, Record Group 16, National Archives.
30. U. S., *Congressional Record*, 63d Congress, 1st Session, 1913, L, 3204–5.

for the average farmer eking out a miserable existence on two dollars a day. The Senator particularly noted the increase in farm tenancy from 28 per cent of all farmers in 1890 to 37 per cent in 1910. He recalled from his own experience that individual initiative could hardly replace numerous greenbacks. The Floridian concluded that America could never fulfill her great promise until these tenants owned their lands.[31]

Fletcher's bill provided long-term loans at 5 per cent interest based on land mortgages. Farmers would join cooperatives to pool mortgagable land, then negotiate loans from twelve land banks located in different sections and supported by private investors. In a curious departure from his earlier pronouncement on government participation, Fletcher proposed the use of federal postal deposits to provide partial capital for the land banks. He also proposed a federal rural banking board to supervise the land banks.[32]

Some conservatives believed that even this bill vested too much authority in the government. David Lubin, a frequent Fletcher adviser after the 1912 Nashville meeting, protested that the bill relied too heavily on the French *Reiffeisen* system. He noted that the French government provided capital, "and such a State-aided system is paternalism pure and simple."[33] Fletcher ignored this protest and sent the bill to President Wilson, who agreed that a remedy should be sought in a separate and distinct financial system.[34]

In late August, 1913, Fletcher again addressed the national conference of governors at Colorado Springs. The governors approved the European commission reports and generally endorsed his credits bill, although some chief executives favored modifications.[35] His address received wide attention in an American press anxious for news about agricultural finance.

President Wilson launched the two-year battle for rural credits in his annual address to Congress on December 2, 1913.

31. *Ibid.*, 3205–7.
32. *Ibid.*, 3208–11. Federal funds would come from United States postal savings stamp funds, a program created in 1910.
33. David Lubin to Duncan U. Fletcher, October 7 and September 3, 1913, Record Group 16, National Archives.
34. Duncan U. Fletcher to Woodrow Wilson, August 14, 1913, and Woodrow Wilson to Duncan U. Fletcher, August 15, 1913, in Wilson Papers, Series II, Box 38.
35. U. S., *Congressional Record*, 64th Congress, 1st Session, 1916, LIII, 3543.

While refusing to extend direct government credit, he pledged federal aid: "We must add the means by which the farmer may make his credit constantly and easily available. . . . We lag behind many other great countries . . . in attempting to do this. Systems of rural credit have been studied and developed on the other side of the water while we left our farmers to shift for themselves. . . ."[36] He urged Congress to implement recommendations of the European rural credit commissions.

Fletcher submitted his credits bill to President Wilson on December 10, 1913. The bill contained all the earlier items plus a provision for federal rather than state charter of land banks. After Wilson endorsed the measure, Fletcher and Representative Ralph W. Moss of Indiana introduced it on January 29, 1914, as the administration rural credits legislation. The European investigating commissions published their reports in early 1914, and since Fletcher chaired both, they predictably advised action similar to his bill. A subcommittee of the Senate Banking and Currency Committee under Senator Henry F. Hollis of New Hampshire conducted hearings on the bill. Instead of reporting the Fletcher measure, Hollis and committee liberals amended it to provide direct government support of land banks in place of private capital. Representative Robert J. Bulkley of Ohio sponsored the Hollis version in the House.

President Wilson quickly rejected the Hollis-Bulkley Bill. He wrote Carter Glass, chairman of the joint committee on rural credits, that he had a "very deep conviction that it is unwise and unjustifiable to extend the credit of the Government to a single class of the community."[37] Glass read the letter to insurgent Democrats who responded with equal intransigence. Stalemate ended hopes for early resolution of the conflict.

Conservative financial interests attacked both the Fletcher-Moss and Hollis-Bulkley bills. Myron T. Herrick, American ambassador to France, warned against government participation allegedly included in the Fletcher bill.[38] The New York *Times* opposed both measures, editorializing that farmer responsibility

36. *Ibid.*, 63d Congress, 2d Session, 1913, LI, 75.
37. Woodrow Wilson to Carter Glass, May 12, 1914, in Wilson Papers, Series VI, Box 205. An even stronger statement of Wilson's opposition to any direct government role in rural credits was included in J. B. Harsh to Woodrow Wilson, May 13, 1914, in Wilson Papers, Series VI, Box 205.
38. Mott, *Myron T. Herrick, Friend of France*, p. 111.

could "best be fulfilled with the least possible intervention of the Government. . . ."[39] The paper speculated that farmers who received loans from New York bankers at 9 per cent interest would spend the money more wisely than if they acquired government loans at 5 per cent. B. F. Harris, chairman of the Agricultural Commission of the American Bankers' Association, deprecated federal efforts to solve agricultural problems. Even Secretary of Agriculture Houston, while generally favoring the Fletcher bill, warned that it would have little effect on tenant farming and contained dangerous precedents.[40]

By 1913 Fletcher was the leading political exponent of rural credits. He conducted a vigorous speaking campaign to counter opposition to his bill; during one week in July, 1913, he addressed the North Carolina and South Carolina Bankers' Associations and the Florida Farmers' Union Convention. He spoke at the 1913 meeting of the American Institute of Bank Clerks in Baltimore, and other senators utilized his research in similar speeches throughout America.[41]

Agrarian radicals remained unimpressed by Fletcher's rhetoric. They demanded direct government action and determined to pigeonhole all bills until Wilson ended his obstinacy and approved the Hollis-Bulkley proposal. Wilson staunchly defended Fletcher's approach and marshaled administration and agricultural spokesmen behind the bill.

Advocates of the Fletcher-Moss Bill included both moderate conservatives and agrarian liberals. The Montgomery *Times* and Atlanta *Journal* praised the measure as far-sighted and progressive.[42] William Jennings Bryan endorsed it in his *Commoner*, and the National Conference on Marketing and Farm Credits favored the legislation. Clarence Poe—editor of *The Progressive Farmer,* most widely circulated southern farm weekly—supported Fletcher's bill and wrote privately that no other American possessed such power to help the farmer.[43] Many leading farm journals endorsed

39. New York *Times*, December 6, 1913.
40. *Ibid.*, November 14, 1915; and David F. Houston to Ralph W. Moss, December 31, 1913, Record Group 16, National Archives.
41. For example see speech text, Senator Morris Sheppard, "Rural Credit," in Wilson Papers, Series VI, Box 205.
42. Jacksonville *Florida Times-Union*, March 8 and February 17, 1914, quoting the Montgomery *Times* and Atlanta *Journal*.
43. Clarence Poe to Duncan U. Fletcher, June 3, 1916; Records of the Farm

the bill including the *Nebraska Farmer, Northwest Farmstead, American Cultivator, New England Homestead, American Agriculturist, Prairie Farmer, Farm and Home, Wallaces' Farmer, Country Gentleman, American Cooperative Journal,* and the *National Stockman and Farmer.*[44] Enthusiasm varied, with some editors predicting a farmers' millennium while others suggested minor alterations in the bill. But all preferred Fletcher's proposal to any other rural credits legislation.

Considerable ambivalence existed even among farm groups often labeled as radical. At a Farm Credits Conference held at Chicago in 1914, Homer C. Price defended the Fletcher bill as an excellent remedy, while a Wisconsin speaker called it excessively liberal, wasteful, and extravagant. The Farmer's *Review* admitted that the National Grange opposed the bill but added that many individual Grangers preferred it.[45] The *Pennsylvania Grange News* reported strong sentiment for the Fletcher-Moss plan in both the Grange and the Farmers' Union despite official opposition by both groups.[46]

Opposition to Fletcher's plan came from poorer farmers in the Midwest and Rocky Mountain states. Most of these exploited yeomen preferred the bill of Ohio's Representative E. R. Bathrick, which provided government loans directly to farmers rather than through banking intermediaries. Organizations representing poorer citizens—the National Grange, Farmers' Union, and the American Federation of Labor—opposed any credit system based on private or semi-private banks. The *National Field* first endorsed Fletcher's bill, then labeled it " a makeshift gotten up for the express purpose of deceiving the farmer and delivering him, bound hand and foot, to the mercy of Wall St."[47] Arthur Capper, later to become leader of the liberal Farm Bloc during the 1920's, maintained that though Wilson, Houston, and McAdoo wanted the Fletcher bill, it had been "shot full of holes."[48]

Many local farm associations attacked the Fletcher-Moss

Credit Administration, Record Group 103, National Archives, Washington, D.C. Hereafter cited as Record Group 103.

44. *References in the Agricultural Press regarding the Fletcher-Moss Land Bank Bill,* Record Group 16, National Archives.

45. *Ibid., Ohio Farmer,* April 25, 1914, and *Farmer's Review,* March 14, 1914.

46. *Ibid., Pennsylvania Grange News,* April, 1914.

47. *Ibid., National Field,* April 13, 1914.

48. *Ibid., Missouri Valley Farmer,* May, 1914.

proposal. One meeting in Portland, Oregon, brought together the Grange, Farmers' Union, Farmers' Society for Equity, and Oregon Federation of Labor. They concluded that neither the Bathrick nor Hollis bills went far enough but heaped particular abuse on Fletcher's recommendation. Anti–Fletcher-Moss petitions rolled in from Granges, Farmers' Unions, and labor organizations in South Dakota, Connecticut, Rhode Island, Maine, Pennsylvania, Michigan, Indiana, Kansas, North Dakota, Wyoming, and California.[49]

The most damaging criticism of the Fletcher-Moss Bill came from an unexpected source, David Lubin. Lubin's private criticism of Fletcher's use of French precedent turned into open opposition. In a widely reprinted letter he asserted that bankers, not farmers, would profit from the bill. This hardly resembled his private objection that the legislation smacked of government paternalism. Arthur Capper and others who opposed the Fletcher plan delighted in utilizing this testimony by the man partly responsible for arousing interest in rural credits. Fletcher publicly ignored Lubin's attack but privately instructed W. W. Flannagan, a close friend and rural credits authority, to refute the charges.[50]

Desperate farmers wearied of the rancorous and sterile debate by early 1916 and demanded that leaders compromise their differences. Prominent agricultural papers advised farmers to end their divisive haggling and direct all efforts toward passing some kind of bill. Pressure groups such as the Rural Credit League, the Northwestern Rural Credit Association, and the National Grange demanded passage of some bill, even if not wholly desirable. During the same period, Fletcher's close advisers suggested that he might strengthen his measure by allowing the government more authority and a larger financial role.[51]

Fletcher had always approached the issue in a conciliatory spirit. As early as October, 1914, he stated that some compromise between proponents and opponents of direct federal aid must and would be made. Fletcher wrote Wilson in October, 1915, that the Hollis-Bulkley measure adopted "the principles of our bill *with a few additional features*," indicating that the proposal was accept-

49. *Ibid.*, *Rural Spirit*, April 15, 1914. Also see petitions in Record Group 46, National Archives.
50. W. W. Flannagan to David F. Houston, August 14, 1915, Record Group 16, National Archives.
51. W. W. Flannagan to Carter Glass, January 28, 1916; and W. W. Flannagan to Charles Hall Davis, January 28, 1916; in Glass Papers, Box 49.

able with certain modifications. He added that despite disagreement over direct government participation, a conclusion could be reached.[52]

Daily negotiations seeking some compromise began in the late fall of 1915. Hollis dropped his provision linking land banks to the Federal Reserve System, and Fletcher recanted on direct government grants. On November 23 Fletcher announced that he would not object to a plan which allowed the government to subscribe half the necessary capital if "local" funds proved insufficient.[53] The Floridian hinted that President Wilson might endorse such a proposal, and the special congressional joint committee accepted this arrangement on December 24, 1915. When completed, the statute adopted the framework of the Fletcher-Moss Bill. Government funds supplied $500,000 in capital to each of the twelve federal banks and purchased bank bonds up to $50 million annually if private investors refused.

Fletcher's concept of farmer cooperatives survived, and only local farm associations consisting of ten or more members could borrow funds. Since each borrower was required to purchase stock equal to 5 per cent of his loan, the farmers became stockholders in the land banks. Gradually, government capital would be replaced and farmers would own the land banks. Fletcher consulted with subcommittee members on December 24 and endorsed the compromise.[54]

President Wilson, facing re-election and desperately needing progressive support, summoned Senator Hollis in early January, 1916, and announced his approval of the modified bill.[55] Conservatives still rejected any concession; Eugenius H. Outerbridge, president of the New York Chamber of Commerce, predicted financial panic if Congress adopted the bill, while the New York *Times*

52. U. S., *Congressional Record*, 63d Congress, 2d Session, 1914, LI, 16299; and Duncan U. Fletcher to Woodrow Wilson, October 21, 1915, in Wilson Papers, Series VI, Box 205. Emphasis that of the author.
53. New York *Times*, November 24, 1915.
54. Jacksonville *Florida Times-Union*, December 25, 1915.
55. Richard M. Abrams, "Woodrow Wilson and the Southern Congressmen, 1913–1916," *The Journal of Southern History*, XXII (November, 1956), 433. Abrams concludes that Wilson compromised because he needed western farm votes in the 1916 campaign; Arthur Link ("The South and the 'New Freedom' ") claims that continuing pressure from southern congressional liberals brought this capitulation. Either view makes the Farm Loan Bank Act extremely important in winning farmer-liberal support in the 1916 presidential campaign.

editorialized that the bill was based on "the socialistic experiments of Europe in cooperative finance."[56] Despite these belated protests, the measure swept through the Senate in May, 1916, by a 58-to-5 vote. Wilson signed the bill in July and presented Fletcher a gold pen in recognition of his leadership in the long struggle.

Progressives considered the act one of the notable achievements of the Wilson years. The St. Louis *Post-Dispatch* summarized that "in the long list of admirable laws . . . under the present administration, perhaps there is none that fills a greater need than this farm bank law." Colonel Edward M. House, Wilson's confidant and adviser, viewed the measure as one of the administration's most liberal accomplishments.[57]

Credit for the bill went largely to Fletcher. A New York newspaper, the Yonkers *News*, called him one of the "progressive and most influential members" of the Senate, who did more to make rural credits a national issue than anyone else.[58] The New York *American*, a Hearst paper which had supported the legislation, editorialized: "To Senator Fletcher . . . is due the greater part of the credit for steering this legislation successfully through Congress. The Senator was a pioneer in the movement . . . and [he] keenly felt the injustice which the existing banking laws allowed to fall upon [farmers]. . . ."[59] John Lee Coulter, agricultural expert and Dean of West Virginia University, confided that Fletcher accomplished more in this one measure than many statesmen achieved in a lifetime; President Wilson recognized passage of the bill by congratulating the senator on "a piece of work well done."[60] In Florida the progressive Sumter County *Advocate* praised his leadership "against all the great moneyed combinations," and observed that his name was "a household word in every farm house in the United States."[61]

56. New York *Times*, May 5, and 22, 1916.
57. St. Louis *Post-Dispatch*, October 10, 1916, and Charles Seymour, ed., *The Intimate Papers of Colonel House* (New York: Houghton Mifflin Company, 1926, p. 344.
58. Jacksonville *Florida Times-Union*, December 13, 1913, quoting Yonkers *News*.
59. New York *American*, July 19, 1916, copy in Record Group 103, National Archives.
60. John Lee Coulter to Duncan U. Fletcher, October 7, 1916, and Woodrow Wilson to Duncan U. Fletcher, October 16 and May 23, 1916, in Wilson Papers, Series VI, Box 205.
61. Jacksonville *Florida Times-Union*, August 16, 1916, quoting Sumter County *Advocate*.

Fletcher justly received credit for the 1916 Farm Loan Bank Act. He generated the original interest which made rural credits a national issue. His energy brought recognition from both political parties, and his indefatigable speaking tours on behalf of the bill publicized it in every part of America. As chairman of both European research commissions, he formulated their final recommendations to Congress. He introduced the first long-term rural credits bill, and the final 1916 measure incorporated the entire structure of his original plan. His willingness to compromise on the issue of federal participation helped break a two-year congressional deadlock and insured conservative Democratic support in the Senate. During the entire contest he demonstrated deep concern for agrarian interests and especially for landless tenant farmers. Recalling his own teen-age experience, he rejected conservative arguments that impoverished farmers should blame themselves for their failure rather than the economic system.

The 1916 act vitally affected American agriculture. Interest rates of 5½ per cent contrasted sharply with pre-1916 rates averaging 10 per cent. The Farm Loan Board received 100,000 letters requesting information during its first month of existence. By 1919 the banks had loaned $182,897,000 to 75,400 farmers. The banks held loans of $1,204,000,000 in June, 1929. Because liberty bond drives absorbed so much capital, private sources subscribed only $100,000 of the original capital, so the government purchased $8,880,000 of Land Bank stock. By 1929 borrower-stockholders had completely repaid the government funds, increased capital stock from $9,000,000 to $65,000,000, and possessed $1,177,000,000 in Land Bank bonds. Former Treasury Secretary William G. McAdoo viewed the program in retrospect: "Not only have these banks done a huge volume of business, but . . . their influence in the field of agricultural credits has been highly beneficial. The activities of grasping money-lenders in the mortgage business have been reduced to a minimum. Any farmer who has good security in land need not pay a higher rate of interest on a first mortgage today than [5½ per cent]. . . ."[62] Leading agricultural historians conclude that the 1916 act accounted for American success in meeting the tremendous agricultural demands of the First World War. Land Banks provided loans to midwestern farmers at half the pre-1916

62. McAdoo, *Crowded Years*, p. 440.

interest rates, resulting in a land boom and general agrarian prosperity.[63]

Fletcher took particular pride in the bill's effect on Florida. He toured the state in 1916 telling farmers how to apply for loans, and he attempted to include citrus in the "agricultural" category covered by the bill. Local farmer cooperatives sprang up across the state, and loan requests flowed into his office from every hamlet and rural community in Florida. State farmers applied for $6 million in loans during the first year of operation, and the Farm Loan Board granted $1 million.[64] Florida farmers complained to Fletcher about the slowness in processing loans. Delay developed because the Federal Land Bank at Columbia, South Carolina, serving four states, received more loan applications than any other bank, an indication of the act's enormous service to southern farmers.[65] Fletcher protested when unscrupulous Florida bankers tried to manipulate the act for their own advantage, and he also advocated a liberal interpretation of the act, which provided millions of dollars to southern tenant farmers.[66]

The Floridian retained his concern for American agriculture throughout his career. W. W. Flannagan, secretary of the Farm Loan Board, considered Fletcher the leading congressional authority on rural credits and consulted him on expansion of the bill. Florida's senior senator successfully opposed a plan to establish different credit rates for the West, East, and South.[67] When conservative Republicans tried to repeal the tax exemption status of the farm loan bonds in 1919, Fletcher joined Representative A. F. Lever of South Carolina to defeat the crippling proposal.[68]

The 1916 Farm Loan Act created no utopia. It left sharecroppers only slightly better than before, while red tape and ad-

63. Saloutos and Hicks, *Agricultural Discontent in the Middle West*, pp. 86, 102–3.
64. Farm Loan Commissioner to Duncan U. Fletcher, December 14, 1917, Record Group 103, National Archives.
65. W. W. Flannagan to Duncan U. Fletcher, July 9, 1917, Record Group 103, National Archives.
66. L. B. Shuler to Duncan U. Fletcher, December 26, 1916; Farm Loan Board to Duncan U. Fletcher, December 8, 1917; and Duncan U. Fletcher to Federal Farm Loan Board, December 5, 1917; Record Group 103, National Archives.
67. W. W. Flannagan to Duncan U. Fletcher, April 20, 1917, and Duncan U. Fletcher to William G. McAdoo, January 3, 1917, Record Group 103, National Archives.
68. Jacksonville *Florida Times-Union*, August 16, 1919.

ministrative delay hindered its operation among more affluent farmers. But the act committed the government to a positive and direct role in agrarian economics, and in that sense it was the forerunner of the broad agricultural experiments of the New Deal. The frustrated, angry cry of destitute farmers compromised Fletcher's conservatism. His persuasive logic contributed to the bill's final structure as a joint venture of private enterprise and governmental initiative rather than a program of federal dole. In later years Fletcher treasured the rural credits system as his greatest congressional achievement.

CHAPTER VI

The People's Ships

AMERICAN ATTENTION shifted from agricultural and domestic reform to foreign affairs in 1916. The United States found it increasingly difficult to maintain neutrality in the face of provocative German action. Administration leaders attempted to avoid foreign confrontation, but ominous European events transcended concern for internal matters. Senator Fletcher, who demonstrated considerable creative genius in formulating rural credits legislation, assumed a new role. Although he did not draft the bill, his adroit senatorial maneuvering won passage for one of Wilson's most important measures, the Shipping Act of September 7, 1916.

Bitter conflict surrounded American maritime policy. While authorities suggested many remedies, none questioned the desperate state of the nation's shipping. In 1846 American ships had transported 81 per cent of the nation's foreign commerce. This figure had declined to 66 per cent in 1860, 26 per cent in 1875, 8 per cent in 1901, and 5 per cent in 1914. Only four American ships plied the trans-Atlantic trade routes when the First World War began. The United States ranked second in total world exports but eighth in merchant marine. She exported twenty-two times as much as Norway, whose merchant marine was twice as large, even allowing for American ferries.[1]

Since 95 per cent of the nation's foreign trade traveled in

---

1. Jacksonville *Florida Times-Union*, May 18, 1915, and New York *Times*, November 8, 1915. For a brief survey of the economic and strategic problems involved in America's maritime deficiency, see Frederick Palmer, *Newton D. Baker: America at War* (New York: Dodd, Mead, and Co., 1931), I, 397–408.

foreign bottoms, the war brought catastrophic dislocation. During the first six months of hostilities, German and Austrian merchantmen disappeared behind a tight British blockade, while the British diverted their shipping to military service. This diversion, coupled with aggressive German submarine action, accounted for two million tons of British shipping. By January, 1915, 13 per cent of the world's prewar tonnage had vanished from trade routes.[2]

Freight rates responded to this decline in available bottoms. Rates on grain shipped from New York to Rotterdam increased 900 per cent between July, 1914, and January, 1915, while freight costs for flour soared 500 per cent. The southern cotton trade suffered even greater dislocation. Cotton shipping rates from Norfolk to Bremen, Germany, rose an astronomical 1,100 per cent. The average expense for sending a bale to Europe climbed from $1.25 in June, 1914, to $25 in January, 1915.[3] Bremen and other German ports paid a spectacular twenty cents a pound for cotton, and southern commerce needed German dyes and chemicals. But prevailing freight costs wiped out possible profits and left cotton bales rotting on southern wharves. Under such adverse conditions, total American exports declined from 5,700,000 tons in July, 1913, to only 3,360,000 in November, 1914.[4] Loud, vigorous protests rolled in from companies unable to export products and from farmers burdened with surplus crops.[5]

Fletcher's Florida constituents suffered heavily. Jacksonville's Schuler Cooperage Company, which exported wrapping paper to Europe, paid freight rates of twenty-three cents per hundred pounds in June, 1914. Between August and late October the company could not obtain shipping at any price. In October the price advanced to thirty cents, then to forty-five cents in December, for a total increase of 96 per cent in six months. This rate drove the company completely out of the foreign market.[6] The president

2. See speech text by William G. McAdoo, "The Shipping Bill," in Wilson Papers, Series VI, Box 326.
3. William G. McAdoo to Duncan U. Fletcher, January 23, 1915, in McAdoo Papers, Box 484, Letterbook 19.
4. Duncan U. Fletcher, "Promotion of Foreign Commerce of the United States By Providing Adequate Shipping Facilities," in Wilson Papers, Series VI, Box 235.
5. William G. McAdoo to Duncan U. Fletcher, December 18, 1914, and J. W. Ashley to William G. McAdoo, December 1, 1914, in McAdoo Papers, Box 483, Letterbook 18, and Box 127.
6. Letter from Schuler Cooperage Company, December 22, 1914, quoted by

of the Pensacola Chamber of Commerce complained that business languished because of the shipping lag, and vessels could not be obtained "even at the piratical prices asked."[7]

The merchant marine also fitted conveniently into Fletcher's overall agrarian scheme. Rural credits provided capital while waterways and canals connected the hinterland to its domestic market. Cheap overseas transportation provided a foreign outlet for America's growing agricultural surplus.

Administration leaders approached maritime problems cautiously. Congress passed a bill encouraging foreign ships to register under the United States flag, but the act proved unsuccessful. When private insurance companies levied prohibitive rates, the shipping industry persuaded Congress to establish federal war risk insurance. Freight rates remained high, and farm prices continued their decline, so Fletcher joined other southern congressmen demanding immediate action.

Treasury Secretary William G. McAdoo suggested a new approach. His plan provided a $30 million government-owned corporation to construct or purchase ships. Wilson won the approval of Democratic congressional leaders in August, 1914, and Senator James P. Clarke of Arkansas, chairman of the Commerce Committee, introduced the ship purchase bill. The bill immediately bogged down in a quagmire of indifference and opposition. Clarke showed little interest, Republicans cried "socialism," and liberals feared that purchase of German ships interned in United States' ports might compromise American neutrality. The opponents combined on the Commerce Committee to sidetrack the bill.

Convinced that the cotton surplus resulted from inadequate transportation, Fletcher viewed government shipping as the only practical solution.[8] Senator William J. Stone of Missouri reintroduced the administration plan on December 9, and Fletcher, acting in place of ailing Senator Clarke as chairman of the Commerce Committee, was selected to manage the bill. He met with the secretaries of Navy, War, and Commerce on December 23 to chart strategy, and assumed a central role in the hardest legislative battle of the Wilson era.

William G. McAdoo, "The Shipping Bill," in Wilson Papers, Series VI, Box 326.
7. C. E. Dobson to Duncan U. Fletcher, December 12, 1914; in Wilson Papers, Series VI, Box 235.
8. Jacksonville *Florida Times-Union*, November 12, 1914.

Opposition to the bill centered in the powerful steamship lines. With their losses insured by the government, these lines tripled freight rates and frequently paid for a ship on two voyages. Conservative newspapers deplored government control as "statism" and "socialism."[9] The United States Chamber of Commerce surveyed its membership and found that seven out of every eight members opposed the bill.[10] The Chamber expressed the general feeling of nonexporting American business: "Government operation is un-American, is likely to be more extravagant and expensive than private control, will seriously interfere with individual initiative and retards the enterprise of our citizens."[11] Republicans countered the McAdoo bill by proposing government subsidies to private shipping companies.

Wilson discussed strategy with Fletcher on January 2 and 3, 1915, and the Floridian assured him that prospects for passage seemed excellent.[12] Fletcher then took his case to the Senate. Countering conservative charges of socialism, he argued that the bill provided only temporary government ownership. After chiding private industry for its failure to build American shipping, he classified the McAdoo bill as "commercial necessity" rather than "government paternalism." He told liberals who feared military involvement that government control would actually reduce international incidents by insuring strict observance of neutrality laws. Introducing an argument which proved more effective two years later, he suggested that merchant ships could be converted to naval auxiliaries in event of war. Finally, he refuted Republican proposals for ship subsidies by calling them a tax on all the people for the benefit of a few businessmen.[13]

Fletcher discovered division within Democratic ranks and called a series of party meetings for January. Some southern conservatives balked at government ownership and announced their opposition to the bill.[14] Fletcher presided over a barren caucus

9. *Ibid.*, June 12, 1915; New York *Times,* November 8, 1915.
10. New York *Times*, November 8, 1915.
11. United States Chamber of Commerce, *Report on the Upbuilding of Our Merchant Marine*, in Wilson Papers, Series VI, Box 326.
12. Jacksonville *Florida Times-Union*, January 3 and 4, 1915.
13. U.S., *Congressional Record*, 63d Congress, 3d Session, 1915, LII, 912–14.
14. Seven Democrats deserted the administration: John H. Bankhead (Alabama), James K. Vardaman (Mississippi), James P. Clarke (Arkansas), Gilbert M. Hitchcock (Nebraska), James A. O'Gorman (New York), Johnson N. Camden (Kentucky), Thomas W. Hardwick (Georgia).

on January 18, and outnumbered Republicans launched a filibuster the next day. He decided to let the filibusterers wear themselves out, but the GOP threatened to debate all session if necessary to kill the bill. Fletcher remained in constant contact with Wilson and held Democratic caucuses on January 20, 21, and 23. On January 23 he proposed binding all Democrats to the majority will, but several senators refused to support the bill regardless of caucus action.

Wilson offered to compromise on January 25, and several Democratic defectors returned to the administration fold. At his weekly cabinet meeting, the President expressed confidence that the bill would pass.[15]

Fletcher, heartened by Wilson's intervention, announced night sessions to exhaust filibustering Republicans. Plunging into the debate, he reveled in conservative inconsistencies and ripped their logic apart. To cries of socialism, he presented a four-part retort: for fifty years there had been no individual initiative by American capitalists to solve the problem, nor was there likely to be any short of government subsidies; the War Risk Insurance Bureau and government operation of the Panama Canal steamship line proved that government ownership could be both inexpensive and successful; the multiplication of government employees was not inherently bad and might be good so long as such operations avoided waste, corruption, and mismanagement; bigness in government was not necessarily bad as proved by the efficient Post Office Department. He reminded liberals that President Wilson could involve the nation in war under the status quo, and authority to purchase ships would hardly increase this danger.[16]

When argument failed, the Floridian turned to parliamentary maneuver. On January 29 he submitted a caucus compromise for the original bill. The modification, backed by some insurgent Democrats, provided for government control only if private capital was unavailable. Republicans, realizing that some independent Democrats might support this version, unsuccessfully tried to block the substitute. This move lost, they gained the floor and talked past midnight while Florida's senior senator snoozed on his desk.

15. E. David Cronon, ed., *The Cabinet Diaries of Josephus Daniels, 1913–1921* (Lincoln: University of Nebraska Press, 1963), p. 94.
16. U.S., *Congressional Record*, 63d Congress, 3d Session, 1915, LII, 1061-62, 1099–1107.

Anti–ship purchase senators sprang a trick of their own three days later. Senator Clarke gained the floor from administration Democrats and moved to recommit the bill. Republicans poured from the cloakroom and joined nine defecting Democrats, including Florida's Nathan B. Bryan, to provide a clear Senate majority. Fletcher happened to be on the floor, sprang to his feet, and moved for adjournment.[17] The motion carried and adjournment saved the bill. Loyal Democrats regrouped at another caucus and launched a counter-filibuster to prevent recommital.

Fletcher switched strategy during the following week and tried to recommit the bill with instructions for specific amendments to make it palatable to bolting Democrats. This effort fell two votes short when illness prevented attendance by a pair of administration senators. Three progressive Republicans agreed to support the amended bill, regaining the initiative and forcing conservatives to resume their filibuster. Fletcher attempted to cut off debate on February 9, but Republicans countered with fifty-four continuous hours of debate, the longest single session in American history to 1915.

Exhausted by the prolonged controversy, Fletcher made one further attempt to pass the bill. He gained the floor shortly before midnight on February 10 and read for some time in a monotonous monotone. Then, without changing pitch, he called for a vote on the pending amendment. An alert Republican discovered the ruse, regained the floor, and resumed the filibuster.[18] After this failure, Fletcher bitterly acknowledged defeat. Throughout the debate he demonstrated a brilliant grasp of parliamentary tactics. His diplomatic negotiation nearly passed the bill, but Wilson's refusal to compromise and his heavy-handed use of patronage alienated several key Democrats.[19]

During the January controversy, McAdoo and Secretary of Commerce Redfield supplied Fletcher with information.[20] The senator determined floor strategy and suggested several minor

17. New York *Times,* February 2, 1915.
18. *Ibid.,* February 10, 1915.
19. Arthur S. Link, *Wilson: The Struggle for Neutrality* (Princeton, New Jersey: Princeton University Press, 1960), pp. 149–50.
20. William G. McAdoo to Duncan U. Fletcher, January 23, 1915; February 16, 1915; December 21, 1914; in McAdoo Papers, Box 484, Letterbooks 19 and 20. See application of these arguments in Duncan U. Fletcher, "Promotion of Foreign Commerce of the United States by Providing Adequate Shipping Facilities," in Wilson Papers, Series VI, Box 235.

amendments to make the bill acceptable to reluctant Democrats. McAdoo retained final authority over changes and vetoed several of Fletcher's modifications. The Floridian conducted a vigorous research program of his own and broadened debate to include several areas not emphasized by McAdoo.[21]

Fletcher's most significant contribution to the discussion concerned Latin American trade. In Congress and before numerous civic groups, Fletcher emphasized the need for an American merchant marine to capitalize on new trade relations. An extensive commercial tour of Latin America had convinced him that normal pre-1914 economic relations could never be restored. He had developed this theme at the 1915 Southern Commercial Congress and won endorsement for a government-owned shipping fleet. While addressing the Florida legislature in 1915, he had predicted that Latin America would soon look commercially to New York rather than London. He interjected this issue into the entire maritime controversy.

Both President Wilson and Fletcher attributed their 1915 defeat to pressure from private shipping lines, and neither man viewed such opposition charitably. Wilson expressed his bitterness to a close friend: ". . . the shipping interest [*sic*] do not want this bill. They will do nothing themselves without a subsidy . . . if they cannot get that . . . they do not mean to let the development take place, because the control of ocean carriage and of ocean rates will pass out of their hands. We are fighting as a matter of fact the most formidable (covert) lobby that has stood against us yet in anything we have attempted; and we shall see the fight to a finish. . . ."[22] Fletcher avoided public accusations until January, 1915. Angered by conservative obstruction, he then charged that steamship lines and Wall Street fought the measure because they feared that successful governmental operation of shipping lines would result in federal ownership of telegraph, telephone, railroad, and other public service corporations.

---

21. William G. McAdoo to Duncan U. Fletcher, December 14 and 24, 1914; January 18, 1915; in McAdoo Papers, Box 483, Letterbook 18, and Box 484, Letterbook 19. Also see Fletcher's requests for information in Bureau of Marine Inspection and Navigation, Record Group 41, National Archives, Washington, D. C.

22. Woodrow Wilson to Mrs. Crawford H. Toy, January 31, 1915, in Ray Stannard Baker Papers, Box 16, Manuscript Division, Library of Congress, Washington, D.C. Hereafter cited as Baker Papers.

In a speech reminiscent of his Populist-influenced rhetoric in the 1890's, Fletcher revealed an alleged rate-fixing cabal. He accused International Mercantile Marine, managed by J. P. Morgan, of owning numerous foreign shipping corporations; in addition, United States Steel, Standard Oil, and the United Fruit Company directed other fleets. He charged that railroads and corporations managed by J. P. Morgan and William Rockefeller controlled nine-tenths of all coastwise shipping. Furthermore, interlocking directorates with the National City Bank, United States Trust Company, National Bank of Commerce, and Guaranty Trust Company, all governed by Rockefeller–Morgan–George W. Perkins interests, dominated practically all American export shipping. Fletcher concluded in the tradition of the New Freedom: "It is against this aggregation that the administration, representing the American people, finds itself. The shipping interests realize that the entrance of the Government into the field will break the chain by which they have the independents shut out."[23]

Fletcher repeated these indictments in a Jacksonville speech. Shipping companies profited from the war, he asserted, with the London Stock Exchange reporting dividends of 10 to 300 per cent. The Senator hurled stinging invective at the private lines: "Objection was made by the shipping interest to the ship purchase bill on the ground that they did not think the government ought to go into any business . . . [in spite of] the fact that they not only failed but refused to build up an American merchant marine and refused to allow independent concerns to do it. These very people appealed to congress to establish a bureau of insurance on the ground that they could not get their vessels or cargo insured by private concerns."[24]

McAdoo and Fletcher agreed that conservative attacks on the alleged socialist implications of the bill damaged their cause. Both men also concurred that an intensive campaign could focus lethargic public opinion, and the Treasury Secretary launched a coast to coast speaking tour to coalesce support.[25] His speeches at Kansas City and the University of Wisconsin sparked lively debate. Fletcher meanwhile answered private criticisms from businessmen,

23. U.S., *Congressional Record*, 63d Congress, 3d Session, 1915, LII, 2458–59.
24. Jacksonville *Florida Times-Union*, May 18, 1915.
25. William G. McAdoo to Duncan U. Fletcher, August 13, 1915; in McAdoo Papers, Box 486, unnumbered Letterbook.

supplied statistical support for McAdoo's speeches, and used his printing committee to distribute ship purchase propaganda to thousands of leading citizens.[26]

This campaign brought the desired result. Resolutions begging deliverance from the "shipping trust" poured into Congress. Thanks to Fletcher's propaganda blitz and soaring freight rates, southerners directed a torrent of abuse at their bolting Democratic senators. McAdoo attributed ultimate passage to this pressure from an aroused public.[27]

Administration forces regrouped in December, 1915, for a final effort. At their organizational caucus, Democrats renominated maverick Senator James P. Clarke as president *pro tempore* of the Senate. Wilson loyalists balked and nominated Senator Atlee Pomerene of Ohio. All of the 1915 shipping defectors voted for Clarke, who also won every southern senator but three, insuring a 28 to 23 victory. Fletcher, angered by Clarke's recalcitrance on maritime legislation, joined Virginia's two senators in support of Pomerene.[28]

Fletcher conferred with McAdoo in December and they approved a revised draft of the bill after several days' work.[29] The administration decided to link the shipping proposal to military preparedness, focusing primary emphasis on an issue suggested by Fletcher in 1915. The revised bill also authorized $50 million for ship construction and established a United States Shipping Board. The Board might lease its fleet to private lines thus erasing some conservative arguments. The measure frankly disavowed purchase of interned German ships. Fletcher announced the revised strategy in a speech to the American Academy of Political Science in November, 1915, and Democrats submitted the new proposal to Congress in January, 1916.

Returning to the congressional wars, Fletcher countered arguments of extravagance by citing 1915 freight costs of $216 million above normal, a figure four times the estimated cost of the shipping

26. William G. McAdoo to Duncan U. Fletcher, September 23, 1915, October 6, 1915, and Duncan U. Fletcher to William G. McAdoo, February 15, 1916, in McAdoo Papers, Box 487, Letterbook 27; and Box 155.
27. See letters to Senator Hoke Smith of Georgia, a Democrat who refused to endorse the ship purchase bill, in Wilson Papers, Series VI, Box 326. Also McAdoo, *Crowded Years*, p. 314.
28. Jacksonville *Florida Times-Union*, December 4, 1915.
29. William G. McAdoo to Duncan U. Fletcher, December 2 and 10, 1915, in McAdoo Papers, Box 488, Letterbooks 29 and 30.

bill. Debate dragged into the summer of 1916, when Democrats attempted to array full strength behind the measure. Fletcher mobilized maximum party unity, aided by Wilson, who agreed to limited compromise and who pressured reluctant Democrats.[30]

Fletcher conferred with Republican leaders on August 15. Placated by modifying amendments, they agreed not to filibuster. He reconciled a lone dissident Democrat, and the bill passed with unanimous Democratic support on August 18 by a 38 to 21 vote.

Passage of the shipping measure evoked mixed reaction. Some Progressives moaned that the long delay had cost millions of dollars because purchasable ships were no longer available.[31] Not all liberals succumbed to such pessimism. The Washington *Post* predicted that "thanks to Senator Fletcher of Florida, who distinguished himself in bringing about the passage of this act, it will not be many years before the American merchant marine will plow the waters of every ocean and add untold millions to the wealth of the nation. . . ."[32] McAdoo telephoned Fletcher from a New Jersey resort, congratulating him on passage of the bill for which he performed such "hard and intelligent" work; years later McAdoo listed Missouri's Senator James A. Reed and Fletcher as the bill's staunchest defenders.[33] Navy Secretary Josephus Daniels also praised Fletcher's vision and termed senatorial rejection of the shipping bill in 1914 the "blunder of our decade."[34]

Since all available ships were in active service, the Shipping Board began constructing new vessels. The necessity for haste created near hysteria, and the government spent seven times more for ships in the next eighteen months than the total cost of the Panama Canal. Shipyard workers labored all night under the glare of electric lights.

When Senator Clarke, chairman of the Commerce Committee, died in September, 1916, Fletcher ascended to this powerful post. For the next two years he presided over the creation of an American merchant fleet. The senator sponsored wartime bills

30. John W. Kern to William G. McAdoo, July 5, 1916, and Woodrow Wilson to Duncan U. Fletcher, August 23, 1916, in Wilson Papers, Series VI, Box 327.
31. McAdoo, *Crowded Years*, p. 315; and Josephus Daniels, *The Wilson Era, Years of Peace—1910–1917* (Chapel Hill: University of North Carolina Press, 1944), p. 421.
32. Jacksonville *Florida Times-Union*, October 5, 1916, quoting Washington *Post*.
33. Telephone memorandum, in McAdoo Papers, Box 491, Letterbook 39; and McAdoo, *Crowded Years*, p. 307.
34. Cronon, *The Cabinet Diaries of Josephus Daniels, 1913–1921*, p. 278.

authorizing the President to nationalize shipbuilding plants, requisition ships and terminals, and control transportation systems near shipyards.[35]

Another controversial expansion of government power involved federal housing. Shipyard officials at Newport News, Virginia, complained that lack of dwellings hindered labor recruitment. The Shipping Board established several investigating committees which promptly bogged down in conferences and red tape. Fletcher tired of the indecision and told shipping officials: "We can not wait upon your developing some plan that you have been at work on for months in the past; there is need for ships now; there is need for housing in order that men can be had. . . ."[36] He took only two days to devise a plan for housing workers, and the Senate passed his $50 million measure on January 18, 1918. President Wilson conferred with congressional and cabinet leaders later that month to determine coordination for the housing project. The cabinet consensus preferred administration by the Department of Labor, but Fletcher feared continued delay and persuaded Wilson to establish independent control of the program.[37]

While seeking efficiency and rapid production, the Floridian maintained his concern for the lowly seaman. After admitting a manpower deficiency in the October, 1918, issue of the *Merchant Mariner*, he argued that seamen could be provided only "when we assure the men fair treatment, wholesome and healthful surroundings, [and] reasonable compensation for services. . . ."[38] He lauded the La Follette Seamen's Act as the first step toward equitable treatment for mariners.

Adequate housing and a rising standard of living for sailors solved the two major labor problems, and by May, 1918, the government was operating 123 shipyards. Fletcher boasted to Wilson that the yards were launching two vessels a day.[39] Between 1916 and 1919 the American government expended $2,645,000,000 to construct 12 million tons of shipping. During these years the nation increased its tonnage from 9 to 25 per cent of the world total. The nation's transoceanic shipping increased from one to seven million

35. U.S., *Congressional Record*, 65th Congress, 2nd Session, 1918, LVI, 621.
36. *Ibid.*, 5213.
37. Cronon, *The Cabinet Diaries of Josephus Daniels, 1913–1921*, pp. 273–74.
38. Jacksonville *Florida Times-Union*, October 20, 1918, quoting *The Merchant Mariner*.
39. New York *Times*, March 16, 1918.

tons. Where only 5 per cent of America's commerce traveled in her bottoms during June, 1914, 55 per cent did so in 1920.[40] American historians date the modern United States merchant marine from 1916.[41]

Such a stupendous project involved inevitable waste, and the cost per ton of construction was the highest in world history. Fletcher argued persuasively that excesses invariably accompanied speed, and the advent of war demanded rapid production at whatever cost. In addition, salaries steadily increased and unskilled workmen required extensive training. Senate Republicans dismissed such explanations and demanded thorough investigation. Fletcher's Commerce Committee and the Justice Department probed charges of excessive profits.

Persistent rumors of profiteering surrounded the complex at Hog Island, Pennsylvania, largest of three fabricating shipyards. The government had let a contract to American International Corporation, and this private company—composed of such powerful financiers as Frank A. Vanderlip, Percy A. Rockefeller, and J. Ogden Armour—had received $6 million to provide technical knowledge. The company's original estimate of $31 million mushroomed to $66 million, and the corporation allegedly furnishing technical advice contained no directors who had ever built a ship. The entire situation proved acutely embarrassing to Fletcher, for Peter O. Knight, his Florida confidant and political ally, was vice-president and general counsel of the American International Corporation. Knight vigorously denied charges of profiteering, but the Fletcher committee found numerous irregularities in the operation.[42]

Reaction to these disclosures varied. The London *Times* defended the Hog Island operation, which launched one ship every twenty-nine working hours during 1919, as the outstanding feature of the entire shipping program.[43] Partisan journals rejoined that enormous volume did not justify waste and fraud.

40. New York *Times*, October 10, 1920, and Jacksonville *Florida Times-Union*, November 20, 1919, quoting *Sea Power*.
41. Arthur S. Link, *Woodrow Wilson and the Progressive Era, 1910–1917* (New York: Harper and Brothers, 1954), p. 192.
42. Scrapbook B, Knight Collection, and Jacksonville *Florida Times-Union*, February 12, 1918.
43. Hog Island *News*, April 1, 1920, quoting London *Times*, in Scrapbook B, Knight Collection.

Even some Democrats privately criticized the yards. Navy Secretary Josephus Daniels suspected excessive profits and recognized wasteful practices; McAdoo admitted unnecessary expenses but attributed responsibility to Republicans who delayed enactment of the shipping bill.[44]

If such indictments tarnished Fletcher's Washington reputation, they hardly clouded his brilliance in Florida. Anxious civic leaders bombarded him with requests for shipyards.[45] Jacksonville—with five railroad lines, abundant cheap labor, and excellent dock facilities—proved ideal for maritime construction. Fletcher allocated weeks of work to bring government contracts to his home city. The Merrill-Stevens Company received many of these contracts, invested $2.5 million in expansion, and became the largest single operating plant in Florida. The government constructed a plant on the St. Johns River which employed 468 men, and three other ship-building plants invested $3 million in local development. Businessmen poured $15 million into Jacksonville's economy during the year ending August, 1918.[46] Northern capital flowed into the city and controlled two of the largest shipyards.

Still unsatisfied, Fletcher insisted that lumber and other Georgia-Florida naval stores be shipped from Jacksonville. The Shipping Board concurred, and 80 per cent of the board's purchases in the area left via the city.[47] This policy further swelled Jacksonville's booming economy. On March 15, 1918, the Shipping Board had 2,225,000 feet of lumber and 250 carloads of piling on the municipal docks awaiting shipment. Jacksonville constructed a $1.5 million terminal to accommodate the additional commerce. Between 1917 and 1919, the city changed from a tourist resort to a manufacturing center with a payroll of $1 million a week. Jacksonville could thank her climate and senior senator for this transformation.

44. Daniels, *The Wilson Era, Years of Peace*, pp. 421–22, and McAdoo, *Crowded Years*, pp. 315–16. Frederick Palmer, biographer of Newton D. Baker, argues that the Hog Island facility was justified and that it prevented the isolation of America's expeditionary army in France; Palmer, *Newton D. Baker: America at War*, I, 401–4.
45. See United States Shipping Board, Record Group 32, National Archives, Washington, D.C. Hereafter cited as Record Group 32.
46. Jacksonville *Florida Times-Union*, August 5, 1918.
47. Duncan U. Fletcher to Edward N. Hurley, March 5, 1918, and Edward N. Hurley to Duncan U. Fletcher, March 15, 1918, Record Group 32, National Archives.

Severe labor shortages developed despite salaries ranging from thirty cents to eighty cents an hour. The government compensated for the drain of Jacksonville Negroes to the North by establishing an industrial school to train unskilled workers. The shipyards employed women, and Fletcher's provision for government housing also helped minimize the labor shortage. The government constructed a $1 million tract containing 158 houses and appropriately named it Fletcher Park.[48]

Other Florida cities enviously eyed Jacksonville. Shipyards were constructed at Miami, St. Petersburg, Tarpon Springs, Pensacola, Apalachicola, and Panama City to compete for government contracts. Some of these shared Jacksonville's good fortune. A company at Pensacola, one of the largest yards on the Gulf of Mexico, received $15 million in government contracts and employed 4,000 men. Several firms in Tampa also received shipping contracts. By June, 1918, Florida yards had contracted to build 68 ships totaling 435,000 tons. State shipbuilders employed 11,157 laborers and constructed $46,500,000 worth of shipping.[49]

Florida's boom ended almost as suddenly as it began. Fletcher, fearing serious labor strife because of reported shipyard reduction, convinced the Shipping Board to curtail Jacksonville operations gradually rather than end them completely in 1919.[50] Gradualism could not avoid significant economic dislocation, and when the government ended all contracts in 1920, the Merrill-Stevens Company sold its yards. Return to "normalcy" and the end of enormous federal spending punctured Florida's artificially inspired boom.

During the entire shipping controversy, Fletcher demonstrated his worth to the administration as a skilled tactician, logical debater, and respected negotiator. He helped defeat bitter conservative opposition, unified Democratic ranks, then endeared himself to Floridians by his vigorous search for government contracts. By his service he won the thanks of a grateful administration, together with the economic plums which he so effectively used to consolidate his political support in Florida.

48. Lewis M. Stoddard to Jesse F. Salyers, October 11, 1918, Record Group 32, National Archives; and Jacksonville *Florida Times-Union*, September 2, 1920.
49. Jacksonville *Florida Times-Union*, June 29, 1918.
50. Duncan U. Fletcher to Charles Piez, March 5, 1919, Record Group 32, National Archives.

CHAPTER VII

A Miscellany of Wilsonian Politics—State and National

A̲LTHOUGH MARITIME AFFAIRS consumed Fletcher's major attention during the war years, he exerted influence on other legislation. His voting record revealed strange contradictions: incisive comment on the dangers of inflammable propaganda coupled with a reactionary view of woman suffrage. Concerned as ever about constituent sentiment, he also maintained a keen interest in Florida's prosperity and contributed to her surging economy.

In 1917 American interest centered on transforming the country from neutrality to active belligerency. The Floridian consistently supported legislation to broaden Presidential emergency authority. He voted for government operation of communication and transportation systems, although he opposed an amendment providing federal control of railroads for an indefinite period of time. Fletcher endorsed the Overman bill reorganizing governmental departments and supported the draft because he feared voluntary enlistment would drain the intellectual elite from American colleges.[1]

The senator's most curious eccentricity was his reticence concerning American propaganda. He warned against emotional persuasion aimed at Germany. Hatred, he contended, helped bring war and would not hasten its end. After the war nations must pursue brotherhood, a feat difficult to accomplish after an acrimonious crusade of hate.[2] Ironically, Fletcher's fear that propaganda would personalize the war and create counter-atrocities was realized in his hometown. In April, 1918, a Jacksonville mob took a German

1. U.S., *Congressional Record*, 65th Congress, 1st Session, 1917, LV, 920.
2. *Ibid.*, 1351–52.

dairyman from his home, accused him of pro-German sympathy, and made him purchase a $100 liberty bond. Without any specific charges, they forced another local German to buy a $500 bond. The citizens threatened to guarantee patriotism with a generous coat of tar and feathers in event of future "disloyalty."[3]

Varied domestic legislation received Fletcher's approval. When filibustering senators killed the 1915 waterway and ship purchase bills, he favored a cloture rule allowing a two-thirds majority to end Senate debate. Most southerners, who used "extended debate" to block anti-lynching and child labor legislation, opposed cloture. President Wilson relied on Fletcher in 1917 for passage of the Alaska General Fisheries bill in order to break a monopoly on the Arctic fishing industry.[4] The Floridian also took a vital interest in conservation, introducing a bill in February, 1920, to provide $140 million for a four-year program of land reclamation in the South and West.[5] The senator supported the graduated income tax but hedged on prohibition. He voted against a 1917 bill which prohibited the use of grains for liquor; then, faced with determined pressure from Florida prohibitionists, he capitulated a year later and voted for the Eighteenth Amendment.

His Wilsonian progressivism received its worst blemish from the issue of woman suffrage. He encouraged female political activity in Florida and endorsed woman suffrage by state enactment, but he steadfastly resisted all congressional attempts to enfranchise women. The Woman Suffrage Association named him to its "blacklist" in 1914, but he ignored this ignominy, zealously defending suffrage as a state prerogative and gloomily predicting that any change would "bring disaster upon the American system."[6] Of course, he was not alone in this opposition. Few southern senators, even nominally progressive ones, dared endorse such "radical" legislation. Florida ladies raged at Fletcher in a barrage of letters,[7] and the senator, shaken but unmoved, confided to an understanding male: "I presume some suffragists will be denouncing me for my

3. Jacksonville *Florida Times-Union*, April 17, 1918.
4. Woodrow Wilson to Duncan U. Fletcher, February 3, 1917, in Wilson Papers, Series VI, Box 281.
5. New York *Times*, February 20, 1920.
6. Jacksonville *Florida Times-Union*, September 6, 1918.
7. Interview with Miss Edith Pitts, October 14, 1964, Gainesville, Florida. Miss Pitts, personal secretary to Fletcher's successor, recalls much bitter correspondence from Florida women on this subject.

vote on the Anthony . . . [woman suffrage] amendment. I can't
help it. If the people of Florida want someone to vote away the
sovereign right of the states to determine who shall exercise the
franchise in that state and to control our own destinies they will
have to get some one else to do it. If the people want woman
suffrage let them change their own constitution. I will not object."[8]
The senator, in another of his paradoxes, cited the implied powers
of the commerce clause to justify government ownership of the
merchant marine; yet he steadfastly adhered to a strict Constitutional interpretation of suffrage restrictions.

Electioneering eclipsed legislative matters in the nation's
attention in the fall of 1918. President Wilson appealed for a
Democratic Congress, and Fletcher labored to insure party success.
He denounced GOP leaders who "have been playing politics to
the limit," and spoke acridly of the opposition party while stumping Florida for the Democrats: "These Republicans represent the
privileged interests, [and] their leader vigorously opposes the league
of nations to give security to the world against another . . . war."[9]

The war emphasized the South's need for expanded agricultural markets and renewed Fletcher's keen interest in Latin
American trade. The 1915 Pan American Financial Conference at
Washington had established an Inter-American High Commission
to eliminate trade barriers and study commercial relations. When
William G. McAdoo, commission chairman, favored the Chamber
of Commerce with appointments to the commission, an angry
official of the Southern Commercial Congress wrote him an insult-
ing letter. Fletcher interceded, explained the antagonism between
the Chamber and the Commercial Congress, and tactfully restored
good relations with McAdoo.[10] During the following months the
senator frequently corresponded with the Secretary of the Treasury,
making some excellent suggestions for the commission. He advised
appointment of a linguist as well as a Latin American cultural-
historical expert. McAdoo, impressed with Fletcher's constructive
ideas, insisted that the Floridian join the commission.[11]

8. Duncan U. Fletcher to Hiram Huddleston, October 7, 1918, in Fletcher
Papers.
9. New York *Times*, October 28, 1918, and Jacksonville *Florida Times-Union*,
November 5, 1918.
10. William G. McAdoo to Duncan U. Fletcher, June 26, 1915, in McAdoo
Papers, Box 485, Letterbook 24.
11. William G. McAdoo to Louis D. Brandeis, August 23, 1915, and William

The commission departed for Latin America in March, 1916. Discussion centered on commercial intercourse: organization of steamship lines, extension of banking facilities, and construction of a transcontinental railroad from New York to Buenos Aires. The commission traveled by train from Argentina to Chile, then up the coast to Peru.[12] Little of consequence was to result from its specific economic observations because America's entrance into the war established new priorities.

Fletcher returned from this trip with both misconceptions and keen insights. Politically, he gained little insight into the *Latino* character. On returning, he favored United States military intervention in Mexico and wrote that most Latin Americans would support such action. He disparaged reports of alleged anti-American feeling south of the border.[13]

Coupled with this political naïveté were some shrewd conclusions about hemispheric economics. The war, he said, had tied down the continent's European suppliers and created a commercial vacuum which the United States should exploit. He predicted financial upheaval after the First World War which would turn the continent commercially northward. To support this theory, he prepared detailed studies of trade potential with Latin American countries and proposed government steamship routes to tap these lucrative markets.[14] William G. McAdoo summarized Fletcher's work on the commission: "He was one of the first to appreciate the importance of bringing the United States closer to the countries of Latin America, and he labored unceasingly to further this important purpose."[15]

A revealing epilogue to the Latin American journey also demonstrated the senator's accessibility and concern for seamen. Fletcher's interest in the U.S.S. *Tennessee*, the cruiser which transported the commission, made the white-haired Floridian a favorite of the crew. On returning to home port, the ship's company learned that Congress had changed the name of their vessel, reserving state names for battleships. The superstitious crew, recalling sailor's

---

G. McAdoo to Duncan U. Fletcher, June 26, 1915, in McAdoo Papers, Box 486, Unnumbered Letterbook, and Box 485, Letterbook 24.
12. McAdoo, *Crowded Years*, pp. 362–63.
13. New York *Times Magazine*, May 21, 1916.
14. U.S., *Congressional Record*, 64th Congress, 1st Session, 1916, LIII, 12359–63.
15. U.S., Congress, *Duncan Upshaw Fletcher*, 75th Congress, 1st Session, 1938, House Document 339, pp. 41–42.

lore that bad luck accompanied such alterations, visited Fletcher and implored him to prevent the conversion. The busy senator called on Navy Secretary Josephus Daniels and tried to persuade him to exempt the *Tennessee*. Daniels was sympathetic but declined. On the ship's next trip to Santo Domingo, a waterspout shot into the air, came down the stacks, and blew the vessel apart.[16]

Another facet of the senator's wartime interests involved home state politics. Fletcher's remarkable facility at manipulating the congressional pork barrel contributed to Florida's booming prosperity. The death of Senator James Clarke in September, 1916, removed a foe of large waterway appropriations and promoted Fletcher to the chairmanship of the Commerce Committee. The senator's ascendancy to committee leadership came at an auspicious moment. Conservatives began castigating the annual river and harbor bills, charging that only this government subsidy made water transportation cheaper than rail. Attacks came from the other ideological direction from liberals who believed that inland waterways should be under governmental control in order to coordinate development.[17]

The 1917 waterways bill faced this angry coalition of conservatives and anti–pork barrel liberals. Fletcher sensed the danger and beseeched President Wilson for aid.[18] With Wilson's help and his own adroit maneuvering, the Commerce Committee sent a $39 million appropriation to the full Senate. Emasculated bills had passed the two previous years only by excluding all specific appropriations, and few senators held out hope for Fletcher's measure which itemized projects. The Floridian tied the measure to national defense and defeated crippling amendments by relying on shrewd parliamentary tactics and his own senatorial popularity. The final $28 million bill flabbergasted even its proponents. Florida received $1 million for major projects at Tampa, Miami, and Jacksonville.[19]

Before Republicans gained control of Congress in 1919, Fletcher won another spectacular victory for his home state. He

16. Judge John W. Holland to author, July 20, 1963.
17. For a sample of the conservative argument, see Harold G. Moulton, et al., *The American Transportation Problem* (Washington: The Brookings Institution, 1933), pp. 505, 511, and the New York *Times*, April 14, 1919.
18. Ray Stannard Baker, *Woodrow Wilson, Life and Letters* (New York: Doubleday, Doran and Company, 1939), VII, 22.
19. Jacksonville *Florida Times-Union*, August 17, 1917.

added $6 million to the House waterways bill, $2.5 million of it for Florida projects, and triumphed by one vote after a bitter Senate floor fight. House conferees rejected the Florida projects, but the salty Floridian replied that they could pass his version or have no bill at all. House members capitulated in February, 1919.[20] When he finally lost control of the committee in 1919, national waterway appropriations declined from $33 million to $12 million.

Fletcher also employed his congressional adroitness on behalf of Florida farmers. When bumper watermelon crops exhausted available railroad cars in 1917, he appealed directly to the Interstate Commerce Commission, which quickly provided transportation. One Florida paper wrote almost in disbelief: "The senator does not delay when matters affecting the people of his state are to be adjusted, and he is one of the best little adjusters we ever knew."[21] Shortly after the war, railroads announced a 15 per cent rate increase; but Fletcher successfully assailed the raise and held rates to a minimum advance.

Construction of army camps and shipyards offered an ideal means for regrouping Fletcher's political fortunes in northeastern Florida. This bastion of his earlier career had deteriorated, and he barely had carried Duval County in 1914. When General Leonard Wood, who commanded the Southern Department under the Secretary of War, reported adversely on a proposed Jacksonville National Guard camp in 1917, Fletcher traveled to Greenville, South Carolina, imploring the General to reconsider. After four days of persuasion, Wood finally agreed; he inspected the proposed site and reversed his decision, attributing his favorable report solely to Fletcher's influence. General Wood wanted to concentrate troops on the Atlantic Coast, but Secretary of War Baker rejected this geographical theory and disregarded the General's report. Baker substituted a camp site in Mississippi.[22]

Fletcher reacted in shocked dismay and staked his legislative prestige in the Wilson administration on acquiring a military base for Jacksonville. Relying on the spoils system and his administration loyalty, he advised Newton Baker that Mississippi senators

20. *Ibid.*, January 28, February 19 and 26, 1919.
21. *Ibid.*, May 31, 1917, quoting Leesburg *Commercial*.
22. Newton D. Baker to Woodrow Wilson, July 14, 1917, in Newton D. Baker Papers, Box 4, Manuscript Division, Library of Congress, Washington, D.C. Hereafter cited as N. D. Baker Papers.

already had received enough in the form of flood control appropriations. He reminded Baker of past services and demanded his just reward:

> Rejection of Jacksonville would place me in a most embarrassing and humiliating position.
>
> It would be a great injustice to reject Jacksonville. It could never be explained. I might as well resign my seat here if that is the treatment we are to have. I have labored as few men in the Senate—no doubt to little effect, but certainly in the best faith and purpose—and I have not been importuning Departments for favors. I want to be helpful at all times and particularly now.
>
> Jacksonville should have a camp site on merit. It can never appear otherwise to the Florida people. I am obliged to feel the same way. I have been willing to yield and stand aside on every occasion. I cannot and ought not on this point.[23]

The Floridian wrote Woodrow Wilson the same day. While somewhat more tactful, his letter remained quite frank. He reminded Wilson of past favors, of Florida's devastating freeze during 1916–17 which had destroyed the citrus crop, and the suffering caused by excessive shipping charges. Jacksonville deserved the camp, he concluded, and it must be established.[24] The President calmed the senator, assured him of Baker's impartiality, and agreed to confer with the Secretary of War on the matter; but the secretary refused to reconsider his decision.[25] Baker did sympathize with Fletcher's predicament: "His constituents are unbelievably annoying to the Senator and unjust to him, and I am afraid his own feelings have been a good deal disturbed . . . but he deserves well at their hands as he has been a most earnest and persuasive advocate of Jacksonville. . . ."[26]

---

23. Duncan U. Fletcher to Newton D. Baker, July 11, 1917, in N. D. Baker Papers, Box 4.

24. Duncan U. Fletcher to Woodrow Wilson, July 11, 1917, in N. D. Baker Papers, Box 4. For a view of Fletcher's influence in the full context of southern political pressure on Wood, Baker, and President Wilson, see Palmer, *Newton D. Baker*, I, 241–43.

25. Woodrow Wilson to Newton D. Baker, July 12, 1917, in Wilson Papers, Series VI, Box 567; and Newton D. Baker to Woodrow Wilson, July 13, 1917, in N. D. Baker Papers, Box 4.

26. Newton D. Baker to Woodrow Wilson, July 14, 1917, in N. D. Baker Papers, Box 4.

Baker and Wilson soothed Fletcher's ruffled political feathers by giving him a choice replacement for the National Guard base. On September 1, 1917, Baker announced the location of a quartermasters' training camp at Jacksonville. The $6.5 million camp brought 25,000 soldiers and 1,000 new homes to Jacksonville. Surrounding timber lands provided construction materials, and North Florida farms fed laborers and soldiers. Fletcher, once more politically secure in Florida's largest city, engaged in a bit of pardonable boasting: ". . . although I have had serious obstacles to overcome, and, at times, the outlook did not seem bright, I have kept working at the matter, and am now glad to say that we . . . get a camp. . . ."[27]

W. R. Carter of Jacksonville, aspiring to Fletcher's Senate seat, minimized the senator's influence in bringing Camp Johnston to Jacksonville. He argued that W. J. Hilands of Washington deserved credit for creation of the camp, not Fletcher. Carter, part owner of the Jacksonville *Metropolis,* reportedly paid handsome prices for information which would minimize Fletcher's influence in the Wilson administration.[28] However, Carter was mistaken concerning the senator's influence on federal projects. Fletcher persuaded Baker to designate Camp Johnston a permanent quartermaster camp after the war; and despite Carter's effort, the incumbent senator subsequently carried Duval County by large majorities. He also devoted attention to other parts of the state, and his influence helped bring two aviation training camps to Arcadia.[29]

Florida's chaotic politics demanded such constant attention. Sidney J. Catts' rise to political power had shaken the state's traditional power structure. Although only a five-year resident of the state, Catts had challenged the Florida Democratic machine in 1916 for the gubernatorial nomination. He had faced almost unanimous opposition from party regulars and narrowly lost the primary. Bolting the party, he had won the governor's chair running on the Prohibition ticket in the general election. Senator Park Trammell, elected to the United States Senate in 1916, could not mobilize Washington patronage sufficiently to isolate Catts, and Fletcher realized that this left him in a strategic position vis-à-vis

27. Jacksonville *Florida Times-Union,* September 2, 1917.
28. Duncan U. Fletcher to Newton D. Baker, December 13, 1917, in N. D. Baker Papers, Box 1.
29. Jacksonville *Florida Times-Union,* January 13, 1918.

state affairs. The new governor had few deep ties with courthouse-level Democrats, and appealed primarily to religious and racial bigotry in the rural areas. Wisely concluding that such emotional issues could not win permanent loyalty, Fletcher tried to isolate Catts by holding his own farm support while attracting strength in the rapidly growing coastal cities.

His strategy to retain agrarian loyalty centered in the farm loan system. Although Secretary McAdoo rejected Fletcher's appeal for a farm bank in Florida, he accepted the senator's nominee, F. J. H. Von Engelken of Palatka, as president of the district bank.[30] In a politically significant decision, the Farm Loan Board permitted Fletcher "to point out to them men qualified for positions in that District. . . ."[31] W. W. Flannagan, Fletcher's old friend and secretary of the Board, consulted the senator on all district appointments. The Floridian thus helped select appraisers, agents, attorneys, and other state farm board employees.

Heated controversy arose from the Board's appointment of a Sidney Catts' aide as land appraiser. Fletcher raged to McAdoo, and the Treasury Secretary complained to the Farm Loan Board.[32] Board officials responded that they had appointed two appraisers, one of them Fletcher's brother-in-law, and both nominated by the senator. One of these appraisers had proven incompetent and had been replaced with a Catts loyalist. A frustrated Board official complained: "As you know, Senator Fletcher is not the best judge of men in the world, and, in this case, I think the Senator has allowed himself to be prejudiced against Scarlett [the Catts lieutenant]. . . ."[33] This incident was an exception to Fletcher's general dominance of Farm Loan Board patronage in Florida.

The senator's work on marine affairs and commerce offered additional job opportunities. He won the post of state internal revenue collector for James M. Cathcart, his secretary; he recommended George W. Allen, a Key West Republican with powerful

30. William G. McAdoo to Duncan U. Fletcher, August 7 and 10, 1916, in McAdoo Papers, Box 491, Letterbook 38.
31. Duncan U. Fletcher to Federal Farm Loan Board, February 20, 1917, and W. W. Flannagan to Duncan U. Fletcher, February 23 and November, 1917, Record Group 103, National Archives.
32. Duncan U. Fletcher to William G. McAdoo, July 25, 1917, Record Group 103, National Archives.
33. George W. Norris to W. W. Flannagan, July 30, 1917, Record Group 103, National Archives.

banking and insurance interests, for the United States Shipping Board; to win Catts' labor union followers, he chose a Tampa union official for a job in the government printing office in Washington.[34] Appointments as commercial attaché and collecting agents further broadened his political base.

A temporary power vacuum in Florida's Washington delegation had been created by the loss of an incumbent senator and the election of the novice Park Trammell. This temporary void allowed Fletcher to settle some old political scores. The first head to roll belonged to P. A. Dignan, Jacksonville's postmaster and Fletcher's sworn enemy after 1914. The Senator triumphantly wrote his brother-in-law during 1918: "I *did* get rid of Dignan. I kept him from being reappointed and that keeps him off the eligible list."[35] The next victim was James B. Hodges, former mayor of Lake City, member of the State Democratic Executive Committee, and chairman of the State Board of Control under Catts. Hodges had supported Fletcher faithfully until 1916, but then had joined the Catts bandwagon. Fletcher retaliated by creating a new base of support in Columbia County (Lake City). He appointed the son of a prominent Columbia County reformer to the United States Military Academy, and the grateful father performed invaluable service in Fletcher's 1920 campaign against Sidney Catts.[36]

Secure in Florida, the senator could concern himself again with national affairs. Republicans firmly controlled both houses of Congress when it convened in May, 1919. Six frantic years of legislative leadership had exhausted Fletcher. He wrote relatives: "I often wish I could run away and spend a week with you and sister and see no one else and hear nothing from the rest of the world during that time. The duties have been and are very exciting and the work exhausting."[37] With Republicans in charge of committees, he hoped to gain needed respite. Tranquility, he discov-

---

34. William G. McAdoo to Woodrow Wilson, May 16, 1917, and Duncan U. Fletcher to Woodrow Wilson, September 22 and March 8, 1919, in Wilson Papers, Series VI, Boxes 283, 329, and 330. For numerous other appointments indicating Fletcher's new political alignment, see Records of Department of Commerce and United States Shipping Board, Record Groups 40 and 32, National Archives. Also Tampa *Morning Tribune*, April 13, 1919.
35. Duncan U. Fletcher to Hiram Huddleston, October 7, 1918, in Fletcher Papers. The emphasis is Fletcher's.
36. J. B. Hodges to Joe L. Earman, August 29, 1919, Box 32, in Hodges Papers.
37. Duncan U. Fletcher to Hiram Huddleston, October 7, 1918, in Fletcher Papers.

ered, was reserved for men of lesser ability. His tireless energy
plunged him into three postwar struggles: the League of Nations,
maritime policy, and a battle for congressional leadership of the
Democratic Party.

Fletcher's role in League ratification reflected his genuine
internationalism, not the party loyalty which motivated many
southern congressmen to support the League. He repeatedly had
prophesied before 1917 that the interdependency of nations precluded disinterested neutrality. After the war ended, the senator
eloquently reaffirmed his elemental faith in man's progress and his
Unitarian humanism with an emotional endorsement of the League
of Nations. America no longer consisted of thirteen isolated colo-
nies, and international realities demanded a new approach:

> New and added responsibilities have come to us. In
> these circumstances peace, just, righteous and permanent
> peace, becomes the concern of all civilized peoples on earth.
> . . . Wars, violence, terrorism, anarchy anywhere, became
> deadly assaults upon democracy throughout the world.
>
> We cannot ignore such disturbances if we would. Other
> civilized nations are affected in the same way. Lawlessness and
> its causes can be removed. An agency can be created through
> the joint efforts of these nations having a common purpose and
> common ideals, can be created and can be made effective. . . .
>
> If [America rejects the League] . . . we proclaim that this
> bloody war has been waged . . . to no purpose. We give notice
> to the world that from now on, every man for himself, and
> God alone help the innocent.
>
> I do not believe we have come to such a pass. I believe
> there is hope for the race and that out of all the suffering and
> sacrifices of the past . . . will come an alliance of enlightened
> purposes formed by the best thought of the age, carrying guar-
> antees that will brighten the future.[38]

When Governor Catts and other Florida isolationists condemned the League, Fletcher stumped the state preaching internationalism with the fervor of a camp meeting evangelist. In Congress he opposed every crippling amendment to the League and,
following Wilson's instructions, voted against any compromise
containing serious American reservations. Fletcher's commitment to
the League finally transcended even his loyalty to President Wilson,

38. Jacksonville *Florida Times-Union*, March 29, 1919.

and he voted for the organization with reservations in March, 1920. The effort failed by seven votes.

American maritime policy vied with the League for Fletcher's attention. Despite the Senator's conservative principles and his theoretical rejection of permanent government ownership, he proposed a long-range program of federal operation. He spoke at opening ceremonies for the Hog Island government shipyard in May, 1918, and said that every ship built there would be a government vessel: ". . . and I think that man has another guess coming to him who thinks at any time in the future this plant will be owned by any private concern."[39] Fletcher encouraged government control of Hog Island following the war.

Private shipping companies expressed a different opinion and received effective assistance from the Republican Congress. Chairman Edward N. Hurley of the Shipping Board endorsed private ownership in a 1919 speech to the National Marine League. A May conference of powerful lobbyists— representing the National Foreign Trade Council, Iowa Federated Farm Bureaus, Illinois Agricultural Association, Mississippi Valley Association, and Pacific Coast Shipowners' Association—also opposed government control.[40] Prominent American shipbuilders met in January, 1919, and called for salary reduction for workers, the cessation of strikes, the repeal of the La Follette Seamen's Act, and "as little government control of any kind as possible. . . ."[41] British interests mobilized to purchase fifty-seven of the newly constructed American vessels at half their original cost.

Josephus Daniels discovered the plan to dispose of government ships and presented the information to President Wilson. The President discussed the question with his War Council in November, 1918, and privately announced his preference for continued government ownership.[42] Fletcher enlisted under Wilson's banner in an address to the Southern Commercial Congress in December, 1918. The future supremacy of America, he argued, would depend on her command of transportation. His final address as chairman of the Commerce Committee contained a withering

39. Hog Island *News*, May 11, 1918, in Scrapbook B, Knight Collection.
40. Jacksonville *Florida Times-Union*, May 23, 1919.
41. *Ibid.*, January 23, 1919.
42. Josephus Daniels, *The Wilson Era: Years of War and After, 1917–1923* (Chapel Hill: University of North Carolina Press, 1946), pp. 573–74; Cronon, *The Cabinet Diaries of Josephus Daniels*, p. 359.

attack on private shipping companies which, according to Fletcher, exploited exporters and restricted commercial growth.[43]

The Shipping Board ignored his opposition and sold nineteen ships in June, 1919. Fletcher, by now the acknowledged Democratic leader on maritime affairs, promptly introduced a resolution halting further sales. To gain popular support for his resolution, he launched a national "Don't give up the Ships" campaign. The primary consideration, he told senators, was preservation of the American merchant fleet. Private enterprise had attempted to build such a fleet for fifty years, yet America possessed 4 million tons less shipping in 1914 than she had in 1861. He proposed continued government operation until a permanent merchant marine was assured, trade routes opened, and adequate personnel provided.[44]

Fletcher's crusade attracted national recognition and support. His penchant for research made him a formidable adversary in public debate. On one occasion Vice President Thomas R. Marshall, presiding over the Senate, asked for certain statistical maritime information. The Floridian paused a moment, then without referring to notes, recited the data.[45] He wrote dozens of magazine articles typified by one in *Sea Power*: "Just why it is considered wise to sell some of our cargo vessels to foreign interests is beyond my comprehension. . . . 'Don't give up the ships' should be sounded in the ears of the shipping board unceasingly. Keep them and operate them. Send them out over new routes. . . . These . . . ships were built with the money of the people. . . ."[46] This campaign evoked favorable response, particularly in the South where the Augusta *Chronicle* reported that "America looks to Senator Fletcher . . . to put a stop to the sale of ships, and to further the building of American tonnage. . . ."[47]

In an effort to counter private ownership, Fletcher offered some expansive alternatives. When insurance companies maintained prohibitive rates after the war, he proposed government insurance for federally operated ships.[48] He favored establishment of government-operated trade routes to Latin America. In early 1920 he

43. New York *Times*, March 28, 1919.
44. U.S., *Congressional Record*, 66th Congress, 1st Session, 1919, LVIII, 1799.
45. Jacksonville *Florida Times-Union*, July 16, 1919, quoting Gainesville *Sun*.
46. *Ibid.*, November 20, 1919, quoting *Sea Power*.
47. *Ibid.*, September 2, 1919, quoting Augusta *Chronicle*.
48. New York *Times*, February 19, 1919.

suggested a five-year continuation of government control to establish new commercial arteries and allow Congress to formulate a permanent federal policy.[49]

During the entire debate, Fletcher faced an intense personal dilemma. Conservative Floridians, led by the *Florida Times-Union*, favored private management. Fletcher's narrow interpretation of constitutional prerogatives and his traditional fear of government usurpation caused him painful soul-searching. But one question gained pre-eminence: what impact would private ownership have on the South's economy in general and Florida's development in particular? In 1915 only four ships had been constructed south of Newport News, Virginia. Under the 1916 Shipping Act, plentiful labor, proximity of natural resources, and mild weather had attracted twelve major shipyards to the Southeast. These twelve yards had produced 100,000 tons of shipping during 1918.[50] Federal activity had brought prosperity and Fletcher desired its continuation. In May, 1919, he conferred with Georgia's Hoke Smith and other southern senators in an attempt to retain this commerce. Under his direction they prepared a letter to the Shipping Board requesting that eight additional ships be allocated to the southeastern United States–Latin American trade.

The Floridian took an even deeper interest in Jacksonville's plight. The Shipping Board desperately wanted to dispose of its operations in the city, and Board officials admitted privately that they would accept a $300,000 loss just to sell the Jacksonville drydock. Fletcher tried to save the government complex by proposing a federally operated shipping line between Jacksonville, the West Indies, and South America.[51] Despite his efforts, government contracts for Jacksonville ended in 1920. He was more successful with the Emergency Fleet Corporation, persuading it to construct a $500,000 drydock at Pensacola in 1919.

Fletcher became embroiled in one additional controversy during 1919. Both Alabama's Oscar W. Underwood and Nebraska's Gilbert M. Hitchcock sought leadership of the Senate Democratic minority. Hitchcock, incumbent Democratic leader, was loosely affiliated with Senate liberals, while Underwood drew support from

49. U.S., *Congressional Record*, 66th Congress, 2nd Session, 1920, LIX, 2831.
50. Jacksonville *Florida Times-Union*, January 18, 1919.
51. H. M. Robinson to Edward N. Hurley, July 24, 1919, and Duncan U. Fletcher to Edward N. Hurley, July 2, 1919, Record Group 32, National Archives.

southern conservatives. Though a personal friend of Underwood's, Fletcher decided it was an inopportune time to elect a new leader and privately counseled postponement.[52] Underwood, desiring the leadership post to help in his 1920 Senate race, considered Fletcher's support imperative.

The Alabamian quickly discovered Fletcher's Achilles heel. The New York *Sun* reported the Floridian's indecision on the leadership fight, and John Clifton Elde, editor of a New York business magazine, responded quickly. After reminding the Senator of the magazine's editorial support in Florida senatorial elections, Elde appealed for Underwood. He considered the Alabamian a "conservative progressive" and urged Fletcher's support.[53] Underwood persuaded J. H. McLaurin of Jacksonville and James L. Giles of Orlando to instigate a letter writing campaign to Fletcher.[54] Senator Underwood also asked Henry Watterson, domiciled in Miami, to contact his Florida associates and request them to pressure the state's senior senator. Watterson induced Frank Shutts, owner of South Florida's powerful Miami *Herald,* to write the senator on Underwood's behalf.[55] Fletcher finally succumbed and backed the Alabamian. The January, 1920, caucus ended in a tie vote, but Hitchcock withdrew in April, making Underwood Senate minority leader.

Fletcher emerged from the Wilson era as a prodigious worker, respected by Democrats and Republicans alike. At a Washington social gathering one senator queried a family friend: "Do you people in Florida realize what a splendid representative you have?"[56] His leadership in the protracted maritime controversy revealed a master parliamentarian and a consummate diplomat. American farmers fondly remembered his work for rural credits. Yet, he also remained an enigma: supporting federal control of shipping and opposing government operation of railroads; humanistically devoted to the League of Nations and oblivious to the injustice of state disfranchisement of women; keenly perceiving

52. M. B. Lane to S. Davies Warfield, December 9, 1919, in Underwood Papers.
53. John Clifton Elde to Duncan U. Fletcher, November 24, 1919, in Underwood Papers.
54. Lloyd M. Hooper to J. H. McLaurin, December 24, 1919; Oscar W. Underwood to James L. Giles, January 16, 1920; in Underwood Papers.
55. Oscar W. Underwood to Henry Watterson, December 22, 1919; Henry Watterson to Oscar Underwood, December 27, 1919; in Underwood Papers.
56. Interview with Miss Sally Puleston, May 27, 1963, Monticello, Florida.

economic changes in Latin America, and naïvely unaware of *Latino* resentment against American presumptions. His contradictory voting record becomes intelligible only when the rationale is not the senator's political philosophy but his party loyalty and constituent orientation.

The Southern Society in Washington tried to persuade Fletcher to run for Vice-President in 1920, and President Wilson's advisers mentioned him as United States ambassador to both Britain and Italy.[57] But by genuine economic service and the judicious use of patronage, he had reconstructed his immense pre-1915 strength in Florida, and the adulation of his constituents proved more attractive than diplomatic service or the political limbo of the Vice-Presidency.

57. Gertrude H. Stephens, "Senator Duncan U. Fletcher—Legislator" (Master's thesis, University of Florida, 1951), p. 91; and Jacksonville *Florida Times-Union*, November 27, 1919.

CHAPTER VIII

Florida and the Politics of Normalcy

FLORIDA WAS A MICROCOSM of America during the early 1920's. Normalcy brought tourists south in droves, making the Sunshine State a mecca for land speculators and legitimate businessmen. The population increased 295,078 or 30.4 per cent between 1920 and 1925. Lower peninsula counties, blessed with mild weather and commercial potential, led the nation in population growth. Dade County spurted from 42,000 in 1920 to 111,352 in 1925, a 160.6 per cent increase. Broward County, located north of Dade, increased an astronomical 177.6 per cent in five years. Florida also became the first southern state to approach urban status. Her population in 1925 of 1,263,549 was distributed in approximate national ratio: 701,000 rural and 562,000 (nearly 45 per cent) urban. The national trek from farm to city reached into Florida, where the rural population in twenty of her sixty-seven counties declined between 1920 and 1925.[1]

While Florida kept pace with national population trends, she raced ahead of America's economic advance. She entered the decade as an underdeveloped state, and her partially artificial economic expansion surpassed that of older, more stable regions. The state adjusted quickly to the loss of military installations and tapped the lucrative tourist trade.

Tourism demanded adequate transportation, and Florida moved rapidly to provide it. By 1926 the state counted 6,000 miles of railroad track, almost twice as much mileage per one thousand

1. Florida, *The Fifth Census of the State of Florida*, 1925, pp. 9–61.

population as any other southern state.[2] The Atlantic Coast Railroad double-tracked its lines from Richmond, Virginia, to Jacksonville, and the Florida East Coast Railway matched this project from Jacksonville to Miami. The Seaboard Air Line extended track to West Palm Beach and Miami. Aided by federal grants, the state boasted 9,200 miles of highway in 1925, with $10,149,000 more under construction. Modernized transportation made tourism Florida's most lucrative economic asset, contributing income of $250 million in 1925 compared to second place manufacturing production worth $150 million. Depressed agriculture lagged far behind in third place at $85 million.[3] Many Floridians considered their state economically diversified by the mid-twenties.

Most economic indicators pointed to unparalleled growth with no end in sight. Banking capital in Florida National Banks rose from $14,765,000 in 1920 to $23,858,000 in 1925; bank deposits increased from $187,286,000 to $375,042,000. Permits for hotel construction in 1923–24 reached $36 million, while motorists increased gasoline consumption from 60 million to 122 million gallons between 1922 and 1924.[4]

Boom times turned the nation politically right, and conservatism also accompanied Florida's prosperity. The state's Republican presidential vote increased steadily: 14,600 in 1916 (21 per cent of total); 44,800 in 1920 (33 per cent); 30,600 in 1924 (33 per cent); and 144,000 in 1928 (a figure of 59 per cent, inflated by Democratic nominee Alfred E. Smith's religion and anti-prohibition sentiment).[5] Senator Fletcher reflected this resurgent conservatism, particularly during the early 1920's.

Only agrarian turmoil checked this move to the right. Agriculture played the same spoiler's role in the Sunshine State as in the nation. Lulled by general prosperity, the state ignored declining farm income until mid-decade. The nation generally disregarded agriculture even longer until 1929, but Florida's 1926 economic collapse brought quicker recognition of the farmers' financial plight.

If Florida's economy soared beyond that of other states, the depression struck earlier and lasted longer. The real estate bust

2. Tallahassee *Daily Democrat*, April 12, 1926.
3. Florida, *The Fifth Census of the State of Florida*, p. 10.
4. Address by Duncan U. Fletcher to the Florida Legislature, May 12, 1925, Box 60, in Hodges Papers.
5. Florida, *Report of Secretary of State, 1916, 1920, 1924, 1928*, inserts.

and Miami's destructive 1926 hurricane plunged Florida's economy into an abyss from which it did not recover until the 1940's. As a result, economic liberalism asserted itself earlier in Florida than in other parts of the nation. Although the 1928 election, replete with the artificial issues of religious intolerance and prohibition, confused election returns, Florida politics drifted left after 1926. Once again the state's senior senator mirrored this shift.

The decade began for Senator Fletcher in frantic fashion. He faced an election challenge from Florida's most prominent representative in the annals of southern demagoguery. Sidney J. Catts had been born in Dallas County, deep in the heart of Alabama's black belt. He had gravitated from law to the ministry to politics. In 1903 he had opposed J. Thomas Heflin, Alabama's bombastic Negro-baiter, for a congressional seat. Heflin won, but Catts had learned a valuable lesson about southern politics: choose a minority group as scapegoat, shout loud enough, and someone will listen. The young minister-politician had become pastor of the First Baptist Church in De Funiak Springs, Florida, in 1911. Low pay had forced his resignation three years later, and he traveled the state selling insurance. Although a resident of Florida for only five years, he had parlayed anti-Catholicism into a winning issue during the 1916 governor's race. He had proposed an advanced reform program, but the legislature, dominated by Democratic loyalists, emasculated it. After four years of frustration, Catts took aim at Fletcher's Senate seat.

The ascendancy of Catts in the years 1916–20 had realigned Florida's Democratic Party structure. The old pro- and anti-Broward dichotomy decreased in importance, and a temporary battle raged between new factions. Jerry W. Carter and other idealistic economic liberals joined Catts, but many progressive loyalists never forgave the governor for bolting the party to run as a Prohibitionist in 1916. Catts' religious and racial bigotry also alienated many philosophically tolerant Floridians. Telfair Stockton, scion of the progressive Jacksonville family, damned both men, calling Fletcher an "autocrat" and Catts a "polecat."[6] The governor relied heavily on state patronage and counted James B. Hodges of Lake City, Jerry W. Carter, and Joe L. Earman, editor of the Palm Beach *Post,* among his prominent followers.

Both men jockeyed for position during 1919, with Fletcher

6. Jacksonville *Florida Times-Union,* August 14, 1919.

using federal patronage to outdistance his future rival. Unlike the senator's earlier campaigns against men he respected, this race involved an opponent that he disliked intensely. He privately predicted a dirty campaign with many "blows below the belt."[7] J. B. Hodges, a power on the state Democratic Executive Committee, used his formidable influence against Fletcher, but newspaper defection from Catts more than balanced this advantage.[8] The senator followed the precedent set in his two campaigns by opening his 1920 race at Live Oak.

Catts relied primarily on peripheral issues. During the war, measles and pneumonia had cost the lives of many Florida servicemen at Camp Wheeler, Georgia. Both Fletcher and Catts had inspected the camp and claimed credit for calling conditions to the attention of Washington authorities. Fletcher's explanation of the epidemic's origin, bad weather and worse food, had the advantage of rationality, but Catts' story certainly attracted more publicity. According to the governor, three German spies had inoculated the food with poisonous germs, and only his timely intervention had saved the camp.[9] Fletcher replied that his opponent suffered from an "overfed imagination."

A second issue involved the paranoic "Red Scare" of 1919–20. In a remarkable defense of free speech, considering his own political career, Catts blasted a bill introduced by Fletcher in 1919. The senator had reacted in horror to the anarchistic outbreaks which had swept America after the war. Following a particularly bitter strike by the Industrial Workers of the World, he introduced a bill to deport to the Island of Guam anyone who tried to overthrow the government. Catts termed the bill an attempt to suppress free speech, adding that not even Congress should expel a socialist.[10] In a paradoxically bigoted defense of free speech, he dubbed Fletcher a "first cousin to the Czar of Russia" and linked the Guam bill to a Catholic conspiracy: ". . . the Catholic Knights of Columbus . . . have taken Senator Fletcher for a soft

7. Duncan U. Fletcher to Joe L. Earman, October 6, 1919, Box 33, in Hodges Papers.
8. J. B. Hodges to Sidney J. Catts, January 9, 1920, Box 33, in Hodges Papers. See also Jacksonville *Florida Times-Union*, July 8, 1919, quoting St. Cloud *Tribune*. The Palmetto *News* and Clay County *Times* supported Catts in 1916 but switched to Fletcher in 1920.
9. Jacksonville *Florida Times-Union*, March 28, 1920.
10. Catts Campaign Pamphlet, in Park Trammell Papers, P. K. Yonge Library, Gainesville, Florida. Hereafter cited as Trammell Papers.

case and are getting him to fix the people of the United States so that they cannot . . . talk; and when they have done away entirely with the 'Freedom of Speech' . . . they will, with Fletcher's aid, hold up the Roman Catholic dogma . . . and say to despised Protestants, 'You worship as the Holy Mother Church says, or you go to . . . the fires of persecution. . . .' Do you think for a moment he can fool the People of Florida into voting for him when he wants to put all of us on the Island of Guam and thus help his Catholic friends to make a conquest of America?"[11] Catts assured Floridians that so long as his trigger finger remained limber no one would send him to Guam.

The governor combined legitimate criticism of Fletcher's economic philosophy with absurd personal references. He combined ridicule of the senator's opposition to child labor regulation with diatribes against Fletcher's fat stomach, "where he carried his beer and champagne."[12] According to Catts, the state's three largest railroads bossed Fletcher, and if the people re-elected him, "they can just say that they have bowed their knee to the corporations . . . of the state." Then in a final appeal to absurdity, he announced that the senator planned to make Florida a dumping ground for lepers.[13]

These personal charges appear mild when compared with Catts' systematic campaign of religious character assassination. The governor's perverted use of the religious issue fulfilled Fletcher's worst prediction of mudslinging. When Catts' campaign began to lag, he relied increasingly on this issue.[14] Anti-Catholicism had reached its zenith in Florida during the 1916 campaign, but Catts, his lieutenants, and the Ku Klux Klan, had kept the issue alive. J. B. Hodges, certainly a sympathizer and presumably a member of the Klan, wrote that Fletcher should be appointed ambassador to Italy "to take up his residence with the Dagos and Catholics. . . ."[15]

Only Jerry Carter's firm rejection prevented Billy Parker,

11. Catts Campaign Pamphlet, in Jerry W. Carter Papers, Tallahassee, Florida.
12. Jacksonville *Florida Times-Union,* May 23, 1920.
13. Catts Campaign Pamphlet, in Trammell Papers.
14. Catts' biographer surveyed limited newspaper sources and concluded that Catholicism played a minor role in the campaign, but additional sources indicate a different conclusion. See John R. Deal, Jr., "Sidney Johnston Catts, Stormy Petrel of Florida Politics" (Master's thesis, University of Florida, 1949), p. 177.
15. J. B. Hodges to Kligrapp of Great Wizard, October 28, 1919; J. B. Hodges to Sidney J. Catts, November 27, 1919, Box 33, in Hodges Papers.

a violent Catholic-baiter, from stumping the state for Catts; but the governor continued to attack the Catholic conspiracy.[16] He predicted victory in every county of the Florida panhandle except Escambia, where Catholics would defeat him. He attributed the opposition of leading Florida papers to their Catholic owners who hated him for fighting the Papal hierarchy.[17] One of the governor's Jacksonville lieutenants attributed anti-Catts sentiment to the Knights of Columbus and called Fletcher a "pope foot-kisser"; the governor told worshipers at Baptist prayer meetings that Fletcher adhered to the Unitarian faith which denied the divinity of Christ and considered Him a bastard.[18]

The League of Nations also emerged as a major issue in the race. Catts championed isolation and deplored Fletcher's concept of the interdependence of nations. James B. Hodges evaluated anti-League opinion in Florida and speculated that Fletcher would not be foolish enough to support the League.[19]

Hodges underestimated Senator Fletcher's devotion to the League just as Fletcher underestimated isolationist sentiment. The senator defended internationalism in every speech. The reaction startled Fletcher aides: a Jacksonville citizen castigated the "pope governed [Wilson] administration" for supporting the League; John S. Beard, leading Pensacolan who had endorsed Fletcher in 1908 and 1914, penned a scathing denunciation of the world organization; a pro-Fletcher paper warned that "if Fletcher don't change his attitude on this league of nations [sic] business, Catts will be the next United States Senator."[20] Jerry Carter, Catts' unofficial campaign manager, persuaded Missouri's isolationist Senator James A. Reed to visit Florida for three anti-League speeches.[21]

Fletcher countered these arguments with his record, superior organization, and Florida's general disaffection with the governor. The senator emphasized his grants for farmers and waterways,

16. Interview with Jerry W. Carter, March 1, 1962, at Tallahassee, Florida.
17. Catts Campaign Pamphlet, in Trammell Papers.
18. P. D. Bullard to J. B. Hodges, May 30, 1920, Box 34, in Hodges Papers; and Catts Campaign Pamphlet, in Trammell Papers.
19. J. B. Hodges to Jerry W. Carter, February 12, 1920, Box 33, in Hodges Papers.
20. P. D. Bullard to J. B. Hodges, May 30, 1920, Box 34, in Hodges Papers; and Jacksonville *Florida Times-Union*, February 25, 1920; *ibid.*, January 17, 1920, quoting Lakeland *Star*.
21. Jerry W. Carter to J. B. Hodges, February 3, 1920, Box 33, in Hodges Papers.

while Arthur T. Williams, his campaign manager, made full use of Fletcher's numerous state appointees. Williams assembled a number of political supporters in Jacksonville for a March, 1920, meeting. He named an executive committee and organized Fletcher clubs on the precinct level. Fletcher also exploited widespread discontent with Catts by blasting the governor's nepotism. Catts had made full use of 1,800 state jobs to reward the politically faithful and provide for his large family. Fletcher discovered that the governor's relatives on the state payroll received $32,000 a year in salaries. His satirical quip that Catts would soon appoint an inspector of icebergs on the St. Johns River proved as effective as it was humorous.

Angered by Catts' extremist rhetoric, Fletcher returned blow for blow. He undermined the Catholic issue by disclosing the governor's appointment of a Catholic sheriff in Brevard County. Joe Earman, a Catts political aide, had persuaded the governor to remove a popular incumbent and appoint a Catholic friend to his place. Catts had not discovered the replacement's religion until Fletcher revealed it, and this issue contributed to the governor's loss of the entire lower East Coast.[22] The campaign compromised Fletcher's ideals and caused him to use the Negro for the first and only time in his political career. During a joint debate at Titusville he disclosed Catts' appointment of R. R. Robinson, a Negro, as assistant probation officer of Duval County. He produced a copy of the Chicago *Plain Dealer*, a Negro paper which advocated social equality, containing pictures of Robinson and Catts side by side.[23]

Such charges carried some influence, but the decisive issue was organized labor. The year 1919 brought a rash of labor violence and projected unions into national attention. Though generally overlooked, labor strife reached into Florida and inspired one of labor's most strenuous political efforts. Three thousand phosphate workers in Polk and Hillsborough counties struck; and before 1919 ended they were joined by 2,500 Jacksonville railroadmen, 250 Jacksonville cigar workers, Miami construction unionists, Sanford railroad employees, and 12,000 Tampa cigar makers. Before the year ended, over 20,000 Florida laborers were out on strike.[24] The

22. Sidney J. Catts to J. B. Hodges, June 16, 1920, Box 34, in Hodges Papers.
23. Jacksonville *Florida Times-Union*, May 7, 1920.
24. See *ibid.*, January-December, 1919. For detailed studies of Florida strife in 1920, see Wayne Flynt, "Florida Labor and Political 'Radicalism,'" *Labor*

state chapter of the American Federation of Labor organized a Florida Political Labor League at its April, 1920, convention in order to wield more effective power in state affairs.

Labor possessed no great love for Senator Fletcher. Railroad workers had opposed his vote to return lines to private control after World War I, and other unions balked at his stand on child labor and woman suffrage. The DeLand *News* reported that national and state labor unions planned to fight Fletcher's re-election, and while unenthusiastic about Catts, would support him over the incumbent.[25] The governor moved quickly to consolidate this labor backing. Tampa unions invited him to speak, and he threatened that if phosphate companies operating in Florida did not meet union demands, he would revoke their charters. He circulated a letter throughout the state announcing his sympathy for the phosphate strikers. Two days later the governor spoke to striking Jacksonville railroad employees, declaring for unionism and against "monarchy." Pensacola unions invited him to speak two months later. The governor also removed the anti-union sheriff of Polk County at the insistence of labor groups. Catts supported Van Cicero Swearingen, attorney-general during the governor's administration and A. F. of L.–endorsed candidate for governor. The two men often campaigned together. The Palmetto *News*, while predicting Fletcher's victory, added that "Catts will carry most of the union vote."[26]

Fletcher considered the labor vote his biggest problem and reserved much of his time for winning defecting unionists. He was not without assets in this undertaking, for his credentials appealed to conservative unionists. He supported the Esch-Cummins Act of 1920, a compromise measure which placed railroads under virtually complete federal control. In April he spoke to shipyard workers at Jacksonville's labor temple. W. E. Terry, one of the city's leading unionists, introduced Fletcher as the man chiefly responsible for Jacksonville's ship-building industry. In his speech the

History, IX (Winter, 1968), 73–90; and Durward Long, "The Open-Closed Shop Battle in Tampa's Cigar Industry, 1919-1920," *The Florida Historical Quarterly*, XLVII (October, 1968), 101–22.

25. *Ibid.*, April 7, 1920, quoting DeLand *News*.

26. Jacksonville *Florida Times-Union*, November 17, 1919, quoting Palmetto *News*. For a brief summary of the campaign from newspaper sources, see Warren A. Jennings, "Sidney J. Catts and the Democratic Primary of 1920," *The Florida Historical Quarterly*, XXXIX (January, 1961), 203–20.

senator advocated a compulsory eight-hour day and praised labor leader Samuel Gompers as a "patriot and statesman."[27]

If labor support generally helped Catts, the reaction against union excesses more than compensated for it. Florida's phosphate strike broke into armed violence, with striking miners killing three nonstrikers and wounding several law officers. Such a storm of protest greeted Catts' removal of Polk County's sheriff that the governor relented. Anti-labor feeling reached a climax in January, 1920, when the Department of Justice arrested eight members of the Communist Labor Party in Jacksonville.[28] The Tampa *Tribune* accused Catts of waving "the red flag of socialism," while progressive spokesman Telfair Stockton attacked Catts' "socialistic doctrine."[29]

Most unionists undoubtedly voted for Catts, but there were significant exceptions, especially among shipyard workers. Labor-endorsed gubernatorial candidate Van C. Swearingen, with little support outside unions, carried 14 of Hillsborough's (Tampa) 55 precincts. Swearingen, though in a three-man race, led Catts in 32 of the 55 precincts. But labor obviously voted for both men, and labor-influenced Hillsborough gave Catts 2,148 votes to 2,207 for Swearingen.[30] Nonunion voters swarmed to Fletcher, and he carried Hillsborough two to one, and Florida by a vote of 62,304 to 25,007.

A respected Republican, Judge John M. Cheney of Orlando, opposed Fletcher in November. He drew wide support and Fletcher became alarmed when a torrent of Negro women registered to exercise their franchise. Women did not have to pay poll taxes because the tax covered only the previous year. Only 7,000 people had voted in Duval County in the all-male Democratic senatorial primary; then 6,500 Negro women registered between July and November. Police stemmed the tide by arresting 500 Negro women for minor registration violations. Fletcher conducted a vigorous campaign to register white women, but partially redeemed his earlier Negro-baiting by protesting the harassment of Negro registrants. He argued that "every person entitled to vote must be permitted to do so, and all valid ballots must be counted and re-

27. Jacksonville *Florida Times-Union,* April 28, 1919.
28. *Ibid.,* January 4, 1920.
29. *Ibid.,* August 2, 1919, quoting Tampa *Morning Tribune;* and October 8, 1919.
30. Tampa *Morning Tribune,* June 10, 1920.

turned without the slightest irregularity or discrimination."[31] Fletcher defeated Cheney by a vote of 98,957 to 37,065, running well ahead of the Democratic presidential ticket, which won 90,515 to 54,971. Conservatism as well as female suffrage obviously influenced the state Republican vote which increased by 40,000 votes or 350 per cent over the 1916 total.

Fletcher returned to Washington missing some of the joy of the Wilson era. The close Fletcher family life ended when his daughters married, Nell moving to Dublin with her Irish husband while Louise resided in St. Louis. Fletcher's wife suffered from arthritis and continued her mysticism, defending spiritualism before a House committee investigating the activities of mediums.[32]

The senator shared in his state's financial prosperity. He bought rental property in Jacksonville by the block and also purchased farms and real estate in Polk County. He amassed property and stock worth $126,000, but had little spare cash. Taxes piled up because Fletcher disliked selling real estate, and he spent one-fifth of his salary each year for tax levies.[33] Most friends and relatives talked of the senator's fortune, but it was modest even by contemporary standards.

Fletcher's increased leisure was turned partly to personal pursuits. With the Democrats out of power and committee responsibilities less demanding, the 1920's saw a renewed affection for historical reading. History had fascinated Fletcher during his undergraduate years at Vanderbilt, and the relative quiet of the early twenties rekindled his ardor. He flavored letters with references to the golden days of Greece and Rome. Government documents took second place in his Senate office to the journals of the Continental and Confederate Congresses, documentary histories of the Constitution, twelve volumes of Confederate military history, and numerous studies of the United States.[34] In 1921 he joined a group of distinguished Floridians in chartering the Florida State

31. Jacksonville *Florida Times-Union*, October 19, 1920.
32. Duncan U. Fletcher to Ruth Huddleston Baxter, undated, in Fletcher Papers.
33. *Last Will and Testament of Duncan U. Fletcher*, Probate Judge's Office, County Courthouse, Jacksonville, Florida; Executors Report of Final Distribution; *Duncan U. Fletcher, Deceased*, Probate Judge's Office, County Courthouse, Jacksonville. Also Duncan U. Fletcher to Hiram Huddleston, February 9, 1921, in Fletcher Papers.
34. Clippings in Fletcher Papers.

Historical Society in order to coordinate research and publish original source materials.[35] In a melancholy private family letter Fletcher revealed a strain of romanticism: ". . . somehow I feel that when the job here is to be laid down, I will still have all that . . . is vitally necessary when I have a wood fire, a flower garden, and a table with two books; Gibbon's *Rise and Fall of the Roman Empire* and Dumas' *Three Musketeers*. I think I would add the Bible and Shakespeare. In the winter the good fire and the novel or history, as the mood strikes me; in the summer and spring, the flower garden and the novel or history."[36]

Such ethereal sentiments could not long submerge the harsh realities of the "flapper age." Fletcher's home state paralleled the nation not only in desirable economic growth but also in the dissemination of hate and intolerance. Rapid political and numerical gains for the Ku Klux Klan marked the resurgence of nativism and bigotry, while fundamentalist religious denominations demanded intellectual conformity. The wide dispersal of Florida's population hindered unified Klan activity, but Jacksonville, Fletcher's hometown, became a Klan stronghold. As many as 5,000 persons attended rallies, and Klansmen captured some local political offices.[37] Governor Catts stirred nativist anti-Catholic sentiment, and Representative Fred H. Davis of Leon County introduced an amendment to deprive "Mongolians and Malayans" of property rights in Florida. State religious leaders damned evolution and conducted investigations of their denominational colleges.

Fletcher had confronted religious bigotry in his race in 1920 and deplored the cancerous spread of prejudice. When the Florida Historical Society invited him to speak in 1924, he pleaded eloquently for greater understanding. Many state leaders attended the speech which was made at the state capitol at Tallahassee. Fletcher assailed intolerance in his historical summary of Florida's past: "Fanaticism, persecution and religious intolerance were exemplified in the earliest days to a degree inconceivable in human beings. All in the name of the King and the Church of God. . . . From

35. See Watt Marchman, "The Florida Historical Society, 1856–1861, 1879, 1902–1940," *The Florida Historical Quarterly*, XIX (July, 1940), 256–63.
36. Duncan U. Fletcher to Cornelia Fletcher Huddleston, August 15, 1921, in Fletcher Papers.
37. See David Chalmers, "The Ku Klux Klan in the Sunshine State," *Florida Historical Quarterly*, XLII (January, 1946), 210.

religious persecution, some found a refuge—such as Ribaut and Laudonniere—only to be slaughtered in the name of religion."[38]

Dogmatic religion found a brilliant champion in the state in the person of William Jennings Bryan. The "Commoner" left his adopted Florida to joust with evolutionists at Dayton, Tennessee, and most Floridians wished him Godspeed. Religious periodicals clamored for Darwin's scalp, and reaction in some areas of the "Sunshine State" exceeded the earlier anti-Catholicism of the Catts era.[39] Fletcher wrote privately to a political ally that he considered the trial unfortunate for the development of Christian education, sympathized with the defendant John Scopes, and deplored the attempt of religious fanatics to force their views on the public.[40] Jacksonville's Unitarian Church, which the Senator helped found, honored his open-mindedness in 1926 by forming a Fletcher Club to discuss contemporary social and political issues.

William Jennings Bryan also figured prominently in Florida politics during the 1920's. In 1916 he had forsaken the Great Plains in favor of Miami. Already a three-time loser in presidential competition, Bryan envisioned a restoration of his national prestige by capturing a seat in the United States Senate. A persistent rumor in 1922 hinted that Bryan would oppose Park Trammell, the state's junior senator.[41] The Tampa *Times* and other state papers coveted the value of a senator with such national recognition. On February 15, 1922, Bryan announced his willingness to be drafted as a candidate, but added that he had "no thought of entering into a contest for the office."[42] Trammell mobilized for an all-out fight, and even papers supporting Bryan's candidacy insisted on an open primary. The "Silver Tongued Orator" made a speaking tour of the state but declined to risk humiliation at the hands of Florida voters.

38. Duncan U. Fletcher, "Address Before the Florida Historical Society," *Florida Historical Quarterly*, III (January, 1925), 22–23.
39. J. B. Hodges to Duncan U. Fletcher, July 22, 1925, Box 60, in Hodges Papers. Bryan had long crusaded against evolution in Florida; see Miami *Daily Metropolis*, February 13, 1922.
40. J. B. Hodges to Duncan U. Fletcher, July 22, 1925, Box 60, in Hodges Papers. Hodges made his peace with Fletcher in 1921, but he could hardly have converted from the "Dago-Catholic" hating Ku Kluxer of 1920 to the tolerant-minded liberal reflected in this letter. It seems more likely that he is agreeing with Fletcher's previously expressed sentiments to regain the senator's favor.
41. J. B. Hodges to Joe L. Earman, April 12, 1922, Box 44, in Hodges Papers.
42. *The Commoner*, February 1922; also see Miami *Daily Metropolis*, February 15, 1922.

Bryan's publicity lapsed until 1925 when political gossip reported his interest in Fletcher's seat. James B. Hodges, rapidly emerging as a major figure in state politics, believed that Bryan had used the Trammell election in 1922 to lay groundwork for his real objective, Fletcher in 1926.[43] During 1925 Bryan sent the editor of the Sanford *Herald* his reasons for desiring the senatorship. "If this matter strikes you favorably," he wrote, "and you have an editorial along these lines, I wish you would send me a number of copies . . . so I can send them to other papers that are friendly."[44] The Tampa *Observer* published an editorial strongly endorsing Bryan, and the editor of the Clay *County Times* joined what he hoped would become a bandwagon.

Across the state in Jacksonville, twenty-one railroad brotherhoods met to determine their preference in the upcoming election. They requested Jerry Carter, state hotel commissioner and pro-union liberal, to find an opponent capable of defeating Fletcher. Carter approached several leading politicians, including former Governor Cary Augustus Hardee. Hardee declined, offering indebtedness to the incumbent senator as his reason. Following these rebuffs, Carter contacted friends of Tampa's Doyle E. Carlton, a highly respected young politician and orator; but Fletcher's aides persuaded Carlton to forego the Senate battle in favor of the 1928 gubernatorial contest. Finally, Carter approached William Jennings Bryan with the proposition. Though noncommittal in his reply, Bryan commissioned Carter to tour the state sampling opinion and provided the necessary funds.[45] While Carter was engaged in this project, Bryan became involved in the evolution controversy and declined to run despite Carter's optimistic report. So the politician-turned-devout headed for his last forensic battle at Dayton, Tennessee, and Carter returned to Jacksonville with a sad report for the railroad brotherhoods.

The railroad workers, still determined that someone should oppose Fletcher, turned to their unsuccessful envoy. Carter, never one to pass up a political hassle, accepted. Since Carter had little money, the unions raised $2,600 for his campaign.[46] By January,

43. J. B. Hodges to Joe L. Earman, April 12, 1922, Box 44, in Hodges Papers.
44. Quoted in Morris Werner, *Bryan* (New York: Harcourt, Brace and Company, 1929), p. 310.
45. Interview with Jerry W. Carter, Railroad and Public Utilities Commissioner, Tallahassee, March 1, 1962.
46. *Ibid.* This amounted to half of Carter's expenditure for the campaign.

1926, rumors spread across the state that Carter would challenge Fletcher for the senatorship.

Jerry Carter was a democrat, a "cracker" in the tradition of Napoleon B. Broward. After his birth in Barbour County, Alabama, on August 11, 1887, his family had moved to Del Rio, Tennessee. He had attended school briefly at Del Rio but was largely self-educated. For Carter, interest in politics was more of a genetic heritage than an acquired interest. He had begun campaigning at eighteen, and before he was twenty-one, angry political opponents had run him out of the state. He had settled at Pensacola in 1908, and returned to his first love eight years later, campaigning from the back of his sewing machine wagon for Sidney J. Catts. The grateful governor had appointed Carter hotel commissioner, a job he maintained under governors Hardee and John W. Martin. In 1924 Florida's "Mr. Democrat" had been elected a delegate to the National Democratic Convention, running second only to William Jennings Bryan. Carter and Fletcher had been distant friends until the senatorial election of 1920, when Carter unofficially managed Catts' unsuccessful race against the senator. The hotel commissioner, an able pamphleteer, had penned satirical cartoons featuring Fletcher, and the friendship cooled.[47]

Reports of Carter's candidacy multiplied after an interview in the Tampa *Morning Telegraph*. According to the hotel commissioner, Florida had "not been represented by a vigorous man of progressive ideas."[48] The interview provoked more criticism than praise. Former Catts lieutenant Joe Earman refused to back Carter and wrote privately, "Jerry must be deluded—IN HIS OLD AGE;" J. B. Hodges, another old friend, warned Carter not to enter the race and threatened to back Fletcher.[49]

The incumbent senator entered the campaign as the overwhelming favorite. J. B. Hodges advised Fletcher that only a major blunder could cost him the election.[50] When state conservatives urged Peter O. Knight to oppose Fletcher, the Tampan replied, "I am not only doing all in my power to have Senator Fletcher re-

47. Interview with Jerry W. Carter, March 15, 1964, Tallahassee. For a more detailed study of the 1926 race, see Wayne Flynt, "Florida's 1926 Senatorial Primary," *Florida Historical Quarterly*, XLII (October, 1963), 142–53.
48. Tampa *Morning Tribune*, in Carter Papers.
49. Joe L. Earman to J. B. Hodges, March 29, 1926; J. B. Hodges to Joe L. Earman, March 30, 1926, Box 65, in Hodges Papers.
50. J. B. Hodges to Joe L. Earman, April 5, 1926, Box 65 in Hodges Papers.

nominated and re-elected without opposition, but I am so proud of Senator Fletcher's work for Florida, that if this high position were tendered me . . . at the expense of Senator Fletcher's defeat, I would not accept it."[51] Fletcher also cultivated female votes lost by his opposition to woman suffrage by sending the ladies copies of his speeches on disarmament.[52]

During the early days of the race, Carter was handicapped by his reputation as a wit. He had founded the "Royal Order of Ancient and Hopping Fleas," an organization which included national political figures such as Tom Watson and numerous Florida politicians. One of his most famous capers had been the nomination of his wife for Vice-President of the United States at the 1924 Democratic National Convention. Although Floridians personally liked Carter, they dismissed his candidacy as just another joke. The Republican editor of the Tampa *Telegraph* called him "a good, genial fellow, a dyed in the wool cracker boy who deserves great credit, but in the United States Senate he would 'rattle like a bean in a bladder. . . .' " The Dunnellon *Truth* praised Carter's record but added that he stood as much chance of beating Fletcher as "would a dog with wax legs of catching an asbestos cat in Sheol."[53] Only fourteen papers extended Carter "equal treatment," and he acknowledged this press opposition in one of his campaign documents: "Fighting to oust the money powers that control the editorial expression of newspapers is the fight of the people and Jerry W. Carter is the natural champion from within their midst."[54]

By marked contrast, Fletcher drew laudatory comment from across the nation. In Washington members of the Democratic Senatorial Campaign Committee backed his re-election; two Georgia papers, the Atlanta *Constitution* and Bainbridge *Post-Searchlight*, called him "the ablest man that the state of Florida has had in public life in the last half century."[55] George W. Bean, Florida's national Republican committeeman, ignored political precedent by endorsing Fletcher: ". . . the Democratic party has not a harder working or more influential senator, and if he lived north of the

51. Scrapbook E, 1926, Peter O. Knight Collection.
52. J. B. Hodges to Joe L. Earman, March 21, 1922, Box 44, in Hodges Papers.
53. Tampa *Telegraph*, January 7, 1926, in Carter Papers; and Jacksonville *Florida Times-Union*, March 3, 1926, quoting Dunnellon *Truth*.
54. *Daily Punch*, May 22, 1926, in Carter Papers.
55. Tampa *Morning Tribune*, May 10, 1926, quoting Bainbridge *Post-Searchlight*.

Ohio River he would be Democratic presidential timber."[56] Such acclaim buoyed Fletcher's confidence, and he predicted a 50,000-vote margin over his opponent.

Carter drew vocal support from organized labor. A. D. Wright, state representative and labor spokesman, endorsed Carter, complaining that Fletcher opposed all legislation advocated by his group. Miami and Jacksonville unions faithfully backed the hotel commissioner, while Charles M. Wood, president of the Florida Typographical Conference and AFL organizer in the Tallahassee area, distributed a letter supporting Carter. Official publications of the Florida Association of Architects and the Tallahassee Typographical Union also endorsed him.[57]

Carter's campaign plugged uncompromisingly for liberalism. He called Fletcher a pawn of Florida railroad interests, accusing the senator of responsibility for a 55 per cent increase in Florida intrastate freight rates. The scrappy hotel commissioner blasted Fletcher's vote against woman suffrage and child labor regulation. Carter attacked Fletcher's internationalism, especially his advocacy of American membership in the World Court. Isolationist Senator James A. Reed conducted a speaking campaign to defeat all incumbent senators supporting the World Court and sent numerous speeches to Carter, who distributed them throughout Florida on Reed's mailing frank.[58]

Fletcher, supremely confident of a smashing victory, largely ignored Carter, and the young progressive conducted an exhaustive grass-roots campaign in every part of the state. Fletcher strategists squirmed uneasily when the senator remained in Washington for the spring congressional session. The Miami *Herald*, though supporting the incumbent, warned that Carter "is known everywhere and is very generally liked"; it "would be suicidal on the part of Senator Fletcher's friends to ignore the candidacy of this gentleman."[59] This warning disturbed the senator and he persuaded his old friend Josephus Daniels, Secretary of the Navy under Wilson, to speak at Jacksonville and defend American membership in the World Court.

56. Jacksonville *Florida Times-Union*, June 5, 1926.
57. Letter from Charles M. Wood, undated; and St. Petersburg *Daily News*, May 15, 1926, in Carter Papers.
58. Interview with Jerry W. Carter, November 21, 1962.
59. Miami *Herald*, in Carter Papers.

Convinced that he had taken Carter's candidacy too lightly, Fletcher returned to Florida on May 25 for strategy conferences with campaign manager Arthur T. Williams. In the next ten days he conducted a whirlwind campaign, emphasizing his seniority and reminding union members that he had opposed only four of the thirty measures favored by the American Federation of Labor. A significant feature of this ten-day swing through Florida was that all major speeches were delivered on or near the coast from Tampa east to Jacksonville. This contest and future races would be decided in powerful Hillsborough, fast-growing Dade, and along the coast. Fletcher could sacrifice strength in north Florida and still win. Carter ignored this demographic change and geared his strategy to the rural psychology of past races.

With all returns tabulated, Fletcher carried the state by a margin of 63,760 to 39,143 for Carter and 4,226 for Dr. John A. Van Valzah, a minor candidate from West Palm Beach. Carter ran well in the old farmer-progressive areas, but carried only two minor counties south of Gilchrist in central Florida. Fletcher lost the labor vote, split farmer ballots, and carried the cities of booming south Florida.

The strenuous electioneering left Fletcher physically debilitated. He became seriously ill with pneumonia and an infected bladder. Physicians rushed him to Battle Creek, Michigan, where two successful operations saved his life. While anxiously awaiting word of Fletcher's condition, Floridians saw the remnants of their declining prosperity vanish. A devastating hurricane packing 100-mile-an-hour winds ripped Miami, killing approximately 400 people, leaving 50,000 homeless, and causing damage in Miami alone of $100 million. Florida's depression began with the real estate collapse and great hurricane of 1926.

Florida's reaction to national politics underwent the same traumatic upheaval as her economy in the 1920's. Fletcher was hard pressed to remain at center stage in the drama of change transforming the state's political milieu. Republicans staged a decade-long challenge to Democratic dominance. They made deep inroads into Democratic strength in 1924, and Fletcher privately advocated elimination of the "dry rot" on the state Democratic Executive Committee.[60] However, even the senator protested the course

60. W. L. Hill to E. D. Lambright, November 8, 1924, Box 60, in Hodges Papers.

of national Democratic politics. In another of his paradoxes, he backed Montana's progressive Senator Thomas J. Walsh, who had exposed the Teapot Dome oil scandal, for the Democratic presidential nomination. When conservative corporation lawyer John W. Davis emerged with the 1924 nomination, Fletcher complained to Florida political intimates that he could see little difference between Calvin Coolidge and Davis; both were very conservative and offered little choice.[61] In 1927 the Floridian urged his party to ignore prohibition and religion at all costs in the forthcoming presidential campaign, suggesting that Governor Al Smith of New York withdraw from consideration.[62] No doubt he was responding to the political climate in Florida.

Sidney Catts returned to Florida politics in 1928 and tried to swing the state's Democratic delegation behind isolationist Senator James A. Reed. Fletcher attended the National Convention, devoting his time to the platform while his state's delegation followed a fruitless "stop Smith" policy. The Floridian accomplished his primary goal at the convention by winning Democratic support for permanent federal control of the merchant marine. When eastern Democrats nominated Smith on the first ballot, Fletcher immediately pledged his loyalty.

Most leading Florida Democrats supported Smith but with singular lack of enthusiasm, and in some cases, with serious reservations. Peter O. Knight advised Floridians to "hold our nose" and vote for Smith, but Sidney Catts led bolting Democrats who refused to back the New Yorker. The Reverend Dr. John Roach Straton toured Florida stirring up anti-Catholicism, and the *Florida Baptist Witness* repudiated Smith's Catholicism and anti-prohibitionism.[63]

Florida Democrats named Fletcher chairman of the Smith forces in the state. A torrent of letters from constituents who vowed to vote for Republican Herbert Hoover deeply disturbed the Senator, and he returned to Florida prepared for a strenuous race.[64] After his arrival on September 15, he launched one of the most

61. J. B. Hodges to W. L. Hill, November 10, 1924, Box 60, in Hodges Papers.
62. New York *Times*, September 18, 1927.
63. *Florida Baptist Witness*, July 14, 1927, Scrapbook F, in Knight Collection. For an excellent summary of this election, see Herbert J. Doherty, "Florida and the Presidential Election of 1928," *Florida Historical Quarterly*, XXVI (October, 1947), 174–86.
64. New York *Times*, September 14, 1928.

vigorous Democratic presidential campaigns in the state's history. He brought Josephus Daniels and vice-presidential nominee Joseph T. Robinson of Arkansas to campaign, along with congressmen from Georgia, South Carolina, and Louisiana. During the week of October 15–21, pro-Smith forces delivered seventy speeches, many over statewide radio networks. Fletcher coordinated the entire loyalist crusade and grew increasingly short-tempered at Park Trammell and other foot-dragging Florida Democrats.[65] He addressed three thousand people at Orlando, telling them a man's religion was personal: ". . . when religion is injected into political discussion people cease to reason and yield only to emotions, prejudice and strange action."[66] All these efforts failed, and Hoover swept to a 144,000 to 101,000 victory.

Fletcher emerged from the 1928 campaign more powerful than ever. As leader of state Democratic loyalists, he appeared particularly strong after the depression destroyed Hoover's luster. In 1931 Fletcher addressed a unity meeting of Florida Democrats at Marianna. He gained the "unanimous approval of his party" and partially healed the devisive breach in their ranks.[67] The Floridian performed the same role as mediator for national Democrats. Jouett Shouse, aide to Chairman John J. Raskob of the Democratic National Committee, invited southern congressmen who had defected in 1928 to a private dinner. The southerners refused to attend, but Fletcher tried to reconcile them: "I want to see the Democrats all get together—let the past be bygone, forget all differences, and stand by the party. . . ."[68]

Such chaotic politics reflected the restlessness of a state undergoing major economic and demographic transformation. She became Dixie's first urban state in 1930 and was more deeply affected by the early years of the depression than most other southern states. Only 355,800 of Florida's citizens lived in towns or cities in 1920, compared to 759,778 in 1930; 51.7 per cent of the state's population in 1930 resided in urban centers, with Texas, 41 per cent urban, a distant second place. Urban residents employed in manufacturing felt the full impact of economic depression. By 1930

65. Duncan U. Fletcher to Park Trammell, May 23, March 1, October 31, 1928, in Trammell Papers.
66. Jacksonville *Florida Times-Union*, September 21, 1928.
67. *Ibid.*, December 11, 1931, quoting Titusville *Star*.
68. New York *Times*, June 9, 1929.

Florida counted 33,000 unemployed, or 5.5 per cent of her work force, compared to unemployment rates of 3.8 in Louisiana, 3.4 in Texas, 2.5 in North Carolina, and 2.4 in Georgia.[69] The severity of the depression in Florida demanded new economic experimentation which accelerated Duncan Fletcher's drift to the political left after 1929.

The senator's political activity in the 1920's is a remarkable tribute to his political insight. Against Catts in 1920 he carried each of Florida's twelve largest counties. In all but one he received over 67 per cent of the vote; only in Jackson County in the panhandle, where he received 52 per cent, was the issue close. Catts managed to get over 40 per cent of the vote in only six counties, all of them in the old populistic rural panhandle of Florida west of the Suwannee River. Jerry Carter mounted a much more serious threat in 1926, but again Fletcher carried every one of the twelve largest counties, with Carter winning over 40 per cent in only one of these. Once again the further north and west one moved, the weaker Fletcher became; but in growing, vote-rich southern and central Florida, the incumbent senator captured insurmountable leads. Carter won 40 per cent or more of the vote in five central Florida counties, eight north Florida counties, and ten panhandle counties, reflecting a primarily rural strength. Eleven predominantly urban counties (Alachua, Dade, Duval, Escambia. Hillsborough, Monroe, Orange, Palm Beach, Pinellas, Polk, and Volusia) gave Fletcher 41,242 votes or approximately 65 per cent of his total vote in the state (63,760). In the same eleven urban counties, Carter received only some 42 per cent of his state total of 39,143.[70]

Following the primary elections, Fletcher switched strategy and appealed to the Democratic strongholds of northern Florida against Republican candidates in the general elections. When one national reporter predicted that the mass migration of eastern Republicans into south Florida might transform it into a Republican state, Fletcher replied that this had never been a Democratic bastion. In an interview on the shifting political balance in the state, the senator chuckled and reminded his questioner that the

69. U.S., *Bureau of the Census, Fifteenth Census of the United States. Population*, III, 29; *ibid., Unemployment*, I, 235.
70. For the undigested statistical data, see Annie Mary Hartsfield and Elston E. Roady, *Florida Votes, 1920–1962* (Tallahassee: Institute of Governmental Research, Florida State University, 1963), pp. 54, 56.

population boom was not changing the Democratic propensity of northern Florida, and "that part of Florida will always be our anchor to windward."[71]

Opposed by candidates championing labor unionism and liberal economics, Fletcher reacted by moving politically right. He correctly sensed the mood of Florida's urban voters who reflected national prosperity and conservatism; but his conservative posture never assumed such dogmatism that he completely alienated cautious laborites or languishing farmers. Even in 1926 he carried many rural northern Florida counties, though his strength in such areas had declined from previous elections. This alteration in his political philosophy also emerged in the area of national affairs, but here too it is mixed with a paradoxical strain of pragmatic liberalism which blossomed after the 1929 crash.

71. Richard L. Strout, "Will Florida Crack the Solid South?" *The Independent,* CXVI (January 23, 1926), 96.

CHAPTER IX

A Cautious Progressive Among "Wild Jackasses"

C HANGES in Duncan Fletcher's national political posture between 1920 and 1932 mirrored the chaotic conditions in Florida. The early prosperous years of the decade reveal a rather conservative philosophy; the latter years are punctuated with an impatient reformism. In view of his increasing "liberalism" after 1926 on such issues as the Muscle Shoals project and federal relief, one might conclude that he lacked a consistent credo, that he had not so much a philosophy of government as a series of responses to national crises. Although there is an element of truth in such a conclusion (perhaps most American politicians respond to specific events rather than to abstract theory), the senator also enunciated a consistent structure of ideas to guide his decision-making. Fletcher, ever the politician, was wary of labels and specifics; so one must cautiously piece together his philosophy from numerous speeches and essays.

While working with the Southern Commercial Congress, he had decided that the South needed new ideas, sharper debate, and new approaches to old problems. He expanded this regional concept to include the entire nation during the 1920's. In a speech in Tampa in 1926 he warned that the "nation in its hobby of standardization is drifting to standardization of thought."[1] In an effort to encourage and foster diversity in the arts, he introduced a bill in 1921 to establish a national, federally financed conservatory of music.[2] Fletcher also questioned the traditional two-year terms in

1. Tampa *Morning Tribune*, June 1, 1926.
2. U.S., *Congressional Record*, 67th Congress, 1st Session, 1921, LXI, 186.

the House of Representatives. He argued that members of the lower House were barely seated before they were forced to begin campaigning for re-election. In 1928 and again the following year he proposed a joint resolution to amend the Constitution to provide four-year terms for representatives.[3]

He believed that the greatest danger of standardization of ideas came from the federal government. In the classical tradition of nineteenth-century liberalism, he argued that government must leave man alone. The centralization of power in Washington represented the most dangerous tendency of the 1920's, and this concentration of governmental authority would bring autocracy if allowed to continue.[4]

Yet, Fletcher's conservative view of man's relationship to government contradicts his specific legislative proposals and even his philosophical precepts. He assailed the laissez-faire Social Darwinism of William Graham Sumner, Yale economist and sociologist. Sumner had warned that federal assistance artificially preserved the weaker elements in society which would normally have fallen victim to stronger economic force. Fletcher rejected this individualistic survival of the fittest for a more congenial, cooperative, and altruistic view of man. Sumner, he argued, overlooked the interdependence of men and nations. No man was self-contained, and every individual should feel responsible for his neighbor. Sumner erred by maintaining that wrong could be remedied by allowing nature to "run its course." Fletcher believed that every good citizen must work positively to alleviate economic and social inequity.[5] Stoical acquiescence was not an acceptable option. The Floridian might disagree with liberals on the objectives of reform, but he conceded that man could progress, that intolerable conditions could be ameliorated, and that positive action could alter environment. By advocating federal-state cooperation in conservation, public health, highway construction, shipping, and agriculture, the senator affirmed that government could extend opportunity and minimize injustice.

Fletcher seemed trapped in a hopeless dilemma. How could

3. U.S., *Congressional Record*, 70th Congress, 1st Session, 1928, LXIX, 8046; and 71st Congress, 1st Session, 1929, LXXI, 107.
4. Address by Duncan U. Fletcher to the Florida Legislature, May 12, 1925, Box 60, in Hodges Papers.
5. Jacksonville *Florida Times-Union*, April 10, 1925.

government provide social equity yet abstain from federal intrusion? The answer lay in Fletcher's concept of centralization. He meaningfully protested the power of government under Calvin Coolidge and the Republicans, while advocating broad expansion of federal prerogatives under Woodrow Wilson and Franklin D. Roosevelt, particularly when used for the public interest. Governmental power was not inherently bad, but only when it was used for narrow special interests. Where opportunity was unequal or where control was vested in a select few of great wealth (as with Secretary Ballinger under Taft or with Florida Bourbon Democrats in the 1880's or with the maritime companies in the 1920's), plutocracy resulted. Democracy existed only when government insured opportunity and fragmented control.[6] Fletcher's voting record in the 1920's reflects support for governmental expansion of opportunity qualified by zealous concern for state and individual rights.

By 1921 only three Democratic senators exceeded Fletcher in seniority. As a result, he served as ranking minority member of the Banking and Currency, Commerce, and Military Affairs committees. Hearings consumed most of his time, and colleagues frequently saw him shuffling to a conference. Balding, with a broad white mustache, pince-nez perched periously on his nose, he usually carried an unlit cigar and a walking cane chosen from his large collection. The senator took his duties seriously and maintained a near-perfect voting record. He privately censured Senate colleagues for their lackadaisical attention to congressional duties: "I don't know how other senators manage to go [home] and stay away as they do. Every day has its calls and demands which I see no way of shirking or putting off on others."[7]

Federal legislation aimed at child labor and lynching demonstrated Fletcher's fear of centralization and his deep conservative strain. He supported the objectives of such laws but insisted that states must assume the initiative. When an angry Florida mother threatened political annihilation if he continued to oppose the Twentieth Amendment abolishing child labor, Fletcher replied with a letter to the Jasper, Florida *News*. If no one under eighteen years of age worked, he predicted that there would be an in-

6. Address of Duncan U. Fletcher to the Florida Legislature, May 12, 1925, Box 60, in Hodges Papers.
7. Duncan U. Fletcher to Cornelia Huddleston, August 15, 1921, in Fletcher Papers.

crease in idleness, immorality, socialism, and communism. Though he desired to end the exploitation of children, he preferred local action to government administration "by selfish persons or by sentimental theorists lacking conception of parental rights, duties, and responsibilities." The proposed Twentieth Amendment was "most revolutionary," and its concentration of power could lead to more socialistic legislation in the future.[8] In an article defending his opposition to federal control of child labor, Fletcher wrote that such congressional legislation undermined the sovereignty of the states, interferred with the right of families to determine the work habits of their own children, and created a vast centralized bureaucracy. He heatedly charged that the proponents of a federal child labor amendment were "surface-minded sentimentalists, unthinking enthusiasts. . . ."[9] On the issue of lynching, he adopted a similar logic; he deplored the murder of Negroes, but vehemently opposed federal legislation, saying that the punishment of crimes committed within a state was the state's responsibility.[10]

Florida politics dictated an even more basic departure from progressivism on the nation's tax structure. Actually, Fletcher had begun the decade in liberal fashion, joining insurgent Republicans to defeat a sales tax bearing heavily on consumers. He also had opposed Republican tax reductions in 1921 which aided the wealthy rather than the public. As late as 1923 he had favored reduced taxes on small incomes and increased levies on larger salaries. But Florida conservatives converted the senator with a well-planned assault on the inheritance tax.[11] To encourage inheritance taxation, the government had allowed an 80 per cent rebate on all receipts collected in states with their own inheritance taxes. Florida sought to attract older citizens seeking to escape high tax rates; hence she was one of only three states which had no state income or inheritance assessments. Since the government collected the tax in Florida but allowed the state no rebate, Fletcher charged that the law was discriminatory. The federal government was attempting by the

8. See reprint of letter to Jasper *News*, in U.S., *Congressional Record*, 68th Congress, 2d Session, 1925, LXVI, 3999.
9. Duncan U. Fletcher, "The Child Labor Amendment–II," *North American Review*, CCXX (December, 1924), 239–42.
10. U.S., *Congressional Record*, 67th Congress, 3d Session, 1922, LXIII, 448.
11. New York *Times*, November 14, 1923. Peter O. Knight and James B. Hodges led the anti-inheritance tax forces. See J. B. Hodges to Joe L. Earman, March 2, 1926, Box 65, in Hodges Collection.

rebate to enforce uniformity of state taxation on inheritances. He defended the constitutional right of a state to decide whether or not it would impose particular kinds of local taxes. Retreating to familiar ground, he acknowledged the value of the estate tax as a wartime emergency measure to produce revenue; but the government no longer needed the money and its continuance was only an attempt by some to implement reforms which they considered socially just.[12] He voted with the Senate majority to repeal the inheritance tax in February, 1926, and in favor of the tax reduction bill of 1928; on both occasions he voted opposite such respected progressives as Robert M. La Follette and George W. Norris.[13]

Senatorial conservatives reciprocated by supporting his waterway bills. Florida received $20,400,000 for rivers and harbors between 1919 and 1926, more in proportion to population than any other state.[14] When floor rebellion threatened the annual appropriation in 1925, he rejected compromise and forced continuous sessions until his opponents capitulated.

Despite this temporary conservative liaison, pragmatism and personal preference dictated a progressive course. Fletcher realized that his party could never move to the right of Calvin Coolidge. Democrats chose Fletcher to serve on the party steering committee in 1921, and he helped formulate congressional strategy and assign committee posts. This position afforded him access to inner party councils, and he assumed a larger role in national planning. At the historic 1924 Democratic convention, he served on the platform committee and helped draft planks on agricultural relief and maritime affairs. He loyally supported the League of Nations but, noting general apathy on foreign affairs, advised party leaders to emphasize the tariff instead.

Unlike many progressives of the "roaring twenties," Duncan Fletcher steadfastly defended internationalism. He stumped Florida on behalf of the League in his 1920 campaign, blaming League inaction on American isolation. No issue affected him so emotionally or perplexed him more deeply, as he revealed in a prophetic New York *Times* interview:

> The rejection of the . . . [League] denies us participation in all those matters which would tend to prevent a re-

12. U.S., *Congressional Record*, 70th Congress, 1st Session, 1928, LXIX, 9162–63.
13. *Ibid.*, 9854; and 69th Congress, 1st Session, 1926, LXVII, 3886.
14. Stephens, "Senator Duncan U. Fletcher—Legislator," p. 105.

currance [sic] of another calamity such as we have just experienced; causes the United States to forfeit moral leadership in the world and lose its power and influence, which it could exert for the good of humanity; places us in a selfish attitude, caring only for what we conceive to be our own little world, 'careless of mankind.'

If America is determined to reject this, then there is nothing to do but to enlarge our military establishment, increase our armament, lay burdens upon the shoulders of our people and prepare for the next war. . . .[15]

Fletcher considered arms limitation an absolute prerequisite to peace. In 1921 he addressed the Senate, deploring the "misgovernment" which allocated 88 per cent of all congressional appropriations to past and future wars, leaving only 12 per cent for constructive programs to aid the people.[16] He chose Armistice Day in 1922 to tell Floridians: "If this world is to be saved . . . each nation must conceive of itself, not as a herd but as a brotherhood. It must realize clearly that materialism [armaments and national greed] is as intellectually wrong as it is morally dangerous."[17] Later in the decade, he voted for the London Treaty limiting naval armaments and advocated American military withdrawal from Cuba and Nicaragua. Perhaps it was his internationalism that first caused him to reject the individualistic Social Darwinism of William Sumner.

As ranking minority member of the Senate military committee, he opposed large standing armies. Since the nations rejected disarmament, he supported a strong navy and high quality army, arguing that adequate preparation might restrain aggression. The senator had taken his first airplane flight with a stunt pilot in 1919 and had become a convert to air power. By 1931 he was advising curtailment of large appropriations for capital ships, and he predicted that future wars would be conducted largely by aircraft.[18]

Fletcher remained the Democratic leader on maritime affairs throughout the decade, and most of his major policy speeches dealt with this subject. His concern for shipping was understandable. The South produced 38 per cent of all American exports in 1924,

15. New York *Times*, October 13, 1920.
16. Jacksonville *Florida Times-Union*, October 24, 1921.
17. *Ibid.*, November 12, 1922.
18. *Ibid.*, September 16, 1931.

and Florida shipping thrived as a result. Fletcher feared that railroads gave preferential treatment to northeastern ports, and he concluded that the Gulf Coast could obtain Mississippi Valley shipping only through government ownership. When the United States Shipping Board constructed the passenger liner *Leviathan* in 1923, conservatives of both parties cried "socialism." Fletcher sailed on the five-day trial run, then praised the government's action as a step "which for some years I have insisted [on] . . . namely, the ownership and operation, aggressively by the government, of needed merchant ships. . . ."[19] He discounted government operational losses, saying it would take time to develop profitable shipping routes. When Fletcher heard that the federal shipping board planned to sell two hundred vessels to private companies in 1925, he threatened a congressional investigation.[20]

The senator flew into a rage when President Warren G. Harding proposed a government subsidy to private shipping lines. When Harding leaders introduced the subsidy in December, 1922, Fletcher led the Democratic assault.[21] He formulated strategy with leaders of the Farm and Progressive blocs, and the two groups substituted the farm credit bill for the subsidy. After passage of the agricultural bill in February, Fletcher launched a vigorous filibuster which killed the subsidy on February 28. Progressive Florida papers celebrated their senior senator as the man who defeated the steamship lobby.[22]

Languishing American agriculture demanded even more attention than maritime policy in the early twenties. Overextension, inflation, decline in foreign demand, and government withdrawal of wheat price supports tumbled farm income from $17 billion in 1919 to $9 billion in 1921. Between 1923 and 1929 total farm income hovered at $11 billion a year. Fletcher considered healthy agriculture a requisite for a strong economy, thus justifying government farm programs. In a comprehensive statement on the American economy, he attributed agrarian difficulties to overproduction

19. *Ibid.*, June 27, 1923; for Fletcher's view of shipping see *ibid.*, February 6, 1921; and Duncan U. Fletcher, "Our Merchant Marine," New York *Times*, October 10, 1920.
20. New York *Times*, August 9, 1925.
21. U.S., *Congressional Record*, 67th Congress, 2d Session, 1922, LXII, 10373–10397.
22. Jacksonville *Florida Times-Union*, March 12, 1923, quoting Bronson *Times-Democrat* and Summerfield *Chronicle*.

and inability to supply foreign markets. Fifteen years ahead of his time, he advocated reduction of agricultural acreage. He favored revitalizing the War Finance Corporation to furnish credit to foreign customers desiring American farm products.[23] Government-owned ships would insure minimum freight rates.

Middle-western farmers suffered even greater dislocation than southerners, causing Senator William S. Kenyon of Iowa to invite twelve senators to a May 9, 1921, meeting at the Washington Farm Bureau Federation. Progressives of both political parties met and established committees to draft agricultural legislation. Fletcher attended this organizational meeting of the Farm Bloc and remained a faithful member.[24] The group was enlarged to twenty-two senators and occasionally included seven more. The Bloc met regularly in Senator Kenyon's office and, aided by a similar group in the House, passed the most advanced agricultural program in American history to 1933.

Between July 5 and August 25, 1921, the bipartisan group blocked congressional adjournment and passed five important measures: the Meat Packers Control Bill, Futures Trading Act, extension of the War Finance Corporation, and two acts increasing capital of the Farm Loan System.[25] Financial interests joined President Harding in castigating the Bloc's activities, and Senator George Moses of New Hampshire branded the mavericks "sons of the wild jackass." Fletcher became a spokesman for the organization and aimed a fiery rejoinder at President Harding. The senator insisted that beneficial agricultural legislation would have died in Congress but for the "energy and insistence" of the Bloc. The bipartisan group, "much abused and vilified," was solely responsible for aid to farmers.[26] He answered senatorial critics in a similar vein: "None of those things would have been accom-

23. Jacksonville *Florida Times-Union*, February 5, 1921.
24. Arthur Capper, *The Agricultural Bloc* (New York: Harcourt, Brace and Company, 1922), p. 9. Other senators present included: Arthur Capper (Kansas), George W. Norris (Nebraska), F. R. Gooding (Idaho), E. F. Ladd (North Dakota), Robert La Follette (Wisconsin), E. D. Smith (South Carolina), J. B. Kendrick (Wyoming), Joseph E. Ransdell (Louisiana), Thomas Heflin (Alabama), and Morris Sheppard (Texas). See also Ray Tucker and Frederick R. Barkley, *Sons of the Wild Jackass* (Boston: L. C. Page and Company, 1932).
25. See Chapter XI, "The Farm Bloc," in Theodore Saloutos and John D. Hicks, *Agricultural Discontent in the Middle West 1900-1939* (Madison: University of Wisconsin Press, 1951), pp. 321–41.
26. New York *Times*, June 29, 1923.

plished if it had not been for the unrelenting energy . . . of . . . the farm bloc. . . . We have the results of that movement here in the Senate, and those results, I submit, are sufficient answer to any slurs or aspersions attempted to be cast upon what is known as the farm bloc."[27] Fletcher considered broadened opportunity central to the agrarian controversy and endorsed federal intervention. He blasted the Republican farm program in 1924, charging that President Coolidge accepted two fallacious premises: that farmers must work out their own problems and that there was nothing government could do to help.

Government agricultural subsidies had gained Fletcher's complete endorsement after the 1916 Farm Loan Act. In 1923 he termed that program "as perfect a piece of legislation . . . as was ever put upon the statute books . . ." and he supported Farm Bloc liberals Arthur Capper, Robert La Follette, George Norris, and Morris Sheppard in extending federal aid to farmers.[28] Old-line Democratic conservatives, such as Virginia's Carter Glass and Alabama's Oscar Underwood, opposed this expansion, and Fletcher-Glass clashes often rocked the Senate. The Floridian recommended in 1923 that farm representatives be allowed a direct voice on the Federal Reserve Board. Glass, one of the fathers of the system, stormed: "I know it is unpleasant to tell farmers they are not bankers . . . but I say here that they are not bankers and they cannot manage banks as bankers can." Fletcher deflated the pontifical Glass by retorting that "they have sense enough to elect members of this body."[29]

Republicans particularly rankled Fletcher by their miserly treatment of his Farm Loan Banks. They provided only $4 million in 1921, and Florida alone had applications for more than this. When Florida farmers complained that local Farm Loan Associations lapsed into inactivity under the Republicans, Fletcher privately inquired about bank conditions and concluded that the GOP was "playing politics."[30] With Farm Bloc aid, he pumped millions into the program during 1922 and 1923.

27. U.S., *Congressional Record*, 67th Congress, 4th Session, 1923, LXIV, 2773.
28. *Ibid.*, 2466; also see votes, pp. 1809, 1879, 1939, 1995, 1996.
29. Rixey Smith and Norman Beasley, *Carter Glass, a Biography* (New York: Longmans, Green and Company, 1939), p. 216.
30. J. B. Hodges to Joe L. Earman, March 6, 1922, Box 44, in Hodges Papers; and Duncan U. Fletcher to Cornelia Huddleston, August 15, 1921, in Fletcher Papers.

Florida's economic decline after 1925 swept Fletcher leftward, and his powerful position as the ranking minority member of the Senate Commerce Committee provided him with an influential forum. In his mind, two of the nation's perplexing problems were interrelated. Agricultural relief could be extended to farmers by controlling exorbitant transportation costs and by providing overseas markets; both of these objectives could be achieved through energetic government use of its merchant marine. The senator charged that railroad freight rates on agricultural commodities were enormous, that lines passed pay increases for their workers on to the shippers. He cited his own experience with a small grapefruit grove which he owned in Florida. After his investment in cultivation, spray, and labor, his net return after paying freight charges to New York was twenty-seven cents a box. He concluded that "excessive express charges and freight rates, the expense of transporting the products to market, as well as the bad system of distribution, constitute the chief evils which afflict agriculture in this country today."[31] Acting on this premise, he fought attempts by railroads to gain control of intercoastal shipping lines, fearing that this would create a transportation monopoly in the hands of a few large railroads.

His maritime policy continued to reflect the pragmatism and expediency which so often lurked behind his public posture. By 1928, 60 per cent of the nation's exports moved through southern ports. The United States Shipping Board operated a total of 290 ships, with 116 of them located in Gulf of Mexico ports. Establishment and maintenance of these lines promised commercial growth for the entire region, a major concern of Fletcher ever since his long affiliation with the Southern Commercial Congress. Many business-minded southerners shared Fletcher's concern that commerce would languish without an active federal maritime policy.

Fletcher conducted an extensive correspondence concerning world maritime affairs and appears to have been the most knowledgeable man in the Senate on such matters. After 1925 he became even more militant about government control of the merchant marine. When T. V. O'Connor, chairman of the United States Shipping Board, advocated private ownership, the senator wrote that he too favored private management; but, "When private enterprise failed, or refused, or neglected, to serve the people, govern-

31. U.S., *Congressional Record*, 69th Congress, 2d Session, 1927, LXVIII, 3422.

ment must act. I do not call that socialism or paternalism. I call it performance of plain duty—incumbent upon the government."[32] In 1926 and again in 1927 he introduced joint resolutions providing "that the United States Shipping Board and Emergency Fleet Corporation shall continue indefinitely in the business of owning and operating merchant vessels in overseas trades and for other purposes."[33] In a speech in 1927 defending his proposal, he argued that government operating costs were going down and that existing federally operated lines should be expanded, especially those involving passenger ships. He predicted that if the government allowed private ownership, the merchant marine would disappear as it had in the era before 1914. The 1920 Merchant Marine Act, which had stated the intent of Congress to return ships to private management, had been misinterpreted by the Harding and Coolidge administrations; in reality Congress had placed first priority on the establishment and maintenance of an American merchant marine and only secondary emphasis on a return to private ownership.[34]

Despite Fletcher's diligent efforts, his resolutions languished in the Commerce Committee, and the Shipping Board continued to dispose of government ships. Between June, 1921, and January, 1928, the Board had sold 1,141 ships for a total of $85 million. By 1928, only 798 ships remained under federal control.[35] This set the stage for a stormy congressional battle over national maritime policy in the Seventieth Congress.

Debate was triggered by the Shipping Board's decision by a split vote to sell thirty-six merchant ships operating in the Pacific. Fletcher opened the attack with a major policy address in the Senate on January 5, 1928. He charged that the Coolidge administration was serving private interests and ignoring the public. His careful research revealed that one ship, the *City of Los Angeles*, has cost $1.6 million to build and $2 million more to recondition into a passenger liner to use on the United States–Latin American route. The government subsequently had spent another $43,000 on hotel supplies. Then, one month later, the Board had sold the ship with all furnishings, supplies, and equipment for $100,000.

32. Jacksonville *Florida Times-Union*, August 22, 1927.
33. U.S., *Congressional Record*, 69th Congress, 2d Session, 1927, LXVIII, 1035.
34. *Ibid.*, 4219–27.
35. U.S., *Congressional Record*, 70th Congress, 1st Session, 1928, LXIX, 2138–39.

Fletcher noted that after five years the private companies that purchased government ships could take the vessels off their former routes, and that the Shipping Board required no guarantee of replacement for ships when they were worn out. Government operating losses presented no reason to sell these ships, for the lines had been designed to open new markets and expand American commerce, not to reap an immediate profit. He noted that during two agricultural crises when European shipping had been tied up by strikes or national emergencies, the Shipping Board had used one hundred of its reserve ships to transport surplus wheat and cotton to Europe. He attributed the decline of America's merchant fleet to private ownership and the sale of government ships: in 1900, United States shipping had carried 9.3 per cent of her overseas trade; due to $3 billion of federal construction funds during the First World War, American shipping carried 42.7 per cent of her foreign commerce in 1920. Under the Board's disposal policy, this percentage had slipped to 36.3 in 1924, 34.1 in 1925, and 32.3 in 1926. The only alternatives to the obliteration of America's merchant marine were a government subsidy to private companies—which Fletcher argued would lead to scandal, favoritism, and special interests—or continued government control. Throughout his speech he used his extensive investigations to quiet conservative critics by challenging their faulty statistics and their knowledge of maritime conditions.[36]

His speech of January 5 provided the reference point for subsequent debate. In a ringing policy statement Fletcher dropped all pretense of temporary federal control:

> . . . if I had the authority, I should not say another word about selling ships. . . . On the contrary, I should announce to the world that private enterprise having failed utterly to take the proper interest in ships . . . the Government is in the shipping business to stay, and the policy shall be from now on to eliminate the words in the merchant marine act, 'ultimately to pass to private hands,' and shall be to aggressively carry out the prime purpose of the merchant marine act. . . . I should make this issue in the next campaign; I should put this pledge in the Democratic platform and go to the country on it, announcing clearly and unequivocally the policy of the Government to permanently own and operate merchant ships in

36. *Ibid.*, 1006–23.

foreign trade, to serve American commerce . . . and serve our country in time of need.[37]

Liberal Senator George W. Norris acknowledged the validity of Fletcher's statistics and the illogic of selling government ships for the losses cited by his Florida colleague. Disclosures such as the case of the *City of Los Angeles* provoked him to demand a congressional investigation.[38] After rallying allies such as Norris, Fletcher swung his support behind Senate Bill 744, which authorized the further development of the merchant marine, guaranteed its permanence, attacked the sale of government ships, and included a provision that such ships could be sold only by the unanimous vote of the seven-member U.S. Shipping Board. Conservatives, raising cries of socialism and bolshevism, tried to kill the measure, or at least amend it to allow action by a simple majority. Fletcher led a coalition consisting of liberals from both parties (Senators Norris, William E. Borah, James Couzens, Robert M. La Follette, Jr., James Reed, and Thomas J. Walsh) which defeated this amendment by 31 to 52, and a similar amendment (requiring a 5–2 vote by the Board) by a 37–47 decision. Senate Bill 744 finally passed 53 to 31.[39]

The House passed a milder bill, and after much wrangling in conference, the Senate acceded to a compromise embodying all the basic elements of the Senate measure but allowing sale of government ships by a vote of five of the seven members of the Shipping Board. Fletcher, who had served on the conference committee, defended the compromise, arguing that while he favored a unanimous vote, the conference report was better than a simple majority. The compromise placated a portion of the liberal coalition, but Borah, La Follette, Walsh, and Reed rejected all modifications and opposed the conference report, which passed the Senate 51 to 20.[40] Public attention had been focused on the maritime crisis primarily by Fletcher, and numerous articles in popular periodicals utilized arguments and information which had been presented initially by the Florida senator.[41]

---

37. *Ibid.*, 1035–36; for summary of this major policy address and a conservative rejoinder, see Duncan U. Fletcher, "Will 1928 Act Aid American Shipping?" *Congressional Digest,* VII (June, 1928), 190–91.
38. U.S., *Congressional Record,* 70th Congress, 1st Session, 1928, LXIX, 2137.
39. *Ibid.*, 2249–50.
40. *Ibid.*, 8044, 8722, 8811.
41. For examples of articles using Fletcher's logic and information, see Franklin

When the Board continued to sell vessels, Fletcher pledged to incorporate a plank in the next Democratic platform guaranteeing federal control and launched a speaking campaign to win popular support. Addressing the Woman's National Democratic Club in Washington, he insisted that government ownership was the best maritime policy. Conservative shippers and Republican officials assailed Fletcher, but one irate New Yorker replied that only interests trying to destroy the government merchant marine attacked Fletcher, who was the major obstacle to their objective.[42] Even after the Shipping Board sold its entire Atlantic fleet to private owners in March, 1929, Fletcher continued his personal feud with the board. He advocated government control in national radio addresses during January and March, 1930.[43] All his efforts were to no avail, and Republicans concluded the liquidation before Hoover left office in 1933. Like many of his constituents, Fletcher's conservatism had been modified by the necessity of federal intervention to provide more economic opportunities for the Gulf South.

Florida's senior senator also widened his agrarian progressivism during the late 1920's. The Farm Bloc merged into an ill-defined progressive coalition while partially maintaining its separate identity. The Bloc regrouped after 1925, uniting in advocacy of the McNary-Haugen and Muscle Shoals bills.

The McNary-Haugen measure was designed to raise farm prices by government support and exportation of American surplus commodities. Midwestern congressmen introduced the bill in 1924, but Fletcher and other southerners opposed it. The inclusion of cotton, tobacco, and rice in the proposed system won southern support, and Fletcher voted for the bill in February, 1927. While denying that attempts to control the costs of production or marketing agricultural commodities would accomplish all that its advocates claimed, he conceded the need for some remedy. Every congressman "must recognize the necessity for a sound and healthy agriculture, and if by experimenting a little we can help maintain

Snow, "American Commerce and Foreign Ships," *The Independent*, CXX (June 2, 1928), 527–28; and "First-Aid for Our Shipping," *The Literary Digest*, XCVII (June 2, 1928), 11.

42. Jacksonville *Florida Times-Union*, May 8, 1929; and New York *Times*, July 20 and 26, 1928.

43. For text, see U.S., *Congressional Record*, 71st Congress, 2d Session, 1930, LXXII, 1802–3.

that industry on a proper footing and in a healthy condition, it seems to me we ought to do it."[44] Insurgent liberals of both parties joined moderates like Fletcher to carry the measure to a 47-to-39 victory.

Fletcher also denounced Republican attempts to transfer control of the Farm Loan Board to the Treasury Department, considering it a move to put New York financial interests in charge of loan rates. He wrote an article warning farmers that this would result in increased interest rates to benefit private lenders. The *Farm Journal,* one of the nation's largest farm periodicals with 1,400,000 subscribers, praised Fletcher's concern: of all ninety-six senators "none had made a closer study of the Federal Farm Loan System than Senator Fletcher . . . and none has been more watchful and energetic in protecting it from attack and advancing its interests."[45] The senator so endeared himself to farmers that the Grange sponsored a national radio address by him on agrarian problems.

Florida's agricultural decline sparked Fletcher's leftward drift. Farm tenancy accurately reflected the state's economic trend: 25.3 per cent in 1920, 21.3 per cent in 1925, 28.4 per cent in 1930. Farm acreage declined from 5,800,000 in 1925 to 5,000,000 in 1930, while the value of land and buildings followed the same pattern: $281.5 million in 1920, $479 million in 1925, $423 million in 1930.[46] The senator damned inequitable marketing costs which brought citrus farmers only $5,623,000 for a crop sold to eastern consumers for $49,000,000. Fletcher expressed the growing frustration of many farmers: ". . . out of what [the farmer] produces the carriers will flourish, the ware house and packing house people, the shippers and sellers, the jobbers and wholesalers . . . and he will be the last to realize any remuneration."[47] He advised Florida farmers to eliminate such exploitation by organizing their own marketing facilities. The Floridian obtained Farm Board assistance for this project, and the federal agency allocated $2,800,000 for a Florida Citrus Exchange. This loan,

44. U.S., *Congressional Record,* 69th Congress, 2d Session, 1927, LXVIII, 3422.
45. Duncan U. Fletcher, "The Land Banks in Peril," *The Farm Journal,* LI (December, 1927), 9, 21, 33.
46. U.S., Bureau of the Census, *Fifteenth Census of the United States: 1930. Agriculture,* II, 739, 684.
47. Jacksonville *Florida Times-Union,* June 4, 1929.

which was the largest of its kind ever approved before 1930, enabled the exchange to construct packing, pre-cooling, and heating plants for cooperative marketing.[48]

The senator's evaluation of the government-built nitrate complex at Muscle Shoals, Alabama, underwent the same traumatic reappraisal. In 1922 Fletcher introduced a resolution offering to sell the facility to Henry Ford for private operation. Ford indicated a willingness to produce agricultural fertilizers, and the plan won solid southern backing as well as support among members of the Farm Bloc. But the determined opposition of Senator George W. Norris blocked passage.[49] The southerners turned to a compromise bill offered by Alabama's Senator Oscar W. Underwood authorizing the government to lease the Muscle Shoals project, or if no satisfactory lessee appeared, to operate the facility as a government corporation to produce chemical fertilizers. In December, 1925, Senator Norris, who had proposed a bill earlier providing for government ownership but not fertilizer production, accepted a compromise including government production of 40,000 tons of nitrogen annually to be used for fertilizers. Many southern senators—including Ellison D. Smith of South Carolina, Morris Sheppard of Texas, Joseph E. Ransdell of Louisiana, and Fletcher—deserted the Underwood bill and entered the Norris camp.

Fletcher's position on Muscle Shoals legislation vacillated. He opposed crippling amendments to the Underwood bill, including one provision for government operation of the complex. When the Norris forces blocked action again, Fletcher switched positions and voted to substitute Norris' bill providing for government construction of dams and the creation of the Federal Chemical Corporation. The measure carried 40 to 39 when all southerners except Underwood and John K. Shields voted for it. When the Administration-Underwood forces rallied (43–38) to substitute the Underwood proposal, Fletcher stuck with the liberal minority of Norris, Walsh, William E. Borah, and La Follette. However, he again reversed himself when the Senate finally voted on the Underwood bill; he voted with the conservative majority (50–30) for

48. *Ibid.*, August 9, October 14, 1929.
49. For a brief explanation and interpretation of the entire controversy, see ch. 6, "The Underwood Bill," in Preston J. Hubbard, *Origins of the TVA: The Muscle Shoals Controversy, 1920–1932* (New York: W. W. Norton and Company, 1968), pp. 147–69.

its passage.[50] This complicated political maneuvering revealed that Fletcher, like other southerners, wanted the Underwood version of the bill; but he also preferred government operation (the Norris bill) to no production.

Actually, the senator's position was not as ambiguous as his voting record indicated. He favored the Underwood bill only because it dealt in specifics on the production of agricultural fertilizers, which Fletcher considered of paramount importance. Influenced by the favorable impact that Muscle Shoals could have on the Florida phosphate industry and on lowering the price of chemical fertilizers, he elevated this issue above the consideration of electric power production. He never employed the conservative issue of alleged socialism in the Norris proposal, an argument which he dismissed in short fashion: "It does not bother me very much about whether the Government performs this work or private parties do it. I never lost much sleep over the question of whether private individuals are conducting a business or the Government is conducting it. The Government's business is to serve the people. If the Government can serve them best and only when private enterprise fails to do it, then let the Government do it. But the Government [in the Norris measure] does not propose to manufacture fertilizer here."[51]

In a major address on March 8, 1928, he praised the efforts of Norris, but again argued that the production of nitrate fertilizers must be included in any measure. If private companies failed to do so, the Government could act on the same principle that it had used to improve harbors and rivers for one hundred years: the national welfare. Government dams constructed for navigation could also produce power and nitrates. He did share Norris' persistent concern for a more inclusive view of Tennessee Valley problems:

> If I were in the place of the Government, with all its resources behind me, I would be disposed to take a broader and more comprehensive view of the whole Tennessee River situation than is attempted at this time. The possibilities for power development on that river are almost unlimited. The navigation of the river is a very important matter to be con-

50. *Ibid.*, 151–54. For test votes see U.S., *Congressional Record*, 68th Congress, 2d Session, 1925, LXVI, 718, 1454, 1726, 1736, 1795, 1805, 1808.
51. U.S., *Congressional Record*, 70th Congress, 1st Session, 1928, LXIX, 4251.

sidered; and, of course, the production of fertilizer is of vast importance to our agricultural interests. . . .

If I had the power to do so and had the resources of the Government behind me, I would consider the whole Tennessee River . . . everywhere from its source to where it empties into the Ohio River.[52]

Despite all his reservations, in March, 1928, Fletcher voted with the majority (43 to 34) to consider Senate Joint Resolution 46, which embodied the Norris proposals. Utah's Senator William H. King represented the conservatives in Congress who damned the measure as "paternalistic and socialistic" and the first step toward a collective society. But the Floridian ignored their charges and voted with Norris, La Follette, Borah, Hugo Black of Alabama, and other liberals to pass the final resolution by a 48-to-25 margin.[53] Later, in March, 1931, Fletcher supported the Norris measure enthusiastically and voted with the majority to override President Herbert Hoover's veto of the Norris plan for federal operation of the Muscle Shoals facility, but the bill was not enacted until 1933.

In 1929 Fletcher joined an insurgent coalition of Democrats and Republicans to win control of Congress. The senator's expanding acceptance of government activity became more apparent after this, and he formed a group of nineteen congressmen in 1931 to draft a program of economic reform. President Hoover appealed to Fletcher's group to help guide his financial program through Congress. Fletcher agreed, placing special emphasis on legislation to provide federal guarantee of bank deposits.[54] He introduced this bill in February, 1932, hoping to restore confidence in the nation's banking structure.[55]

Unemployment understandably drew Fletcher's attention during the same years. Florida's financial collapse convinced him that a major overhaul of America's economy was essential. Prosperity confined to the few "enjoying special privilege and special favors" from the government had failed, he said, adding sarcastically, "prosperity seems to be obstructed on its way trickling down"; the people "would be better satisfied with the prosperity that begins at the bottom and builds up."[56] General reform gained pre-

52. *Ibid.*, 4308–9.
53. *Ibid.*, 9842.
54. Burdetter G. Lewis to editor, New York *Times*, June 23, 1936.
55. U.S., *Congressional Record*, 72d Congress, 1st Session, 1932, LXXV, 4751.
56. Jacksonville *Florida Times-Union*, August 21, 1928.

eminence after 1933, but for the time being, he proposed more immediate action.

A conference committee agreed in 1931 to House insistence on rejection of two Senate initiated unemployment measures. Fletcher helped a coalition, led by Norris, La Follette, and Hugo Black, defeat the conference report. The vote (39 to 42) indicated that the liberals in Congress and their moderate allies desired some kind of positive action from the Hoover administration.[57]

On August 7, 1931, the Floridian again attacked the nation's seeming indifference to her six million unemployed. Insisting that government must provide every man an opportunity to work, he favored a broad program of federal expenditures. Fletcher joined liberals to enact a $2 billion public works bill in 1932, then blistered Hoover for delaying projects to aid unemployed Floridians.[58] In a Jacksonville speech entitled "Progress in Social Welfare," the senator advocated state-federal legislation compelling industry to insure employees against unemployment.

Senator Fletcher's vigorous labor on behalf of depressed farmers and laborers brought him popular acclaim. When he toured the state in 1930, the Avon Park *Times* called it more a triumphal procession than a tour. In 1929 John Temple Graves II conducted a survey to determine the greatest living Floridian, and Fletcher won without serious competition.[59] The Senator's loyalty to Al Smith made him the state's unquestioned Democratic leader. Georgia's Bainbridge *Post-Searchlight* paid him its supreme compliment: "Duncan Fletcher is the most outstanding man that Florida ever sent to the nation's capitol. He is the best known nationally of any Florida man that ever went on the hustings. . . . Away from his state he is looked on with higher regard and respect perhaps than in his own state. . . ."[60]

As conservative as his constituents demanded in the early twenties, he quickly adjusted to the economic realities of the depression. His compassion for suffering people fanned his anger at a system which served the wealthy while ignoring the poor.

57. U.S., *Congressional Record*, 71st Congress, 3d Session, 1930, LXXIV, 953.
58. New York *Times*, August 8, 1931, and St. Augustine *Record*, in Fletcher Papers.
59. Scrapbook H, in Knight Collection.
60. Jacksonville *Florida Times-Union*, June 18, 1930, quoting Bainbridge *Post-Searchlight*.

CHAPTER X

Duncan Fletcher and the New Deal

DUNCAN U. FLETCHER spent the last years of his public career the same way as he had the early ones, championing the economically disinherited. Fear of agrarian radicalism had made him a reformer in the 1890's, and fear of revolutionary change by the impoverished masses made him a New Dealer in the 1930's. The senator's advocacy of direct government action after the 1929 crash re-established his political strength with Florida unionists and farmers. Floridians tendered their overwhelming support, and he won the 1932 Democratic senatorial nomination without opposition. This statewide consensus reinforced his leadership of the party and allowed him to devote major attention to national politics.

Democrats anticipated victory in the 1932 presidential contest; consequently, prospective candidates fought hard for the nomination. Democratic National Chairman John J. Raskob, who favored Alfred E. Smith, hoped to cripple Franklin D. Roosevelt's chances by encouraging southern favorite sons. Jouett Shouse, Raskob's assistant, used his southern influence to promote uninstructed delegates to the Democratic convention in hopes of keeping the section out of Roosevelt's corner.[1] Oklahoma's Governor William H. Murray and Representative John Nance Garner of Texas actively solicited southern votes and were joined by favorite sons such as Virginia's Harry F. Byrd.

1. Frank Freidel, *Franklin D. Roosevelt: The Triumph* (Boston: Little, Brown and Company, 1956), pp. 178, 244–245.

166

Most southern states joined the Roosevelt bandwagon, but his forces met stubborn resistance in Florida. Harllee Branch of the Atlanta *Journal* toured Florida in the fall of 1931 officially surveying presidential sentiment but unofficially assessing Roosevelt's strength. Branch reported political apathy among rank and file voters, with powerful financial support for a conservative candidate. One Jacksonville-Miami coalition—consisting of lawyers, bankers, power company officials and corporation owners—was encouraging Newton D. Baker, former Secretary of War under Woodrow Wilson. S. E. Thomason of Chicago, co-publisher of the *Tampa Morning Tribune*, favored industrialist Owen D. Young, with Baker a second choice. Peter O. Knight, dubbed by Branch "the best known political manipulator" in Tampa, privately endorsed Baker; lawyers in Lakeland also indicated substantial interest in the former War Secretary.[2]

Branch also discovered some notable Roosevelt strength, and the New York governor moved quickly to exploit his opponents' disarray. He shrewdly chose campaign managers both from among Florida Democrats who had opposed and those who had supported Al Smith in 1928. Bryan Mack, a progressive newspaper publisher who had fought Smith, endorsed Roosevelt and strengthened the New Yorker's chances among state liberals. D. B. McKay, who published the Tampa *Daily Times*, enthusiastically endorsed the governor, and Roosevelt clubs were organized in Miami, Tampa, and St. Petersburg. According to Branch, Roosevelt sentiment centered in the Tallahassee–Pensacola–West Florida region and around Lakeland.

Branch advised Roosevelt of Fletcher's prestige in Florida politics,[3] and Roosevelt wrote the senator on November 16, 1931. He asked the Floridian to visit him at Warm Springs in Georgia, and Fletcher obliged on December 1.[4] Since Roosevelt strategists viewed Florida as politically doubtful, national newspapers placed great significance on Fletcher's visit. Roosevelt told reporters the trip was purely social and that he would not discuss politics with

2. Harllee Branch to Louis M. Howe, November 18 and 20, 1931, Papers of the Democratic National Committee, Official File 300, Franklin D. Roosevelt Papers, Hyde Park, New York. Hereafter cited as Roosevelt Papers, OF.
3. Harllee Branch to Louis M. Howe, November 18, 20, and 30, 1931, in OF 300, Roosevelt Papers.
4. Franklin Roosevelt to Duncan U. Fletcher, November 16, 1931, Group 12, Box 59, Roosevelt Papers.

his "old friend."[5] Actually, Fletcher spent three hours with Roosevelt discussing little else; they talked of proposed legislation and the Florida political climate. The senator assured Roosevelt that sentiment in his state strongly favored FDR and was steadily growing. He pledged his own loyalty and suggested that he personally head the state's Roosevelt delegation to the national convention.[6]

During the next few weeks, Fletcher helped representatives Tom Yon and Ruth Bryan Owen swing Florida into the Roosevelt camp.[7] Anti-Roosevelt forces centered their activity on the Florida Democratic Executive Committee, hoping to persuade its members to choose the national convention delegates in lieu of a statewide primary. When the committee met in February, 1932, Jouett Shouse was present to urge a slate of unpledged delegates. J. B. Hodges, now solidly committed to Fletcher after his apostasy in the early 1920's, was the new state Democratic chairman and presided while pro-Roosevelt members adopted a presidential preferential primary.[8]

Florida conservatives, outflanked by Fletcher, launched a short-lived drive to get John Nance Garner on the state ticket, but soon acknowledged defeat. Oklahoma's William ("Alfalfa Bill") Murray announced for the Florida contest and scheduled speeches in Lake City, Jacksonville, Pensacola, Ocala, and Tampa. Murray drew 1,000 curious auditors at Ocala and Tampa but generated little enthusiasm. Roosevelt won the state primary in spectacular fashion, 203,372 to Murray's 24,847.

Fletcher continued his active support of Roosevelt during the general election. As a member of the Democratic "Truth Squad," he blasted Hoover's farm policy.[9] He returned to Florida in September and spoke at Democratic rallies in West Palm Beach, Fort Lauderdale, and Eustis. George B. Hills of Jacksonville, who headed the state Roosevelt organization, helped the senator organize Democratic forces in every county, and Roosevelt swept the state.

The new President enjoyed enormous congressional support during the so-called first New Deal from 1933 to 1936. Democrats

5. New York *Times*, November 28, 1931.
6. Franklin Roosevelt to Harllee Branch, December 5, 1931, in OF 300, Roosevelt Papers.
7. See Jacksonville *Florida Times-Union*, December 16, 1931, quoting Lakeland *Ledger*.
8. *Ibid.*, February 20, 1932.
9. See New York *Times*, September 30, 1932.

controlled the 1933 Senate by a margin of 60 to 35, and following the 1934 off-year elections, the Senate was Democratic by a majority of 69 to 25. Only Idaho's William E. Borah and Utah's Reed Smoot had served longer in the Senate than Fletcher, and rumors predicted that the Floridian would parlay his seniority into chairmanship of the Commerce Committee. Roosevelt apparently persuaded him to forego the commerce post in a conference on January 19, 1933.[10] The President installed Fletcher instead as head of the Banking and Currency Committee in order to outmaneuver conservative Carter Glass and insure friendly control of that powerful committee. In reality, Glass surrendered control of banking matters in name only, since he continued to head a subcommittee which maintained full authority in all vital banking matters.[11] Fletcher announced his decision to become chairman of the Banking and Currency Committee on February 25.

Americans demanded revision of the nation's shaky financial structure. In 1929, 659 banks had closed, followed by 2,294 closings in 1931 and 1,456 in 1932. The new President conferred with Fletcher and Alabama's Representative Henry B. Steagall, chairman of the House Banking Committee, in April and outlined his proposals for banking reform. This legislation consumed Fletcher's energy for the next four years and dominated the early New Deal.

Herbert Hoover had inaugurated the investigation of American banking practices in 1932. The committee conducting the inquiry made little headway until 1933 when Fletcher became chairman and employed Ferdinand Pecora as chief council. Roosevelt conferred with Fletcher on March 13, 1933, and requested him to broaden the probe to include private banking operations and investment houses. The Senate adopted Fletcher's resolution empowering the committee to subpoena private records. For the next two years this committee revealed practices which thoroughly discredited the American financial structure and laid the groundwork for New Deal reform.

The committee usually met in Room 301 of the Senate Office Building from 10 A.M. to mid-afternoon. In addition to Fletcher, members included Carter Glass (Virginia), Alben W.

10. Jacksonville *Florida Times-Union*, January 3 and 21, 1933.
11. Marriner S. Eccles, *Beckoning Frontiers* (New York: Alfred A. Knopf, 1951), p. 180. Eccles concludes the aged Fletcher was content with merely the symbols of power.

Barkley (Kentucky), Edward P. Costigan (Colorado), John G. Townsend (Delaware), James Couzens (Michigan), and Peter Norbeck (South Dakota). Chairman Fletcher normally arrived before the cleaning woman and was known to sift testimony until 2 A.M. The senator refused to amend his day for golf or other Washington pastimes, causing one Senate colleague to warn that he was "working himself almost to death."[12] Thomas L. Stokes, who later won a Pulitzer Prize for his political reporting in the Scripps-Howard newspaper chain, penned a vivid description of Fletcher as he presided over the hearings: "His eyes might be closed as the swarthy man with the protuberant jaw at his side [Pecora] pushed questions at a gentleman sitting across the table. Then, all at once, open pop the eyes. Out comes, easily and casually, a penetrating inquiry. If the answer doesn't satisfy a gruff:—'Well I can't see—.' . . . Some painter should have perpetuated the combined scene of the masters of finance, with Senator Fletcher sitting there apparently dozing, Pecora pointing eternally with his cigar at the assembled giants of money."[13]

Never before in the nation's history had such a procession of financial giants been held accountable by Congress. The list of witnesses constituted a who's who of American finance: J. P. Morgan along with most of his partners; Otto H. Kahn and his colleagues of Kuhn, Loeb and Company; Charles E. Mitchell and partners of National City Bank; Albert H. Wiggin and his co-officers of Chase National Bank; Clarence Dillon and associates of Dillon, Read and Company; Richard Whitney, president of the New York Stock Exchange; former Vice-President Charles G. Dawes. Others included financiers and industrialists such as Owen D. Young, Samuel Insull, John J. Raskob, and Winthrop W. Aldrich.

The May, 1933, investigation began in spectacular fashion when J. P. Morgan and four partners left New York in separate automobiles accompanied by fifteen private bodyguards. Conservative Carter Glass tried to limit Pecora's questioning of Morgan before the committee, but Fletcher supported a sweeping inquiry of the Morgan empire. Pecora made some astounding disclosures: that J. P. Morgan had paid no income taxes during 1930, 1931,

12. *Memorandum*, July 28, 1933, in Trammell Papers. For Fletcher's remarkable schedule, see *United States News*, April 30, 1934, in Fletcher Papers.
13. Thomas L. Stokes, "Men of Congress," New York *World-Telegram*, June 20, 1934, in Fletcher Papers.

and 1932; that all members of the Morgan firm had paid less than $50,000 income taxes in 1930.[14] The committee also discovered an ingenious device for avoiding taxation; financiers sold stock to near relatives at reduced figures, declared a loss on their income tax, then repurchased the stock at the original sale price. One Morgan partner had sold 4,987 shares of stock to his wife at a tremendous "loss" in 1930, then had repurchased the shares in April, 1931. This technically legal maneuver had allowed a tax savings of $20,000. Charles E. Mitchell had claimed a "loss" of $2,872,305 on 18,300 shares "sold" in a similar transaction.[15]

The inquiry into Morgan's empire revealed an enormous concentration of wealth and its unsavory influence on politics. In 1929 seventeen J. P. Morgan partners held 99 directorships in 72 corporations with combined assets of $20 billion. Fletcher's probing disclosed that only certain personal friends could invest in Morgan's banks and that a number of investors so favored were officials of both the Republican Party and the U.S. Chamber of Commerce.[16]

Testimony at the hearings intensified Fletcher's opposition to financial monopoly. While questioning Morgan partner George Whitney, the senator insisted that holding companies operated selfishly to aid specific businesses and not for the public interest. He coined the term "concentration of control of wealth" in referring to instances where a well-organized Morgan faction controlled a company though possessing only a small percentage of the stock.[17] Speculating on the need for regulation, he noted, "Some of these corporations are growing enormously and are becoming very powerful. They are run by a handful of men without regard to the stockholders. . . . Proper regulation of corporations and the practices and operations of such corporations, and securing the rights of stockholders . . . might reach all the way along the line of our inquiry here even to the stock exchanges. . . ."[18]

Carter Glass opposed the inquiry and frequently clashed with Fletcher. But Senator James Couzens, Michigan multi-millionaire who contributed liberally to the poor, delighted in helping Pecora draw and quarter financial titans and supported Fletcher

14. U.S., Congress, Senate, *Hearings, Stock Exchange Practices*, 73d Congress, 1st Session, 1934, Part 1, pp. 47, 53. Hereafter cited as *Hearings*.
15. *Hearings*, pp. 781–82.
16. *Ibid.*, Part 2, pp. 849, 178–80; Part 9, p. 4504.
17. *Ibid.*, Part 2, pp. 483–84, 857.
18. *Ibid.*, Part 4, pp. 1886–87.

in his exchanges with Glass. Fletcher infrequently lost his temper in the face of conservative recalcitrance. When Richard W. Whitney, who presided over the New York Stock Exchange, refused to distribute a committee questionnaire to members of the exchange, Fletcher threatened to subpoena all 1,375 exchange members.[19]

The investigation took two years and filled 11,000 pages of testimony in 25 volumes. It revealed how banks had joined the speculative hysteria before the depression, how they had diverted Federal Reserve Credit to the stock market, and had become pawns of bank-holding companies. One economic historian concluded that the inquiry "laid bare financial practices which were generally legally permissible but were . . . abhorrent to a people caught in the backwash of depression."[20] Another keen observer of the New Deal summarized that committee disclosures destroyed the moral and political authority of the business community.[21] The investigation was unquestionably the most thorough ever made of stock exchange practices.

Public reaction to the disclosures demonstrated the depth of protest against such practices. The daily testimony made national front-page newspaper copy for weeks. When some commercial leaders attacked the committee proceedings, the Cleveland *Press* replied, "Many members of the Stock Exchange must know, even if its governing board does not, that the vigorous support of the public, congress and the Roosevelt administration is behind this investigation."[22] Even the conservative *New York Times* deplored the "imprudence and irregularities" revealed by the committee.[23] Citizens often addressed their private protests to Fletcher: a sophisticated businessman called the stock market "the greatest single source of misfortune and disaster in the history of the American people"; Jack Churiva, a Nogalis, Arizona, Indian, sent Fletcher a walking cane for "uncovering the truth" about bankers which "saved us from greasing up our Winchesters and coming down . . . to clean out this whole gang."[24]

19. Jacksonville *Florida Times-Union*, October 17, 1933.
20. Broadus Mitchell, *Depression Decade: From New Era Through New Deal, 1929–1941* (New York: Rinehart and Company, 1947), p. 155.
21. Arthur M. Schlesinger, Jr., *The Age of Roosevelt: The Coming of the New Deal* (Boston: Houghton Mifflin Company, 1958), p. 434.
22. New York *Times*, October 22, 1933, quoting Cleveland *Press*.
23. *Ibid.*, February 28, 1933.
24. George D. Hirst to Duncan U. Fletcher, February 12, 1934, *Hearings*, Part 13, p. 5986; and Jacksonville *Florida Times-Union*, November 16, 1933. For

Charles E. Mitchell, former chairman of the National City Bank, became the financial community's scapegoat. He stood trial for income tax evasion and resigned as chairman of his bank. Financiers hoped his resignation would minimize public resentment, but Mitchell's sacrifice produced no such effect.

Fletcher contributed significantly to these revelations. Ferdinand Pecora, the Sicilian immigrant who served as chief counsel, dedicated his book on the investigation to "the late Senators Duncan U. Fletcher, Peter Norbeck, James Couzens, and Edward P. Costigan, whose steadfast support . . . greatly contributed to putting Wall Street Under Oath."[25] Journalist Thomas L. Stokes, a New Deal liberal, summarized Fletcher's role: "You imagined that he would grace a rocking chair, on a sunny porch, with a soft hat lying across his lap. But he was not that kind. He was tough and of hard fiber. He kept the investigation going when those who would squelch it brought pressure wherever they could."[26] A liberal Florida editor noted in similar if less erudite fashion, "Our good old friend Senator Duncan U. Fletcher is having the time of his life calling all the big bugs up on the 'carpet' before his investigating committee."[27]

Fletcher blasted "New York big bankers," and provoked one member of the New York Stock Exchange to confide that his financial associates considered the Floridian an enemy of Wall Street.[28] The senator soon earned their wrath by aiding the passage of four measures which altered America's financial structure—the Banking Act of 1933, the Securities Act of 1933 ("Truth in Securities" Act), the Securities Exchange Act of 1934 (Fletcher-Rayburn Act), and the Public Utility Holding Company Act of 1935. In addition, impetus for the 1935 Banking Act came from Fletcher's Senate investigation.

---

the widespread public media reaction to the Pecora revelations, see P. W. Wilson, "The House of Morgan," *Review of Reviews*, LXXXVIII (July, 1933), 15–19 ff.

25. Ferdinand Pecora, *Wall Street Under Oath* (New York: Simon and Schuster, 1939), p. vii.

26. Thomas L. Stokes, *Chip Off My Shoulder* (Princeton: Princeton University Press, 1940), p. 346.

27. Jacksonville *Florida Times-Union*, February 2, 1934, quoting Frostproof *News*.

28. Interview in Washington *Star*, December 31, 1933, in Roosevelt Papers, President's Personal File 1358. Hereafter cited as PPF; and Henry Goldman, Jr., to Duncan U. Fletcher, November 3, 1933, *Hearings*, Part 7, p. 3446.

Fletcher had sent Roosevelt a copy of his bill to guarantee bank deposits in March, 1932, and asked the then governor of New York for comments. Roosevelt had referred the bill to Joseph A. Broderick, New York Superintendent of Banks, and Broderick replied that there was a wide division of opinion on the matter which was "fraught with political dynamite."[29] Roosevelt informed Fletcher that the government must have additional supervisory power if such legislation were enacted, and the senator amended his bill to provide regulation by the comptroller of the United States.

Spurred by the disclosures of Fletcher's committee, Congress pushed through the Glass-Steagall Banking Act of 1933. The bill contained four provisions: the guarantee of bank deposits; regulation of bank investments; control of speculation using Federal Reserve credit; and the divorce of investment affiliates from commercial banks. Conservatives, led by the American Bankers' Association and the New York Federal Reserve Bank, attacked this moderate measure. Senator Glass drafted the bank guarantee provision, which was much more conservative than Fletcher's earlier proposal to protect all bank deposits. Had it not been for the more "radical" proposals of Fletcher and others, conservatives might have killed the entire bill.[30]

The Securities Act of 1933 or "Truth in Securities" Act also resulted from revelations of the Fletcher committee. Roosevelt brain-trusters Benjamin V. Cohen, Thomas G. Corcoran, and James M. Landis drafted the measure which insured accurate information about securities. The banking community assailed the bill but to no avail. When different bills passed the Senate and House, Fletcher dominated Senate conferees by virtue of his conduct of the banking hearings and his unwavering support of Pecora. Fletcher's gracious deferment of leadership to Sam Rayburn, who chaired the House banking committee, greatly facilitated passage.[31]

The next step in federal regulation of finance was the Securities Exchange Act of 1934, also known as the Fletcher-Rayburn Act. Roosevelt appointed Cohen, Corcoran, Landis, and several

29. Duncan U. Fletcher to Franklin D. Roosevelt, March 5, 1932; *Memorandum* from J. A. Broderick to F. D. Roosevelt, March 15, 1932; Group 18, Box 12, Roosevelt Papers.
30. H. Parker Willis, "The Banking Act of 1932—An Appraisal," *American Economic Review*, XXIV (March, 1934), 105.
31. James M. Landis, "The Legislative History of the Securities Act of 1933," *George Washington Law Review*, XXVIII (October, 1959), 44–45.

other advisers to draft the measure. Their intricate proposal established federal supervision of securities, limited speculation, and regulated stock exchanges.[32] Fletcher and Rayburn introduced the bill on February 9, 1934. Brain-truster Raymond Moley directed the congressional battle by telephone, but Fletcher almost lost control of his banking committee.[33] In his desire to permit full discussion, he allowed conservatives to remove effective enforcement by the Federal Trade Commission.

Conservative protests against the Fletcher-Rayburn bill presaged a long debate. Wall Street spokesmen described the measure as a "long step toward nationalization of the security markets"; stock exchanges advised clients to wire their opposition to congressional delegations; and one California firm reportedly issued twenty million circulars attacking the bill.[34] This campaign angered the Floridian, and he directed a verbal fusilade at his conservative critics:

> The president of the New York Stock Exchange should explain why it was that the Exchange not only did not prevent but by its actions . . . enabled . . . corporation executives to run pools and to make enormous personal profits at the expense of their own stockholders. . . .
>
> The facts have demonstrated that the power of Stock Exchange authorities to subject the interests of the nation to the purposes and profits of stock brokers . . . must be ended. . . .
>
> In the face of the evidence they will need something more than propaganda to satisfy the public that they furnish an open and free market for securities.[35]

Roosevelt vigorously attacked the bill's critics in a letter to Fletcher designed for publication. He praised the Fletcher-Rayburn bill and deplored what he called the most "definite and . . . highly organized drive . . . against effective legislation" of his

32. For a detailed study of the bill, see Charles H. Meyer, *The Securities Act of 1934* (New York: Francis Emory Fitch, Inc., 1934).
33. Raymond Moley, *After Seven Years* (New York: Harper and Brothers, 1939), pp. 285-286; and Duncan U. Fletcher to Franklin D. Roosevelt, January 27, 1934, OF 34, in Roosevelt Papers.
34. New York *Times*, February 10, 1934; and *Hearings*, Part 15, pp. 6892-6893; Part 16, p. 7744.
35. New York *Times*, February 22, 1934.

career.[36] The senator finally silenced opposition by a brilliant maneuver; he directed his Senate banking committee to investigate stock market propaganda. The ensuing report revealed that New York Stock Exchange members had made $833,167,686 between 1928 and 1933, while spending $1,674,000 for 5,337,354 pamphlets, speeches, and books designed to influence public opinion.[37] Incensed Americans, apprised of Wall Street manipulation, rallied behind the Fletcher-Rayburn bill and it won a narrow victory. One southern liberal summarized the struggle:

> Somewhat surprising, on casual survey, is the fact that the reform was put over by two gentlemen [Fletcher and Rayburn] from the South who have been known as conservatives.
>
> Senator Fletcher reminds one of some grey-moss-covered rock that stands the wear of ages in the way he resisted Wall Street attack.
>
> History will show only the final result. It will not record, perhaps, the way Mr. Fletcher kept the stock market inquiry going when powerful influences sought to stop it. . . .[38]

He concluded that the Senator's career had made "Fletcher synonymous with Florida."

The Banking Act of 1935 involved Fletcher in another bitter controversy with his old antagonist Carter Glass. Roosevelt had offended the Virginian deeply by ignoring him in nominating Marriner Eccles as governor of the Federal Reserve Board. When Glass blocked the nomination, Roosevelt asked Fletcher if there were "some way in which you can get Eccles confirmed?"[39] Fletcher promptly issued a ringing endorsement of Eccles which crippled Glass' opposition. This skirmish deepened the chasm between Roosevelt and Glass and intensified the impending clash over banking reform.

Marriner Eccles was chiefly responsible for formulating the 1935 Banking Act. Believing that Federal Reserve banks served the interests of private financial institutions rather than the

36. Franklin D. Roosevelt to Duncan U. Fletcher, March 26, 1934, OF 34, in Roosevelt Papers.
37. Jacksonville *Florida Times-Union*, May 2, 1934.
38. Stokes, "Men of Congress," New York *World-Telegram*, June 20, 1934, in Fletcher Papers.
39. Franklin D. Roosevelt to Duncan U. Fletcher, March 26, 1935, PPF 1358, Roosevelt Papers.

national interest, Eccles centralized power in an expanded Federal Reserve Board. He shrewdly combined titles badly needed by the banking community with his controversial Title Two which strengthened federal control. The Senate customarily had extended Glass virtual veto power over banking legislation, and the Virginian was angered when Roosevelt again bypassed him. Roosevelt sensed the danger and implored Fletcher to keep the bill away from Glass' subcommittee.[40] The Floridian was pessimistic though he did vow to mobilize administration forces on the committee. He contacted Senators Joseph T. Robinson of Arkansas and James F. Byrnes of South Carolina who approved his strategy.[41]

Glass and Fletcher had often tested their political acumen. The seventy-seven-year-old Virginian was a vehement debater; during one of his oratorical philippics he had banged his desk with such force that he split his knuckles and ended the debate with a bleeding hand. Fletcher, seventy-six years old, relied on parliamentary skill and patient persuasion to carry his logic. The two aged antagonists struggled valiantly for mastery of the banking committee. Glass campaigned vigorously to wrest control of the bill and was able to get the measure into his subcommittee. But Fletcher checked him by enlarging the subcommittee with administration senators.

Conservatives bitterly denounced the bill. Bankers distributed over 100,000 copies of a letter attacking "Fletcher Title II," and newspaper opposition included the Boston *Post,* Philadelphia *Inquirer, New York Times,* Baltimore *Sun,* and Columbus *Dispatch.*[42] The Florida Bankers' Association and the state Chamber of Commerce assailed Title II, while local bankers in Blountstown, Bonifay, Crestview, Malone, Greenwood, Havana, Marianna, Panama City, Pensacola, Quincy, River Junction, Tallahassee, Valparaiso, and Wewahitchka pressured Fletcher to drop the bill.[43]

40. Franklin D. Roosevelt to Duncan U. Fletcher, May 14, 1935, PPF 1358, in Roosevelt Papers. For a discussion of the Banking Act by its author, see Eccles, *Beckoning Frontiers.*
41. *Confidential Memorandum* from Henry B. Steagall to Franklin D. Roosevelt, February 5, 1935; Duncan U. Fletcher to Franklin D. Roosevelt, PPF 1358, in Roosevelt Papers.
42. R. H. Sparkman to Duncan U. Fletcher, May 21, 1935, Box 344, File 2; and Box 317, File 1, in Glass Papers.
43. W. O. Boozer to Duncan U. Fletcher, July 19, 1935, Box 344, File 2; G. J. Avent to Duncan U. Fletcher, July 20, 1935, Box 344, File 2; and Box 317, File 1; in Glass Papers.

Such opposition only increased the Floridian's determination. He answered Wall Street critics by contending that "bankers as a whole are not qualified to determine nor competent to administer our monetary policy."[44] He pleaded for the bill in a national radio address, pressured Glass to end debate, and persuaded President Roosevelt to accept minor compromises. Glass's subcommittee finally reported the bill on June 28, 1935, and the modified measure retained all three original titles. On the floor Fletcher voted with the liberals to broaden the bill; but opposition from southerners—including Trammell, Virginia's Harry Byrd and Glass, and Georgia's Walter George—defeated the effort. Despite this failure the final act was Eccles's in philosophy if not in detail.[45]

Although Fletcher neither formulated legislation nor directed strategy, he skillfully handled administration forces. He faithfully implemented Roosevelt's directions without alienating conservative senators. If he moved slowly, it resulted from advanced years and considerable congressional skill, not from restrained enthusiasm. Roosevelt praised the senator's role in the banking struggle and flattered him: "Take care of yourself—you know how greatly I count on you. . . ."[46]

Influential Florida businessmen had little use for Franklin D. Roosevelt or his New Deal and deplored Fletcher's solid support of administration policy. The *Florida Times-Union*, maintaining its conservative tradition, opposed virtually all New Deal measures, while railroad and public utility companies also looked askance at Roosevelt's legislation. Facing a seldomly seen conservative-liberal dichotomy in Florida, Fletcher abandoned the conservatives. This decision entailed considerable soul-searching and private reservations; but he acted forcefully and consistently.

Fletcher's correspondence with Roosevelt reflected his neo-liberalism. Convinced that the Democratic administration insured

44. Duncan U. Fletcher to Hamilton F. Kean, June 6, 1936, Box 345, File 4, in Glass Papers; and Jacksonville *Florida Times-Union*, April 21, 1935.
45. Carter Glass to Duncan U. Fletcher, May 15, 1935, Box 345, File 4, Glass Papers; John M. Blum, *From the Morgenthau Diaries*, vol. I (Boston: Houghton Mifflin Company, 1959), 351; Arthur M. Schlesinger, Jr., *The Age of Roosevelt: The Politics of Upheaval* (Boston: Houghton Mifflin Company, 1960), p. 301.
46. Franklin D. Roosevelt to Duncan U. Fletcher, September 23, 1935, PPF 1358, in Roosevelt Papers. It was widely recognized that Fletcher exercised no real power in conceiving banking legislation and that his primary role was one of political implementation. See *Time* (July 29, 1935), p. 48.

the public welfare, he proposed government shipping subsidies to maintain maritime supremacy.[47] After passage of the 1935 Banking Act, he privately cautioned Roosevelt about appointments to the Board of Governors of the Federal Reserve System. He strongly advised the President to "select men who believe in the public control of credit." The Senate banking investigation had persuaded him that a handful of self-seeking financiers controlled America's banking and credit structure. He candidly revealed his convictions to Roosevelt: "I don't think he should select a man on that Bd [Board of Governors] who doesn't believe in [public control of credit] if he can avoid it. That's all I say about that—it's vital. If he should get the wrong man on the Board, all the good that can be accomplished by the Act of 1935 will be gone."[48]

Fletcher's New Deal voting record reflected near perfect support of the administration. On twenty-seven roll calls between 1933 and 1936 which dealt with New Deal legislation, Fletcher voted with liberals on twenty-five and with conservatives on just two bills. He voted with Wisconsin's liberal Senator Robert La Follette, Jr., on twenty-two measures, and against him on three; he voted with Virginia's conservative duo of Harry Byrd and Carter Glass only six times and against them thirteen times.[49] Fletcher backed labor legislation establishing maximum hours and minimum wages and finally endorsed federal child labor prohibition at the end of his career.[50]

Pragmatism once again dictated change and Fletcher responded. His private secretary recalled that the senator sometimes questioned the constitutionality of New Deal legislation though voting for it.[51] Fletcher's own explanation of his altered philosophy was simple—extraordinary times called for new solutions: "We are in the midst of problems today with which we were

47. Duncan U. Fletcher to Franklin D. Roosevelt, June 6, 1933, OF 99, in Roosevelt Papers.
48. *Memorandum* from Duncan U. Fletcher to Franklin D. Roosevelt, January 1, 1936, PPF 1358, in Roosevelt Papers.
49. *Yea and Nay Votes in the United States Senate on Important Legislation*, 73d and 74th Congresses, in Hodges Papers. Key votes included Social Security, Tennessee Valley Authority, Home Owner's Loan Act, Black Labor Bill, Farm Bankruptcy Act, etc.
50. Duncan U. Fletcher to Franklin D. Roosevelt, August 2, 1935, OF 526, in Roosevelt Papers.
51. U.S., Congress, House, *Duncan Upshaw Fletcher*, 75th Congress, 1st Session, 1938, House Document 339, pp. 51–52.

never before confronted. In the beginning of 1933 we had 13,000,000 people unemployed. Other conditions prevailed which made it necessary to enact legislation to remedy and cure the situation as far as we could. We have enacted legislation which is out of the ordinary. I grant that. But the legislation was needed and was necessary at the time and has been found to have cured and to have saved a situation which otherwise would have brought on chaos and disaster."[52]

Bitter Florida conservatives received similar answers to their queries. Laurence F. Lee, president of Pensacola Life Insurance Company, privately deplored economic "pump-priming" and public relief, calling such measures "more socialistic political propaganda lashing out at industry as a part of the attempt to socialize the heavy industries." Fletcher defended the New Deal in his reply to Lee, and concluded curtly, "You evidently have no conception of the Unemployment and other problems which have to be dealt with."[53]

Fletcher's sudden affinity for liberalism puzzled Peter O. Knight, Tampa's financial wizard and the senator's lifelong friend. To Knight, the depression constituted a necessary deflationary trend; common sense and private initiative would soon restore America's Golden Age, epitomized for Knight in the years between 1880 and 1917. He viewed growing federal control as little better than communism. Knight recognized that Fletcher's age precluded another Senate term and concluded correctly that Fletcher must therefore be voting his convictions: "You were always such a sound, conservative man, always had the courage of your convictions; believed in the sanctity of contracts, the protection of the inalienable rights of the individual, that fact that under our form of government all the people of the United States combined can not infringe upon the inherent rights of the humblest citizen of

52. U.S., *Congressional Record*, 74th Congress, 2d Session, 1936, LXXX, 381. Certainly Frank Freidel's generalization that conservative southern congressional leaders supported F. D. R. out of a sense of party loyalty, desire for regional economic progress, association of his program with the New Freedom, and his personal charm were all factors in Fletcher's support. But Freidel does not emphasize enough the genuine alteration of philosophy and policy necessitated by the depression crisis. For Freidel's analysis see Frank Freidel, *F. D. R. and the South* (Baton Rouge: Louisiana State University Press, 1965), pp. 35–70.
53. Laurence F. Lee to Duncan U. Fletcher, November 20, 1935, and Duncan U. Fletcher to Laurence F. Lee, November 21, 1935, Box 107, in Hodges Papers.

the land, that, watching your vote upon various and sundry impractical and moon-shooting bills that come before the senate, I am amazed."[54]

Fletcher included a penetrating self-analysis in his reply to his old friend. Knight's argument, he wrote, characterized "big business, special interests, and privilege" which cared for "ninety percent of the people" only "to use and exploit for their own benefit." The senator deplored an economy where 2 per cent of the people owned 60 per cent of the wealth:

> It may be that I feel an overzealous sympathy, and keen desire to be helpful, for the great majority of our people who are living on the margin of the poverty line. It is not altogether their fault or blame that they are in that situation. . . .
>
> This disparity of wealth, the inequality of distribution, is disturbing. It looks like everything is passing into the hands of financiers. *Talk* about liberty, freedom, the guarantees of the Constitution and individual rights, in this situation—with nine million people unemployed . . . with want and suffering on every hand. . . . We must *do* something.
>
> Our 'rights' must give way, temporarily, at least, to our duties.[55]

Fletcher refused to give an inch in defense of Roosevelt and the New Deal despite the criticism of his old friend: "I have endeavored, when I could, to support the Administration. I have regarded President Roosevelt as a great leader in whom the people had confidence and whom they trusted. It is inexcusable, unpatriotic and treacherous, in my judgment, to attack, condemn and oppose his policies and plans, some of them admittedly experimental, until they have been given a chance to demonstrate their wisdom and effectiveness, or failure. Even though they may not conform to our views, they should, since no one proposes other policies or plans, be allowed to prove their efficacy. Certain good results have already followed."[56] This letter also revealed the

54. Peter O. Knight to Duncan U. Fletcher, April 11, 1934, Scrapbook K; also see Peter O. Knight to Duncan U. Fletcher, November 10, 1932, Scrapbook J; and Peter O. Knight to Walter L. Reynolds, December 2, 1933, Scrapbook K; in Knight Collection.
55. Duncan U. Fletcher to Peter O. Knight, April 16, 1934, Scrapbook K, Knight Collection. The emphasis is Fletcher's.
56. *Ibid.*

rationale of the conservative as reformer; reform could be conservative, could sometimes short-circuit more drastic and iconoclastic change:

> I will admit that I have voted for measures I never expected to vote for and hope I will not feel obliged to favor again. I have done so because of this *emergency* and as *emergency* measures.
>
> You have rested snug and contented at home, surrounded with plenty, comfortable and serene. I am afraid you are not advised as to what has been going on, experienced and threatened in other portions of the country.
>
> Do you want strikes, riots, revolutions?
>
> I think not.
>
> Just let things move along and work themselves out without *doing* anything that might overcome this depression, and you will have what you do not want. . . .
>
> We ought to endeavor to cure, help and give relief, even at the risk of doing things not conservative.[57]

Fletcher's appeal to expediency does not sufficiently explain his actions. Surely the senator realized that such sweeping proposals as the 1935 Banking Act, the Wagner Labor Relations Act, the Tennessee Valley Authority, and the Social Security Act were not "emergency measures" but major departures from the status quo. He must have foreseen the permanency of such legislation, yet he enthusiastically endorsed it. Even his phraseology, with its denunciation of vested interests, revealed a relapse to his quasi-Populist oratory of the 1890's.

Florida politics reflected the senator's altered views. In 1932 Fletcher departed sharply from his previous neutrality in state politics by endorsing an obscure liberal in the gubernatorial race. David Sholtz, a native New Yorker of Jewish ancestry, campaigned on an anti-establishment platform against two former governors, Cary A. Hardee and John W. Martin. The Daytona Beach resident promised a full nine-month school term, free textbooks, workingmen's compensation, child welfare, agricultural aid, and reduction of small homeowners' taxes. Though completely unknown at the first of the race, he won a runoff spot opposite John W. Martin, Fletcher's arch enemy. On June 17, 1932, the senator issued a ringing endorsement of Sholtz, who went on to win a smashing runoff

57. *Ibid.*

victory.[58] The new governor worked closely with Fletcher for the next four years, and they frequently conferred in Washington.

The bitter 1934 Senate campaign between Claude Pepper and Park Trammell again drew Fletcher into state affairs. Jacksonville interests wanted a cross-Florida ship canal and backed Pepper when incumbent Senator Trammell appeared less than enthusiastic about the project. Fletcher, who never worked closely with Trammell, assured Pepper of his neutrality. Labor unions endorsed Trammell, and Eli Futch, a veteran AFL campaigner, came from Washington to spearhead the senator's race. Futch noted labor defection to Pepper and advised President William Green of the AFL to hold Florida unions in line with national pressure.[59] R. L. Glenn, another union leader aiding the incumbent's forces, urged Fletcher to intervene. He reported Trammell's endorsement by the AFL and questioned rumors that Fletcher was supporting Pepper. Pepper's lieutenants claimed to have the senior senator's endorsement, and the assertion was crippling Trammell's campaign.[60] Fletcher, who profited from labor backing after 1926, buckled under the strain and issued an innocuous endorsement hedged with qualifications. He encouraged Floridians to decide for themselves, adding that he personally would vote for Trammell because of their long association.

Pepper telephoned Fletcher seeking an explanation, and the senator attributed his statement to hounding newsmen. He denied any enthusiasm for his junior colleague, restated his personal friendship for Pepper, and wished him a successful political career.[61] Labor exploited Fletcher's controversial "endorsement." The Brotherhood of Locomotive Engineers and Firemen sent Floridians 100,000 copies of their national publication during the last five days of the contest. The issue, which cost $20,000 and was especially prepared for the election, contained equal praise for Fletcher and abuse of Pepper.[62] The combination of Fletcher's statement and labor support carried Trammell to a narrow 4,000-vote victory.

58. See Merlin G. Cox, "David Sholtz: New Deal Governor of Florida," *Florida Historical Quarterly*, XLIII (October, 1964), 142–52; Jacksonville *Florida Times-Union*, June 18, 1932.
59. Eli Futch to Joe [?], June 11, 1934, in Trammell Papers.
60. R. L. Glenn to Duncan U. Fletcher, June 11, 1934, in Trammell Papers.
61. Interview with Representative Claude Pepper, September 1, 1964, Washington, D.C.
62. Kenneth Ballinger, "Side Glances at State Politics," Miami *Herald*, undated, in Trammell Papers.

The new political realities also altered Fletcher's relationship with old antagonists. He made his peace with Jerry Carter, and liberal Floridians groomed the former hotel commissioner for the governorship in 1936.[63]

Florida's economy consumed as much attention as her politics, and the two interests frequently coincided. Patronage remained a principal concern, and Fletcher gained final veto power over Jacksonville applicants to the Works Progress Administration; government officials also allowed him to suggest local attorneys for WPA litigation. When an anxious Floridian decided to ignore Fletcher in quest of a federal judgeship, State Democratic Chairman J. B. Hodges warned that such action would prove disastrous.[64]

President Roosevelt and Postmaster General James Farley kept a tighter rein on state patronage than previous administrations, and Fletcher lost some influence over appointments. Senator Trammell protested that Farley ignored the Fletcher-Trammell nominee for collector of Internal Revenue in favor of J. Ed Larsen. Trammell speculated that some Florida Democrats wanted to build a Tammany-like political machine.[65] When Trammell died in 1936, influential businessmen pressured Governor Sholtz to appoint Peter O. Knight as interim senator. Sholtz traveled to Washington, presumably talked with Fletcher, then conferred with Farley and Roosevelt, who vetoed the appointment because of Knight's opposition to the New Deal and his affiliation with public utility companies. According to Knight, the President threatened to suspend Florida public works if Sholtz insisted on appointing him.[66]

Faced with patronage competition, Fletcher utilized public works projects to maintain his political base. Florida's unenviable unemployment rate continued, and 85,000 residents were hunting work by November, 1933. Unemployed Floridians filled the senator's Washington office and caused him genuine concern.[67] Fletcher,

63. Interview with Jerry Carter, May 15, 1964, Tallahassee, Florida; and telegram from W. G. Curry and King Parrot to Franklin D. Roosevelt, January 7, 1936, OF 300, in Roosevelt Papers.
64. Carl F. Jones to J. B. Hodges, November, 1935; George B. Hills to J. B. Hodges, November 15, 1935; J. B. Hodges to Linton B. Collins, May 2, 1936; Box 107, in Hodges Papers.
65. *Memorandum*, July 28, 1933, in Trammell Papers.
66. Peter O. Knight to James W. Morris, May 27, 1936, Scrapbook M, Knight Collection.
67. Interview with Mrs. Harry E. Graham and Miss Ella Creary Thompson, May 21, 1963, Tallahassee.

acting as spokesman for the Florida congressional delegation, labored diligently for federal appropriations. His persistence brought to Florida twenty-five Civilian Conservation Camps which employed 2,800 men.[68] When the administration began the gradual reduction of relief programs, Fletcher countered by proposing a quasi-permanent Public Works Administration with a five-year appropriation of $500 million.[69]

Fletcher's long-time dream of a trans-Florida ship canal provided the perfect project for unemployed laborers. He did not originate the idea; Florida canal companies had flourished in the 1880's, and the project had excited periodic interest for the next five decades. Twenty-eight surveys of possible routes had been conducted by 1933, but the Public Works Administration had rejected the proposed cost of $208 million. Floridians persuaded Roosevelt to conduct one additional survey which reduced the estimated cost to a manageable $146 million.[70]

The President's pro-canal position met mixed reaction in Florida. The Geological Survey reported that a sea-level canal would create serious problems for south Florida's fresh water supply. The proposed canal would drain north Florida's underground springs, the source of south Florida's drinking water. In late August, 1935, the Associated Citrus Growers and Shippers condemned the project. Roosevelt dismissed these protests and, under prodding from a group of pro-canal senators organized by Fletcher, appropriated an initial $5 million on August 30, 1935.[71] North Florida residents credited Fletcher with success when excavation began in September.

Reaction to the canal intensified during 1935. One powerful south Florida Democrat warned Roosevelt that he would lose Florida in 1936 if he insisted on pushing the canal; he reported

68. Louis M. Howe to Duncan U. Fletcher, November 16, 1933, PPF 1358, Roosevelt Papers; and Jacksonville *Florida Times-Union*, April 29, 1933, and April 30, 1934.
69. New York *Times*, December 12, 1935.
70. For an excellent survey of the trans-Florida ship canal, see Benjamin F. Rogers, "The Florida Ship Canal Project," *Florida Historical Quarterly*, XXXVI (July, 1957), 14–23.
71. Letter to Franklin D. Roosevelt from Senators Fletcher, Trammell, H. D. Stephens, John H. Overton, Morris Sheppard, Huey Long, J. H. Bankhead, September 12, 1934, PPF 1358, in Roosevelt Papers. Roosevelt responded to this pressure by instructing his secretaries of Treasury and Interior to discuss the project with adviser Harry Hopkins; *Memorandum*, November 12, 1934, PPF 1358, in Roosevelt Papers.

that Democrats in his area were as "sore as boiled owls."[72] Secretary of the Interior Harold L. Ickes received similar reports while touring the state. In addition to these ominous rumblings, Republican Senator Arthur Vandenberg threatened to make the project a major campaign issue in the approaching presidential election.

Ickes, a chief Roosevelt adviser, also opposed the canal. He recorded that Roosevelt began to question the project's feasibility in a conference on December 19, 1935, and had concluded by January, 1936, that the estimate of canal costs was "cockeyed."[73] The President decided to drop the politically explosive measure and wrote Fletcher that future action must originate in Congress. The senator tried to reverse Roosevelt's decision or at least win his active support for a congressional appropriation. He called at the White House on January 1, 1936, warning that congressional rejection of the canal would be considered an administration defeat and begging Roosevelt to pressure Democrats on the appropriation's subcommittee: ". . . insist that they stand by the Administration and support the President—demand it—. . . ."[74] He told Roosevelt in February that it would take his "every effort" to get the bill through Congress, and without additional funds, 800 to 1,000 men would be laid off.

Fletcher attempted to force the President's hand by telling Floridians that some agency would allocate funds to continue the canal. Jacksonville Mayor John T. Alsop telephoned Harllee Branch, Roosevelt's southern confidant, that unless the President backed the canal there would be a "very bad political effect."[75] James Farley became even more concerned when rumors spread in Florida that Roosevelt refused to see Fletcher or discuss the canal. John H. Perry, who owned four Florida papers and a radio station, wrote angrily, "Senator Fletcher has been blindly loyal and devoted to Roosevelt from [the] beginning. . . . It is incomprehensible to Fletcher's countless personal and political friends in Florida that [the] President would use him for three years and fail to

72. Dudley V. Haddock to Steve Early, February 14, 1936, OF 300, in Roosevelt Papers.
73. Harold L. Ickes, *The Secret Diary of Harold L. Ickes: The First Thousand Days, 1933–1936* (New York: Simon and Schuster, 1953), pp. 488–89, 513–14.
74. *Memorandum*, January 1, 1936, PPF 1358, in Roosevelt Papers.
75. Duncan U. Fletcher to Franklin D. Roosevelt, February 19, 1936, and December 23, 1935; *Memorandum* to James Farley from Harllee Branch, March 5, 1936, OF 635, in Roosevelt Papers.

appreciate, reciprocate or cooperate with Fletcher. . . . Fletcher's voice is the official voice of Florida and his constituents resent the treatment being accorded him . . . by the Executive whom he has served perhaps too faithfully for his own good."[76]

When the influential liberal journal *New Republic* endorsed the canal, Roosevelt weakened. After advising Fletcher in mid-February, 1936, to expect no more work relief funds, the President relented. He sought advice from Harry Hopkins and then allocated an additional $200,000 for temporary continuation of the project. The President privately assured Floridians that he held Fletcher in the highest esteem, as did everyone in Washington, and conferred with him frequently.[77] Despite these peace overtures, Roosevelt reiterated his determination to end work on the canal if Congress failed to appropriate funds.

Fletcher lumped a $29 million canal appropriation with four other scattered waterway projects designed to draw maximum strength from states where the other projects were located. He tied the package to the War Department Appropriation bill and asked Roosevelt to intervene on behalf of the rider.[78] Roosevelt faced a difficult dilemma, pressured on one side by Fletcher, his southern colleagues, and north Floridians, and on the other by Secretary Ickes, Republicans, and south Floridians. He decided on a cautious middle course, advising close friends that by sending the bill to committee, he did everything he could until the committee acted.[79] The subcommittee handling Fletcher's amendment rejected it 6 to 5; the senator then took his case to the full committee where it lost 12 to 11. When he carried the struggle to the floor and lost by a vote of 39 to 34, a young Missouri Senator who sided with Fletcher, Harry S. Truman, moved to reconsider; but this move lost 36 to 35 when critically ill Park Trammell could not attend. Roosevelt finally broke his silence in late May, and the measure passed the Senate 35 to 30.

Fletcher did not live to see his canal project collapse. During

76. Telegram from John N. Perry to James A. Farley, March 14, 1936, OF 635, in Roosevelt Papers.
77. Harry Hopkins to Franklin D. Roosevelt, January 31, 1936, and *Memorandum* for James A. Farley, March 20, 1936, OF 635, in Roosevelt Papers.
78. Duncan U. Fletcher to Franklin D. Roosevelt, February 27, 1936, OF 635, in Roosevelt Papers.
79. *Memorandum* from Marvin H. McIntyre, February 10, 1936, OF 635, in Roosevelt Papers.

the two-year banking struggle, he had kept his Senate committee in almost continuous session. He devoted enormous energy to the trans-Florida canal fracas, and colleagues, noting his declining strength, advised him to rest. Fletcher agreed to reduce his work after completing the canal fight, but added, "I had rather wear out, than rust out."[80] He died of a heart attack on June 17, 1936, only a month and nine days after the death of his colleague Park Trammell. The next day, June 18, the House killed the Florida ship canal by a 108 to 62 vote.

Roosevelt made a flowery—and sometimes undeserved—tribute reserved for American public servants, paying the highest compliment when summarizing Fletcher's motivation: "Throughout a long and distinguished career in the Senate he was ever actuated by motives of high patriotism and unselfish devotion to the public welfare." In private correspondence Roosevelt more candidly mourned the passing, of a "loyal and steadfast friend."[81] Florida mourned his passing, and one paper eulogized: "The life of such a man is an inspiration to the young men of this day who are excusably cynical about politicians. If more men in public life would measure up to Senator Fletcher in integrity and ability, the word politics would not carry the opprobrium with which we so commonly associate it. If even a small minority of politicians could be as good as he was, it would still be considered an honor to be in politics."[82] The New York Times, whose editorials had often criticized the senator's policies, revealed deep respect for its old antagonist: "Florida possesses the excellent art of electing competent Senators, giving them an opportunity to broaden their experience in national affairs and the mysterious ways of the Senate, and enabling them to acquire influence and power. The chairmanship of the Committee on Banking and Currency is one of the great prizes of the Senate. Whatever may be the judgment of time on the changes in fiscal and banking policies made by Mr. Roosevelt and guided through the Senate by Mr. Fletcher, their sincerity of motive will not be questioned."[83]

Five thousand Floridians filed past Fletcher's bier in Jacksonville's city hall, and radio stations in Jacksonville and

80. Jacksonville *Florida Times-Union*, June 19, 1936.
81. Franklin D. Roosevelt to W. J. Sears, June 23, 1936, PPF 1358, in Roosevelt Papers.
82. Unidentified Florida newspaper in Fletcher Papers.
83. New York *Times*, June 18, 1936.

Gainesville broadcast the funeral service statewide. He was buried near the resting place of two other Florida Senators, William J. Bryan and Nathan P. Bryan.

Ironically, the political upheaval of the depression years had tempered his conservatism and made him spiritually kin to the liberal Bryan brothers. Political expediency inadequately explained this change, for Fletcher faced no significant competition in Florida. Nor can one explain his political activities during the 1930's solely in terms of party loyalty, an argument advanced by many historians to rationalize the support of New Deal measures by other essentially conservative southern congressional leaders. His spirited defense of the New Deal (both its legislative tinkering and its reform philosophy) in private correspondence to faithful conservative friends was unnecessary if only loyalty to his President and party were at issue. Rather, two lifelong and consistent factors explain the transformation of the conservative reformer into the New Dealer: his fear of revolutionary change based on the altered attitudes of his constituents, and his abiding sympathy for oppressed people.

CHAPTER XI

The Career of a Conservative-Progressive

ONE OF THE MOST damning indictments of political bi-
ographies is the charge that they reveal policy-makers but not
real men. While exploring the political dimensions of a personality,
they lose the man, his humanity, family life, and non-political
interests. Alas, this biography admits that it suffers from such a
flaw. In the scant records of his life, his simple humanity appears
for a moment, then recedes into the pragmatic and sometimes
misleading world of Senate roll calls. Yet, concern for other people
did permeate his private life. While visiting Jacksonville on one
occasion, he found a purse and returned it to a tearful little girl.
The next Christmas, without fanfare or publicity, he sent the
child an expensive bag.[1] When his brother's farm declined in
1921, he offered funds to save the homestead. He quietly paid the
real estate taxes for financially impoverished relatives and celebrated
his birthday by sending gifts to his daughters.[2]

Part of the reason for the obscurity of the senator's private
life can be found in the lack of personal family correspondence,
but a more basic problem is the personality of the man himself.
To our age, weaned on political charisma, Fletcher is enigmatic.
Like so many conservative southern Democrats, he lacked personal
magnetism and his strength was the subcommittee, the party caucus, and the Congressional pork barrel; he "got things done." Po-

1. Duncan U. Fletcher to Ruth Huddleston Baxter, December 3, 1921, in
Fletcher Papers.
2. Duncan U. Fletcher to Hiram Huddleston, October 7, 1918, and February 9,
1921; Nell Smith-Gordan to Duncan U. Fletcher, January 21, 1921; in Fletcher
Papers.

litical editorials commented on his service to Florida and the South, his interest in constituent problems, and his service on behalf of American farmers and shippers. They did not mention any warmth of spirit or overwhelming personality. Perhaps behind his cool exterior there was warmth; at least, some of his private correspondence suggests this inner dimension. But such self revelation is so rare that it almost resembles a political faux pas, an unguarded moment when Fletcher briefly forgets that he is first and always a public figure. The people who were his constituents respected him, acknowledged his skill and his service to Florida, and voted for him. They did not love him as if he were really one of them.

Nor was this personal obscurity altogether accidental. He chose to reveal only the public man for many reasons. The shyness of his formative years which was finally overcome only with great effort may offer a clue to his reserve. So may his wife's "peculiarities." This remarkable woman was kept, or kept herself, at the periphery of his political career, and her mystical and flighty religious interests constantly threatened to embarrass him in religiously orthodox Florida. His education and temperament made him logical, precise and rather aloof on the stump. His contempt for religious and political demagoguery, both of which enjoyed periods of popularity in Florida during his career, necessitated caution in expressing his private feelings on personal faith and conviction.

Another difficult problem in summarizing the senator's career is the complex motivations for his positions on policy. Historians searching for the reasons why southern Congressmen supported the New Freedom and New Deal have demonstrated the important role of party loyalty and the desire of southern Democrats to present a constructive legislative record after years of Republican control.[3] They have not adequately explored the essential ambivalence of southern politicians. From agrarian roots they brought conservative concepts of society; yet, they oftentimes voted as pragmatic liberals prodded by their search for advancement in a region which had a paucity of financial capital and therefore needed all the federal help that it could get. They were quick to protest invasion of sacred spheres of state rights

3. For elaboration of this point, see Arthur S. Link, "The South and the 'New Freedom,'" pp. 315–16; and Freidel, *F. D. R. and the South*, pp. 48–49.

in matters of race and social change, but they were just as quick to seek federal relief for their farmer and laborer constituents. Perhaps most importantly, they were forced to react to changes in voter attitudes.

Judged solely by legislative enactment, Fletcher's career was significant. He provided both the impetus and the detailed structure for the Farm Loan Bank Act of 1916, directed administration strategy during the battle for government maritime control, presided over the 1930's exposé of Wall Street, and guided Roosevelt's banking reforms through the Senate. Regionally, he tried to project the South into the mainstream of American life through the Southern Commercial Congress. In Florida he won millions for waterway development and provided a major stabilizing force against religious and political demagoguery.

Fletcher made the solution of everyday human problems the rationale of his actions. Biographers often ignore the Duncan Fletchers of American politics; their careers minimize spectacular debate and maximize the plodding committee. Because of the state they represent or their own unambitious personalities, they work unobtrusively. The measure of Fletcher was his willingness to serve in the political shadows. Only the final product concerned him in the 1914–16 merchant marine struggle or the 1933 Securities Act. If others received the honor of drafting legislation, Fletcher would insure its passage. It was no accident that Woodrow Wilson chose him to manage the most controversial New Freedom legislation or that Roosevelt picked him to head the key Banking and Currency committee. Exhaustive labor, skillful debate, and congressional tact became the senator's hallmark and resulted in passage of many a hard-pressed measure.

He was one of only eight Democratic and two Republican senators whose tenure spanned the years from Wilson's New Freedom, through the "Republican ascendancy" of the 1920's, and into the early New Deal; by 1936 only Senator William E. Borah of Idaho had served longer than Fletcher.[4] Several of the senator's contemporaries, notably Borah and George W. Norris, cut a deep trace in American political history. Their genius, however, lay in inspiring and leading the American people; Fletcher usually was content to reflect the people's collective will.

4. See U.S., Congress, *Congressional Directory*, 64th Congress, 1st Session, 1915 and 1933.

Since his tenure included both of the great reform eras of the first half of the century, his reaction to the progressive movement and the New Deal is instructive. Historians have demonstrated that although the two reform periods had certain characteristics in common, they were basically different from each other in leadership, motivation, and program. Professor Otis L. Graham, Jr., has observed that most of the leaders of the reform movements of Theodore Roosevelt and Woodrow Wilson who lived into the 1930's opposed the New Deal. A minority of the older progressives supported President Roosevelt, and a still smaller group desired even more basic change.[5] Fletcher really fits none of these patterns exactly. One can make a case for the argument that the senator, judged by his voting record, was a better New Dealer than he had been Wilsonian reformer. Though he served Wilson faithfully, even initiating important New Freedom legislation, he had serious reservations concerning the relationship of the Federal Government to the individual, and he hedged on many prominent reforms of the day—prohibition, child labor reform, and woman suffrage to cite three obvious examples. During the 1930's, though he authored no major legislation, his voting record was consistently favorable to the New Deal. His earlier fear of federal power had given way under the stress of national calamity and his confidence in President Roosevelt. The President's pragmatism and his lack of consistent objectives, which alienated so many of the older progressives and drove them into the opposition, apparently bothered Fletcher little if any. Perhaps, had he lived beyond 1936, the court-packing scheme or other New Deal measures might have finally driven him into the opposition camp, but there are no signs of it before his death in 1936. To understand his stance during both periods, one must always refer to local conditions.

The senator mirrored the average Floridian's opinion, and this largely explained his occasional senatorial inconsistency, as well as his long tenure. Fletcher's career was a classic example of the interaction of politician and local constituent and the way this interaction can determine a man's national posture. Infrequently, Fletcher led the people, as against the religious exclusiveness and racial bigotry of Sidney Catts, William Jennings Bryan,

5. For an excellent study of continuity and discontinuity in the modern reform tradition (1900–1938), see Otis L. Graham, Jr., *An Encore for Reform: The Old Progressives and the New Deal* (New York: Oxford University Press, 1967).

and the Ku Klux Klan; but his leadership consisted of cautious innuendo rather than bold proclamation. His paradoxical career—urban reformer in the 1880's, pseudo-Populist in the 1890's, middle-class spokesman during the New Freedom, conservative in the early 1920's, liberal during the New Deal—reflected the curious meanderings of Florida voters. He possessed an intuitive grasp of political transition—the decline of Broward's progressive mandate in 1908, political realignment under Catts, urbanization in the 1920's—and he elevated the study of constituent problems to an art. The senator was never far from his people—either ahead or behind.

To the degree that one can attribute an element of consistency to Fletcher, it is related to the economic progress of his agrarian–small business constituency. In the 1890's his flirtation with Populist principles involved the need to regulate large corporations and railroads. During the New Freedom, he supported the Smith-Lever Act, the Clayton Anti-Trust Act, the Federal Trade Commission Act, rural credits, and merchant marine legislation, to aid the same groups. His alliance with the Farm Bloc in the 1920's continued this tradition, and his support of the New Deal climaxed it.

Even Fletcher's apparent inconsistencies acquire meaning when evaluated in this context. Philosophically, he favored private capitalism as the source for construction of the merchant marine, provider of rural credit, and manufacturer of chemical fertilizers at Muscle Shoals. When congressional deadlock threatened these projects, however, he altered his stance. His economic and political pragmatism caused him to favor government involvement to help farmers obtain credit, transportation, and fertilizers rather than forego their healing balm just to please his theoretical preference for laissez-faire. Fletcher was a master of the politics of the possible, and he favored action to solve problems even if the action came at the expense of his conservatism.

This responsiveness to constituent pressures made him difficult to locate on the political spectrum. Jacksonville, the senator's Florida citadel, was the center of Democratic financial conservatism, and his hefty campaign chests were filled by many conservative contributors. Yet, he drew strong moderate-progressive backing in every election and could not have won his initial 1908 victory without splintering Napoleon Broward's progressive coalition. His elastic voting record confused even his associates and close friends:

one biographer and a family friend call him a conservative; his secretary's assistant recalls his progressivism; a life-long associate writes that Fletcher's statesmanship clouded all trace of political philosophy.[6]

Certainly his own background was rooted in the soil; the rural society which valued a stable social order, conservative institutions, and fiscal conservatism shaped his life. In the fashion of nineteenth-century liberalism, he feared tyranny, whether from an unrestrained majority or a centralized government; he repudiated extravagance and damned big government, at least until 1933. Despite such precepts, however, he championed man's inevitable progress and equality of opportunity. His religious views were decidedly liberal, and his intimate friends included members of many churches and creeds, poor and rich, black and white.[7] In an era of demagoguery and intolerance, he appealed "to the reason of men—rather than to their prejudice or to their emotions."[8] His politics reflected a potpourri of philosophical conservatism and pragmatic liberalism, supported by his faith in the people:

> There is no barrier between me and . . . [the people]; no conflicting spectre stalks between the interests of the people and the objects of my service. There is no call which has a clearer, dearer sound to my ears than the voice of the people . . . and whatever works for their good will have my support, and whatever works for their harm, I shall combat. . . .
>
> The people as a whole are patriotic, public-spirited and are moving onward and upward. . . . Our public officials are generally conscientious and capable. There is no occasion for harrowing gloom or for the agonizing iconoclast. Our eyes should turn to the front; our movement should be forward, and our courage and hope should rally for humanity's march. . . .[9]

Even Andrew Jackson would have applauded such a credo.

---

6. Stephens, "Senator Duncan U. Fletcher—Legislator," p. 116; interviews with Miss Sally Puleston, Monticello, May 27, 1963, and Miss Edith Pitts, Gainesville, October 14, 1964; Judge John W. Holland to author, October 9, 1963.
7. U.S., Congress, House, *Duncan Upshaw Fletcher*, 75th Congress, 1st Session, 1938, House Document 339, p. 51.
8. Speech text by Governor Spessard L. Holland, in Fletcher Papers.
9. Text of Fletcher's Senate acceptance speech to the Florida Legislature, in Jacksonville *Florida Times-Union*, April 22, 1909.

A keen observer penetrated to the crux of Fletcher's political philosophy; Florida's liberal Senator Claude Pepper, Fletcher's successor in the Senate, wrote, "I would attribute to Senator Fletcher what I would define as a reasonable and reasoning liberalism. I have used those words advisedly—a man whose feet were on the ground, and yet whose mind penetrated into the ethereal realms of idealism; a man whose heart beat in unison with the pulsations of the great masses of mankind . . . a man who in the latter years of his life had such a fresh outlook . . . that instead of lagging behind he was in the forefront of those fighting for that kind of liberalism."[10]

Fletcher's "liberalism" came from an open and honest mind that committed him to no fixed method of problem solving. His "conservatism" was based on his desire for order, not on specific programs. He was equally at home when opposing political experimentation (woman suffrage) during times of stability, or while advancing liberalism (government maritime control, social security) in periods of social and economic upheaval. In his lexicon of conservatism, relevance ranked ahead of property, opportunity above unrestrained individualism, progress before tradition. Private property could only be secure, he believed, in a society characterized by broadly based social and economic mobility. Fletcher was convinced that people burdened by social ostracism or economic peonage would someday destroy the most treasured possessions of the genuine conservative.

One cannot help feeling that excessive concern about locating him properly on the political spectrum would have wearied Duncan Fletcher. His world consisted of activity, pragmatism, and constituent needs, not rigid philosophical postures or combative political jargon. He felt most at home addressing a Florida Grange picnic, or shuffling down the corridor to a subcommittee meeting, or bargaining in the Senate cloakroom on the annual waterway appropriations bill.

10. U.S., Congress, House, *Duncan Upshaw Fletcher*, p. 47.

Bibliography

PRIMARY MATERIALS

Manuscript Collections

Albert W. Gilchrist Papers. Reproductions at Florida State University.
Correspondence in this collection by Florida's Governor, 1908–12, indicates the continuity of the Broward Era and concerns Fletcher and Everglades' drainage.

Austen Shuey Mann Papers. P. K. Yonge Library of Florida History, University of Florida.
Mann was a Florida Populist leader who corresponded with Governor William S. Jennings during the early years of the century.

Bureau of Marine Inspection and Navigation. Record Group 41, National Archives, Washington.
These records are invaluable for the 1914–16 maritime controversy.

Carter Glass Papers. University of Virginia Library.
The extensive Glass papers reveal much of Fletcher's tactics and opposition in the 1914–16 farm credit struggle, as well as conservative antagonism to his banking reforms during the New Deal.

Duncan Upshaw Fletcher Papers. In possession of Mrs. Fred G. Yerkes, Jacksonville, Florida.
More than a dozen private letters and a number of clippings concern Fletcher. Hundreds of boxes of Fletcher's letters were destroyed by his private secretary after the senator's death. Letters to his daughter were destroyed in a St. Louis, Missouri, flood some years ago. Other than letters to, from, and about him in other manuscript collections, only these few letters remain.

Edwin Hansford Rennolds Diaries. P. K. Yonge Library of Florida History, University of Florida.
These daily accounts by a northeastern Florida farmer-preacher reveal his impressions of Jacksonville politics.

Federal Farm Loan Board. Record Group 103, National Archives, Washington.
Fletcher's correspondence with the Loan Board indicates his role in 1916 Farm Loan activities, agricultural patronage in Florida, and his suggested modifications of the system between 1916 and 1936. This collection contains much

correspondence by Secretary of Agriculture David Houston with and about Fletcher.

Franklin D. Roosevelt Papers. Franklin D. Roosevelt Library, Hyde Park, New York.
This collection is extremely valuable for all phases of Fletcher's career from 1932 through 1936. The National Democratic Committee Papers for the 1930's which are included in the collection indicate the senator's role in Roosevelt's 1932 Florida race.

General Records of the Secretary of Commerce. National Archives, Washington.
These papers hold limited Fletcher correspondence on maritime affairs.

James B. Hodges Papers. P. K. Yonge Library of Florida History, University of Florida.
These papers are exceptionally valuable and extensive. Hodges was a prominent political leader in Florida who served as ally to Sidney J. Catts and later as member and chairman of the Florida Democratic Executive Committee. He supported Fletcher from 1908 until 1916, and from 1921 until 1936, but followed Catts in the 1916–21 period.

Jerry W. Carter Papers. Florida State University, Tallahassee, Florida.
Scrapbooks and political pamphlets compose most of this collection. Carter was active in politics beginning in 1908 and his papers contain material on Fletcher's 1920 and 1926 campaigns.

Napoleon Bonaparte Broward Papers. P. K. Yonge Library of Florida History, University of Florida.
This is an excellent collection of correspondence by the leader of Florida progressivism and Fletcher's 1908 opponent; principally 1904–10.

Newton D. Baker Papers. Manuscript Division, Library of Congress, Washington.
Baker, Secretary of War under Wilson, played a large part in the location of military bases in Florida. His correspondence reveals Fletcher's industrious struggle on behalf of Florida's economy during World War I.

Oscar W. Underwood Papers. Alabama Department of Archives and History, Montgomery, Alabama.
Underwood's papers reveal Fletcher's role in the 1912 presidential primaries and the 1919 Democratic leadership battle in the Senate.

Park Trammell Papers. P. K. Yonge Library of Florida History, University of Florida.
Six largely unsorted boxes contain some important material on recent Floridiana, especially political campaigns.

Peter O. Knight Papers. P. K. Yonge Library of Florida History, University of Florida.
This collection contains scrapbooks and correspondence of a powerful Tampa political and business leader, a close Fletcher confidant and adviser.

Ray Stannard Baker Papers. Manuscript Division, Library of Congress, Washington.
The Baker collection contains material of limited benefit taken from the Woodrow Wilson Papers for the official biography of the President.

Records of the Office of Agriculture. Record Group 16, National Archives, Washington.
These papers include considerable Fletcher correspondence concerning the Farm Loan system. This collection is especially rich in letters from Secretary of Agriculture David Houston regarding the concept of agricultural credit.

Thomas E. Watson Papers. Southern Historical Collection, University of North Carolina.
Some correspondence by the Georgia Populist leader concerns the 1908 Florida Senate race.

United States Shipping Board. Record Group 32, National Archives, Washington.
These extensive records indicate Fletcher's continuing interest in merchant marine affairs and his valiant struggle to maintain government ownership after 1916.
William G. McAdoo Papers. Manuscript Division, Library of Congress, Washington.
McAdoo played a major role in Wilson era maritime policy and patronage. The collection reveals a great deal about Florida patronage and administration strategy in the shipping battle.
William S. Jennings Letterbooks. P. K. Yonge Library of Florida History, University of Florida.
Correspondence by Florida's Governor (1900–1904) to and from Fletcher is especially valuable for 1900 Democratic politics and state aid after Jacksonville's 1901 fire.
Woodrow Wilson Papers. Manuscript Division, Library of Congress, Washington.
This collection is invaluable for Fletcher's role in the Wilson administration, 1913–20, especially concerning agriculture and maritime policy.
Manuscript collections of other political contemporaries proved disappointing since Fletcher apparently confined his correspondence to those with whom he had direct dealings. Therefore collections such as the John Bankhead and William Bankhead Papers at the Department of Archives and History in Montgomery were examined but not included in this Bibliography.

Newspapers and Journals

Unless otherwise noted all newspapers on microfilm are located at Florida State University.
Daytona *Gazette-News.* April 1–May 31, 1908.
Gainesville *Daily Sun.* April 1–June 14, 1908. On microfilm at the University of Florida.
Jacksonville *Daily Florida Union.* November 20, 1881–November 10, 1882.
Jacksonville *Daily News-Herald.* June 1, 1887–May 31, 1888.
Jacksonville *Evening Telegram.* January 1, 1891–December 31, 1893.
Jacksonville *Florida Times-Union.* November 20, 1881–June 31, 1936.
Jacksonville *Florida Weekly Times.* January 1, 1884–December 31, 1890.
Jasper *News.* January 3–June 19, 1908.
Miami *Daily Metropolis.* February 1–28, 1922. On microfilm at the University of Florida.
New York *Times.* January 1, 1913–June 30, 1936.
Panama City *Pilot.* April 1–May 31, 1908.
Pensacola *Journal.* January 1–November 7, 1908. On microfilm at the University of Florida.
St. Louis *Post-Dispatch.* August 1–31, 1913; January 1–February 28, 1914; July 1–31, 1916; October 1–31, 1916.
Tallahassee *Daily Democrat.* February 1–December 31, 1926.
Tallahassee *Smith's Weekly.* April 1–June 30, 1926.
Tallahassee *Weekly True Democrat.* January 10–June 12, 1908.
Tampa *Morning Tribune.* December 25, 1907–June 30, 1908; January 1–December 31, 1919; May 1–June 30, 1920; March 17–June 8, 1926.
The Commoner. February, 1922. In New York Public Library.
The Jeffersonian. April–June 30, 1908; June 1–August 31, 1914. In the Flowers' Collection, Duke University.

Personal Interviews

Carter, Jerry W. Tallahassee, Florida, March 1, 1962; November 21, 1962; and May 15, 1964.
Dodd, Dr. Dorothy. Tallahassee, Florida, June 22, 1964.
Fletcher, Mrs. Tom. Forsyth, Georgia, October 27, 1964.
Graham, Mrs. Harry, and Thompson, Miss Ella Creary. Tallahassee, Florida, May 21, 1963.
Pepper, Representative Claude. Washington, D.C., September 1, 1964.
Pitts, Miss Edith. Gainesville, Florida, October 14, 1964.
Puleston, Miss Sally. Monticello, Florida, May 27, 1963.
Yerkes, Mrs. Fred. Jacksonville, Florida, July 7, 1964.

Private Letters

Fletcher, Jack K., to author. October 31, 1964.
Holland, Judge John W., to author. July 20, 1963.

Public Documents

American Commission. *Agricultural Cooperation and Rural Credit in Europe.* Senate Document 261. 63d Congress, 2d Session, 1914.
Deed Book W, 1889, Monroe County, Georgia. County Court House, Forsyth, Georgia.
Executor's Report. *Final Distribution. Duncan U. Fletcher, Deceased.* Probate Judge's Office, County Court House, Jacksonville, Florida.
Florida. *Journal of the House of Representatives, 1893.* Tallahassee: State Printing Office, 1893.
Florida. *Report Secretary of State, 1916, 1920, 1924, 1928.* Tallahassee: State Printing Office.
Florida. *The Fifth Census of the State of Florida, 1925.* Tallahassee: State Printing Office, 1925.
Jacksonville. *Minutes City Council, Books 4–17.* City Hall, Jacksonville, Florida.
Last Will and Testament of Duncan U. Fletcher. Probate Judge's Office, County Court House, Jacksonville, Florida.
Monroe County, Georgia Tax Digest, 1854–1861, 1863–1883, 1868–1870, 1872–1873. County Court House, Forsyth, Georgia.
U.S. Bureau of the Census. *Fifteenth Census of the United States: 1930. Unemployment, Agriculture,* and *Population,* vols. I, II, and III.
U.S., Congress. *Duncan Upshaw Fletcher.* Document No. 339. 75th Congress, 1st Session, 1938.
U.S., Congress. *Investigation of the Department of the Interior and of the Bureau of Forestry.* 61st Congress, 3d Session, 1910-1911. Vols. I–XIII.
U.S. *Congressional Record.* Vols. XLIV–LXXX.
U.S., House of Representatives, Committee on Expenditures in the Department of Agriculture. *Everglades of Florida.* Report No. 12, 62d Congress, 1st Session, 1912.
U.S., Senate. *Hearings on Stock Exchange Practices.* 73d Congress, 1st Session, 1934. Vols. 1–25.
U.S. *War of the Rebellion: A Compilation of the Official Records of the Union and Confederate Armies.* Washington: U.S. Government Printing Office, 1880–91, Series I, vols. XI, XIX, XXV, XXXI, XXVII.

SECONDARY MATERIALS

Monographs

Baker, Ray Stannard. *Woodrow Wilson, Life and Letters.* Vol. VII. New York: Doubleday, Doran and Company, 1939.

Blum, John M. *From the Morgenthau Diaries.* Vol. I. Boston: Houghton Mifflin Company, 1959.

Capper, Arthur. *The Agricultural Bloc.* New York: Harcourt, Brace and Company, 1922.

Cash, William T. *History of the Democratic Party in Florida.* Live Oak, Florida: Florida Democratic Historical Foundation, 1936.

Cronon, E. David, ed. *The Cabinet Diaries of Josephus Daniels, 1913–1921.* Lincoln: University of Nebraska Press, 1963.

Daniels, Josephus. *The Wilson Era, Years of Peace—1910–1917.* Chapel Hill: University of North Carolina Press, 1944.

Daniels, Josephus. *The Wilson Era: Years of War and After, 1917–1923.* Chapel Hill: University of North Carolina Press, 1946.

Davis, T. Frederick. *History of Jacksonville, Florida, 1513 to 1924.* St. Augustine, Florida: Florida Historical Society, 1925.

Eccles, Marriner. *Beckoning Frontiers.* New York: Alfred A. Knopf, 1951.

Freidel, Frank. *F. D. R. and the South.* Baton Rouge: Louisiana State University Press, 1965.

Freidel, Frank. *Franklin D. Roosevelt: The Triumph.* Boston: Little, Brown and Company, 1956.

Graham, Otis L., Jr. *An Encore for Reform: The Old Progressives and the New Deal.* New York: Oxford University Press, 1967.

Grantham, Dewey W., Jr. *Hoke Smith and the Politics of the New South.* Baton Rouge: Louisiana State University Press, 1958.

Hendrick, Burton J. *The Life and Letters of Walter H. Page.* Vol. I. Garden City, N.Y.: Doubleday, Page and Co., 1922.

Houston, David F. *Eight Years with Wilson's Cabinet, 1913–1920.* Garden City, N.Y.: Doubleday, Page and Company, 1926.

Hubbard, Preston J. *Origins of the TVA: The Muscle Shoals Controversy, 1920–1932.* New York: W. W. Norton and Company, 1968.

Ickes, Harold L. *The Secret Diary of Harold L. Ickes: The First Thousand Days, 1933–1936.* New York: Simon and Schuster, 1953.

Johnson, James Weldon. *Along This Way.* New York: The Viking Press Edition, 1968.

Key, V. O., Jr. *Southern Politics in State and Nation.* New York: Alfred A. Knopf, 1949.

Link, Arthur S. *Wilson: The New Freedom.* Princeton: Princeton University Press, 1956.

Link, Arthur S. *Wilson: The Road to the White House.* Princeton: Princeton University Press, 1947.

Link, Arthur S. *Wilson: The Struggle for Neutrality.* Princeton: Princeton University Press, 1960.

Link, Arthur S. *Woodrow Wilson and the Progressive Era, 1910–1917.* New York: Harper and Brothers, 1954.

McAdoo, William G. *Crowded Years.* New York: Houghton Mifflin Company, 1931.

Martin, Sidney W. *Florida's Flagler.* Athens: The University of Georgia Press, 1949.

Mason, Alpheus T. *Brandeis: A Free Man's Life*. New York: The Viking Press, 1946.

Meyer, Charles H. *The Securities Act of 1934*. New York: Francis Emory Fitch, Inc., 1934.

Mitchell, Broadus. *Depression Decade: From New Era Through New Deal, 1929–1941*. New York: Rinehart and Company, 1947.

Moley, Raymond. *After Seven Years*. New York: Harper and Brothers, 1939.

Mott, T. Bentley. *Myron T. Herrick, Friend of France*. Garden City, N.Y.: Doubleday, Doran and Company, 1929.

Moulton, Harold G., et al. *The American Transportation Problem*. Washington: The Brookings Institution, 1933.

Palmer, Frederick. *Newton D. Baker: America at War*. Vol. I. New York: Dodd, Mead and Company, 1931.

Pecora, Ferdinand. *Wall Street Under Oath*. New York: Simon and Schuster, 1939.

Proctor, Samuel. *Napoleon Bonaparte Broward: Florida's Fighting Democrat*. Gainesville: University of Florida Press, 1950.

Rerick, Rowland H. *Memoirs of Florida*. Edited by Francis P. Fleming. Atlanta: The Southern Historical Association, 1902.

Rossiter, Clinton. *Conservatism in America*. New York: Random House, 1962.

Saloutos, Theodore. *Farmer Movements in the South, 1865–1933*. Lincoln: University of Nebraska Press, [1964?]; reprinted from the University of California Press 1960 edition.

Saloutos, Theodore, and Hicks, John D. *Agricultural Discontent in the Middle West, 1900–1939*. Madison: University of Wisconsin Press, 1951.

Schlesinger, Arthur M., Jr. *The Age of Roosevelt: The Coming of the New Deal*. Boston: Houghton Mifflin Company, 1958.

Schlesinger, Arthur M., Jr. *The Age of Roosevelt: The Politics of Upheaval*. Boston: Houghton Mifflin Company, 1960.

Seymour, Charles, ed. *The Intimate Papers of Colonel House*. 4 vols. New York: Houghton Mifflin Company, 1926.

Smith, Rixey, and Beasley, Norman. *Carter Glass, A Biography*. New York: Longmans, Green and Company, 1939.

Stokes, Thomas L. *Chip Off My Shoulder*. Princeton: Princeton University Press, 1940.

Tucker, Ray, and Barkley, Frederick R. *Sons of the Wild Jackass*. Boston: L. C. Page and Company, 1932.

Werner, Morris. *Bryan*. New York: Harcourt, Brace and Company, 1929.

Wilson, Woodrow. *The New Freedom*. New York: Doubleday, Page and Company, 1914.

Woodward, C. Vann. *Origins of the New South, 1877–1913*. Vol. IX of *A History of the South*, edited by Wendell Holmes Stephenson and E. Merton Coulter. Baton Rouge: Louisiana State University Press, 1951.

Periodicals

Abby, Kathryn T. "Florida Versus the Principles of Populism, 1896–1911," *The Journal of Southern History*, IV (November, 1938), 462–75.

Abrams, Richard M. "Woodrow Wilson and the Southern Congressmen, 1913–1916," *The Journal of Southern History*, XXII (November, 1956), 417–37.

Chalmers, David. "The Ku Klux Klan in the Sunshine State," *The Florida Historical Quarterly*, XLII (January, 1964), 209–15.

Cox, Merlin G. "David Sholtz: New Deal Governor of Florida," *The Florida Historical Quarterly*, XLIII (October, 1964), 142–52.

Doherty, Herbert J. "Florida and the Presidential Election of 1928," *The Florida Historical Quarterly*, XXVI (October, 1947), 174-86.

"First-Aid For Our Shipping," *The Literary Digest*, XCVII (June 2, 1928), 11.

Fletcher, Duncan U. "Address Before the Florida Historical Society," *The Florida Historical Quarterly*, III (January, 1925), 22-30.

Fletcher, Duncan U. "The Child Labor Amendment—II," *North American Review*, CCXX (December, 1924), 238-44.

Fletcher, Duncan U. "The Land Banks in Peril," *The Farm Journal*, LI (December, 1927), 9 ff.

Fletcher, Duncan U. "Will 1928 Act Aid American Shipping?" *Congressional Digest*, VII (June, 1928), 190-91.

Flynt, Wayne. "Florida's 1926 Senatorial Primary," *The Florida Historical Quarterly*, XLII (October, 1963), 142-53.

Grantham, Dewey W., Jr. "Southern Congressional Leaders and the New Freedom, 1913-1917," *The Journal of Southern History*, XIII (November, 1947), 439-59.

Jennings, Warren A. "Sidney J. Catts and the Democratic Primary of 1920," *The Florida Historical Quarterly*, XXXIX (January, 1961), 203-20.

Landis, James M. "The Legislative History of the Securities Act of 1933," *George Washington Law Review*, XXVIII (October, 1959), 29-49.

Link, Arthur S. "The South and the 'New Freedom': An Interpretation," *The American Scholar*, XX (Summer, 1951), 314-24.

Long, Durward. "Florida's First Railroad Commission, 1887-1891," *The Florida Historical Quarterly*, XLII (January, 1964), 248-57.

Marchman, Watt. "The Florida Historical Society, 1856-1861, 1879, 1902-1940," *The Florida Historical Quarterly*, XXVI (January, 1948), 256-63.

Proctor, Samuel. "The National Farmers' Alliance Convention of 1890, and its 'Ocala Demands,'" *The Florida Historical Quarterly*, XXVIII (January, 1950), 161-81.

Rogers, Benjamin F. "The Florida Ship Canal Project," *The Florida Historical Quarterly*, XXXVI (July, 1957), 14-23.

Snow, Franklin. "American Commerce and Foreign Ships," *The Independent*, CXX (June 2, 1928), 527-28.

Strout, Richard L. "Will Florida Crack the Solid South?" *The Independent*, CXVI (January 23, 1926), 95-96.

Willis, H. Parker. "The Banking Act of 1933—An Appraisal," *American Economic Review*, XXIV (March, 1934), supplement, 101-10.

Wilson, P. W. "The House of Morgan," *Review of Reviews*, LXXXVIII (July, 1933), 15-19 ff.

Unpublished Studies

Carper, N. Gordan. "The Convict Lease System in Florida." Ph.D. dissertation, Florida State University, 1964.

Cory, Lloyd Walter. "The Florida Farmers' Alliance, 1887-1892." Master's thesis, Florida State University, 1963.

Deal, John R., Jr. "Sidney Johnston Catts, Stormy Petrel of Florida Politics." Master's thesis, University of Florida, 1949.

Flynt, J. Wayne. "The 1908 Democratic Senatorial Primary in Florida." Master's thesis, Florida State University, 1962.

Green, George N. "Florida's Politics and Socialism at the Crossroads of the Progressive Era, 1912." Master's thesis, Florida State University, 1962.

Johnson, Evans C. "Oscar W. Underwood: The Development of a National Statesman." Ph.D. dissertation, University of North Carolina, 1953.

Link, Arthur S. "The South and the Democratic Campaign of 1912." Ph.D. dissertation, University of North Carolina, 1945.

Proctor, Samuel. "Napoleon Bonaparte Broward: The Portrait of a Progressive Democrat." Master's thesis, University of Florida, 1942.

Scott, Anne Firor. "The Southern Progressives in National Politics, 1906-1916." Ph.D. dissertation, Radcliffe College, 1957.

Stephens, Gertrude H. "Senator Duncan U. Fletcher—Legislator." Master's thesis, University of Florida, 1951.

Wells, William James. "Duncan Upshaw Fletcher: 'Florida's Grand Old Man.'" Master's thesis, Stetson University, 1942.

Index